The Gendering of Global Finance

Also by Libby Assassi

GLOBAL REGULATION: Managing Crises after the Imperial Turn
(edited with D. Wigan and K. van der Pijl)

AFTER DEREGULATION: The Global Financial System
(edited with D. Wigan and A. Nesvetailova)

The Gendering of Global Finance

Libby Assassi

palgrave
macmillan

First published 2009 by
PALGRAVE MACMILLAN

Palgrave Macmillan in the UK is an imprint of Macmillan Publishers Limited, registered in England, company number 785998, of Houndmills, Basingstoke, Hampshire RG21 6XS.

Palgrave Macmillan in the US is a division of St Martin's Press LLC, 175 Fifth Avenue, New York, NY 10010.

Palgrave Macmillan is the global academic imprint of the above companies and has companies and representatives throughout the world.

Palgrave® and Macmillan® are registered trademarks in the United States, the United Kingdom, Europe and other countries.

ISBN: 978–0–230–51793–6 hardback

This book is printed on paper suitable for recycling and made from fully managed and sustained forest sources. Logging, pulping and manufacturing processes are expected to conform to the environmental regulations of the country of origin.

A catalogue record for this book is available from the British Library.

A catalog record for this book is available from the Library of Congress.

10 9 8 7 6 5 4 3 2 1
18 17 16 15 14 13 12 11 10 09

Printed and bound in Great Britain by
CPI Antony Rowe, Chippenham and Eastbourne

Contents

Preface

The one area which consistently remains almost totally devoid of feminist literature in terms of not only asking 'where women are' but in critiquing how mainstream and heterodox International Political Economy consistently marginalises or insists on women's invisibility is within the field of global finance. Interestingly it is only now in the midst of a financial and credit crisis are questions being asked as to whether it is the very characteristics associated with masculine behaviour in terms of high risk, speculation and competitive behaviour, that has in significant part led to chaos on the international scene. This book then is timely in terms of using gender as a starting point for analysis within the international political economy so as to make visible the inherently gendered structures that inhabit financial markets. It can only be the very start of such an exploration because as I have stated in the introductory chapter, research in this area has been extremely challenging due to the paucity of work not only in the contemporary world, but also in terms of its historical context. Despite tantalising but rare glimpses of women's involvement within the financial sector in past centuries, finance and banking have remained an overwhelmingly male domain from the emergence of the modern financial system, through to today's financial scene. The invisibility of women particularly in earlier centuries necessitated an eclectic methodology and in this respect I have likened the project to a gigantic jigsaw puzzle with so many of the pieces still missing. However, it is hoped that this will provide the basis of other research to go forward in analysing the gendered nature of global finance, not least in terms of assessing its relevance to the nature of the financial crisis of 2008/2009.

I have received much support throughout this research, initially as part of my doctoral thesis. In this respect, I am very grateful to Jan Aart Scholte, one of my early supervisors in encouraging me to take on this task and also John Maclean who bravely continued his supervision to the very end. I would also like to thank the many colleagues and friends at the University of Sussex who provided me with feedback and encouragement, and in particular Gurminder Bhambra and, although now at some distance, Heloise Weber. Further, I owe a debt of gratitude to colleagues and friends at the Centre of Gender Studies at Sussex for their unwavering support and to my many students whose insightful contributions on gender allowed me to constantly evaluate, question and reassess my own position.

Lastly, although I owe my family in general a debt of gratitude for their patience over the length of this project, it is to my daughter, Gigi, that I owe that special word of thanks. Our many conversations and her insights into the world of marketing have been immensely valuable in terms of the ultimate direction of the final chapters.

1
Introduction

The consequences of the global 'credit crunch' (2007–2009), the latest but most serious financial crisis since the interwar years, continue to unfold at the time of writing, causing havoc to the lives of millions of people across the world. There have been sharp falls in volatile stock markets, a contraction of credit markets with increasingly precarious outcomes for firms and individuals and a series of significant interventions by central banks and governments. Big names in the financial system have all but disappeared as lenders have gone out of business, been taken over by other financial entities or partially nationalised, with many of these amalgamations and interventions directly instigated by governments. The virtues of the previously extolled free market are now being severely questioned by economists, governments and society at large as the financial system and society more generally come to terms with the inherent dangers of financialisation and the deregulated market. 'Innovative products'[1] began to unravel, leading to increasing fissures in the system and the apparent bursting of the 'credit boom' bubble. The far-reaching effects of such securitisation have not only spread those losses around the global financial system, but have also caused a fear of bankruptcy to both states and firms. The causes of the widespread contagion effects are various and complex but more often than not are placed under the general description of 'globalisation'. In terms of the financial system, Will Hutton has stated that we live in a world where, as a result of financial deregulation and the global ambitions of American and European banks, discrete financial markets no longer exist. There is one system he argues '...that operates around

1

the same principles, copying each other's methods, making the same mistakes and exposing themselves to each other's risks' (Hutton, 2007). It is also a system, and another crisis which is 'man' made. Financial markets, from the outset, have remained a male-dominated sphere of activity characterised by boasts of aggressive risk taking, speculation and vast profits. It was somewhat ironic, as a feminist, to read recent media reports which appeared to naturalise the perceived innate characteristics of men and so seemingly excuse the reckless risk-taking behaviour of predominantly male market traders in a variety of financial markets. Testosterone, it has been suggested, has had serious implications for decision-making. 'Any theory of financial decision-making in the highly demanding environment of market trading now needs to take these hormonal changes into account. Inappropriate risk-taking may be disastrous... [as this] may be biased by emotional and hormonal factors...' (Joe Herbert, cited in *ScienceDaily*, 2008). So it seems that financial markets are dominated not by rational economic men, as we have long been led to believe by neo-classical economic theorists, but by subjective emotions. Well, this comes as no surprise to feminists, who have long argued that dominant understandings of the workings of the market, resting as they do on masculinist notions of 'rational economic man', are inherently flawed.

This book, then, sets out the argument that the organisation of global finance has a gendered structure. In this respect, it forms the first tentative steps in an extremely complex but, until now, relatively unexplored territory. It argues that modern systems of finance, banking and credit are based on private property forms which historically involved limiting the direct access of women to financial security. In exploring the gendered character of the transition from feudalism to capitalism, and the emergence of formal financial markets, connections can be made with women's inequitable access to financial resources in diverse territorial and cultural locations as a result of the development and expansion of finance and credit markets across the global political economy. The possibility of gendered and subordinating structures being present in the workings of global finance is an area which has been consistently overlooked by international relations (IR) scholars and particularly those focusing on the global political economy (GPE). Although there has been much excellent research by feminists and other critical theorists dealing with or touching on aspects of gender and finance, including microfinance schemes (Cohen, 2002; Goetz & Gupta, 1996; Guérin, 2006; Mahmud, 2003) the impact of the South East Asian crisis (Aslanbegeui & Summerfield, 2000; Floro & Dymski, 2000), the gendered nature of International Monetary Fund (IMF) and World Bank policies (Benería, 2003; Elson, 2002; Elson & Çagatay, 2000) and the gendered culture of the City and financial firms (Kwolek-Folland, 1994; McDowell, 1997; McDowell & Court, 1991), generally the foundations of such masculinised and so gendered financial structures have remained unexplored and consequently invisible.

Because of the paucity of studies in this area, the methodology utilised here has been somewhat eclectic in that trying to find meaning and evidence for the historical exclusion of women from formal financial markets has necessarily meant drawing support from whatever source could be found. This task has been the equivalent of constructing a gigantic jigsaw with many pieces still missing and can form only the prelude to further extensive research projects. Making women visible in history has always been problematic: making women visible in terms of the emergence of finance has been doubly problematic and has meant examining the structures of global finance in a new way. Because of the lack of research in the field of finance and gender in a substantive form or in terms of meso- and macro-levels of finance, as van Staveren (2002) warns, caution is needed. However, in taking a more comprehensive, cultural and historical approach towards the structures of global finance, rather than studies specifically relating to micro- and macro-levels, much of the argument in this book has been built by implication and inference. In part it has meant structuring the analysis on the possibility of recreating that which was included by focusing not on presence, but absence; not on inclusion, but exclusion; not on the masculine but the feminine. It is the very absence of women and the absence of documentation that constitutes the reality of gender subordination. In this respect, this is just the start of unearthing the connections between global finance and gender, inequality and subordination.

Gendered history

Despite tantalising, but rare, glimpses of women's involvement in the financial sector in past centuries, the globalisation of economic processes, particularly through financial institutions, has a gendered history. That history has been made invisible through assumptions and constructions of the 'nature' of women and men and their supposed proper place in the socio-economic and political order, and in this respect global financial markets have played a critical role in shaping the structure and dynamics of that order. Since gender is a constitutive element of social relationships rooted in perceptions of difference between the sexes, as well as a crucial element in signifying relationships of power, shifts in the organisation of social relationships are closely related to shifts in representations of power. In this respect, although the roots of international or cross-border finance carry a much longer history, the formalisation of financial markets in the eighteenth and nineteenth centuries carried values and assumptions associated with a specific masculinised hegemonic ideology (Connell, 1995: 77) which prioritised the individual, efficiency, self-interest and competition in the pursuit of capital accumulation. This was in opposition to ideological constructs of 'woman', which became redefined in relation to her role as carer and nurturer, and placed within the private sphere of the household.

This contention is not new, being the foundations of much feminist scholarship, but within the context of this book, it will be related directly to the ways in which such understandings historically became naturalised and operated as a further constraint to women participating in formal financial activities. There is an implicit – and on occasion explicit – assumption, particularly with the construction of the conceptual separation of productive from reproductive activities, that women were historically absent from social relations of credit and finance. This is where constructions and abstractions of state and market, formal versus informal markets, as well as the private sphere of the household versus the private sphere of the economy are complicit in making women's economic activities largely invisible. The value, content and use of finance and credit within the household both before and after the emergence of capitalism can be seen as a function of production *and* welfare, not necessarily in liberal market terms of individual choice, but in terms of social security, stability and reproduction of the domestic unit.

Despite the relatively rare glimpses of women's financial activity in earlier centuries (W. C. Jordan, 1993; Lemire, 1997, 1998; Tebbutt, 1983), historical research continues to unearth evidence which indicates an early, strong and substantial presence in Britain and elsewhere of small-scale credit transactions and pawnbroking. This pattern of communal female lending within traditional and informal markets has also been evidenced in many 'pre-capitalist' or developing societies throughout the world, and in many societies still continues today. Historically these 'traditional' and mostly localised markets have always existed in one form or another, providing opportunities for economic exchange among individuals, enterprises or communities, but such localised patterns of exchange underwent significant change during the emergence of the Industrial Revolution. The subsequent rise of 'formal markets' and the general nature of the market system were characterised by the classical political economists, Adam Smith, David Ricardo and Karl Marx and such characterisations formed the basis of contemporary – and masculinist – approaches to international political economy (IPE). However, the very real constraints on women participating in the activities of financial markets as they became more formalised in the formative years of the emergence of capitalism in England were considerable. These gendered structures translated historically not only into inequitable access to 'formal' financial resources for many women but also contributed to the specific gendered impacts of, for example, financial crises (Elson, 2001; Floro & Dymski, 2000; Ling, 2002). Yet financial institutions have long been assumed to be vehicles for transmitting value-free exchanges so as to facilitate more efficient capital markets, not least in terms of global financial markets, which have had – and indeed continue to have – a critical role in shaping the structure and dynamics of the emerging global political and economic order (Helleiner, 1994: 173). In this order, the majority of the world's women do not equitably own, inherit or control property, land or wealth in relation to men (Seager, 1997: 120),[2] thus global finance and gender subordination may be centrally embedded within the development of more general global inequalities and stratification. It must be emphasised that by using the term 'subordination' – making subservient, placing in a lower or inferior rank or class – does not in any way imply that women do not resist and use a multitude of everyday strategies to counteract and battle against the injustices which befall them and their households. Nor does it suggest that shifts in the representations of power during times of social change do not impact on gender relations and consequently offer opportunities for the reorganisation of social relationships. However, the consequences of such global inequalities have crucial relevance as to how we analyse the nature and development of the global political economy which is a central element of this book. Since global finance is central to the gendered and inequitable distribution of power and poverty in the world, it is imperative to make visible the systemic effects of its embedded gendered practices so as to open up opportunities for challenge and radical agency.

The substantive concern here is the systematic exclusion of women from benefits that may have resulted from the expansion of financial markets. It is also accepted that is not only 'women' who may have been excluded, as gender cross-cuts both class and ethnicity. What is distinctive about women's exclusion however is that, as a group, shifting legal, ideological and social constraints founded upon perceptions of a woman's 'natural' role in society were built into and upon existing subordinations at a specific historical juncture, but in new forms. For particular groups of men who participated in trade and commerce more generally, however, the emergence of capitalism facilitated new opportunities for capital accumulation and wealth creation. An important process in freeing up capital was through the alienation of property from its social relations – of which gender was prominent – so as to construct new intangible and mobile forms, which enabled a new expansive dynamic in the production of financial resources for investment at a time of monetary scarcity. In other words, gender subordination may well have been historically necessary in part to enable the enormous expansion in financial, monetary, investment and credit flows, and to the construction of specific, now global, modes of social organisation and capital accumulation.

In terms of studies relating to contemporary global financial issues, despite the centrality of the role and power of finance not least in terms of discussions on 'globalisation', there is still much realist/neo-realist interpretation of finance and the political management of the prosperity of the state in relation to the ordering of its economic affairs (Gilpin, 1987, 1996, 2001; Spero, 1997). Others seek to understand the roots or influences of the contemporary global political economy within the context of Adam Smith's perception of trade and industry as being the basis of national wealth. The fundamental assumption of Smith's system which has been incorporated into neo-classical economic models is that of a relationship between individual self-interest and the collective needs of the community, in that rational egoism will enable the 'invisible hand' of the market to ensure the pursuit of self-interest, and in and of itself, will then lead to the public good (Smith, A. 1723–1790 [1776]). Such assumptions underpin the discourse of globalisation in that 'States willy-nilly became more effectively accountable to forces inherent in the global economy; and they were constrained to mystify this accountability ... through the new vocabulary of globalisation, interdependence, and competitiveness' (Cox, 2006: 59–60), with technology and autonomous market forces being typically identified as the causal factors behind the tremendous explosion of financial markets across the world (Stubbs & Underhill, 2006: 103). However, although there has been increased recognition of the importance of feminist contributions in the field of IR more generally, as well as a growth in feminist literature relating to the global political economy, global finance continues to receive little attention in terms of gender analysis. This is despite many scholars expressing a profound interest in seeking to explain global inequalities aggravated or deepened by forces of globalisation. However, considerations of the gendered nature of global finance (as opposed to those studies identified earlier and mostly arising from the area of development studies) are beginning to emerge. The gender invisibility within dominant approaches – often perceived as neutrality – is also revealed in most (if not all) of the standard texts relating to the history of finance and banking, credit and the expansion of international/global finance. This underlines the problems faced by feminist researchers, in that part of the condition of gender subordination is the manner in which women are rendered invisible as a result of the ways in which IR and IPE/GPE are theorised (Peterson, 1992: 183–206). In this context, such literature is not alone in being constitutive of the conditions of gender subordination, with its focus on specific forms of finance and credit practices. In this respect, a further contribution of this book to the field of GPE and global finance, in drawing upon and critiquing mainstream and critical understandings of the expansion and workings financial markets (both historically and contemporary) through a gendered lens, is to disrupt both orthodox and heterodox understandings of the financial system, allowing space for challenge.

The questioning of the political and social implications of the role and workings of financial institutions has rarely been so relevant in recent decades as at this particular time. Although the differential aspects of wealth and power of finance have been explored, within which studies particular gendered [male] ethnic and social class dominance is often implicit – but disregarded – the differential aspects of poverty and powerlessness within which women are overwhelmingly represented, remain largely unanalysed. Yet one set of hierarchies must presuppose and countenance the other. Here it must be recognised that the measurement of wealth, more particularly in relation to gender, is problematic but this, too, is a reflection of the androcentric nature of the various disciplines involved in analysing the nature of the social world. For example, for economists, personal wealth consists of assets that have a market value and take the form of 'real' property (such as buildings, land or machinery), and financial assets (including stocks and bonds) which imply a share of ownership in real wealth or a claim on income. Since such understandings of wealth and property are valued in terms of the market, women's unpaid work in reproduction and subsistence activities remains ignored and unvalued and is a further aspect of gender inequality.

Further, Warren et al., in researching poverty and wealth in Britain, have argued that little attention has been paid to the gendering of assets as opposed to income. Oliver et al. is cited as stating 'analyses of income only capture the current state of inequality, while wealth embodies the potential for examining accumulated and historically structured inequality' (1993: 75 cited by Warren et al., 2004: 51). This is precisely the challenge that this book intends to take on in terms of exploring processes which have resulted in the accumulated and historically structured inequality within the structures of finance. Wealth accumulation through income is also heavily gendered in its consequences since in every country of the world women as a group earn less than men (United Nations Development Report (UNDR), 2003 but also see Chen et al., 2005), which then has direct repercussions in terms of accumulation of assets, including pensions. An illustration of this is set out by Warren et al. (2004): of working-age women and men in Britain in 1995–1996, women had saved an average of only £2,000 compared with men's £13,000 and held slightly more of their assets in state pensions and less in occupational pensions. However, the conditions under which employers in many industrialised countries are prepared to offer occupational pension benefits to their employees as state benefits continue decline in value and form, are currently undergoing significant normative revision. Such revisions Condon argues are creating new forms of gender inequality (2007: 94). Rosenblatt and Rake (2003) also support the contention that the pension system in Britain (and in other developed countries) compounds the inequality women experience in the workplace and the failure to recognise their role of carers. This maldistribution within society is compounded by women being vastly underrepresented in decision-making positions in government (UNDP, 2003: table 1.5) and indeed within international financial institutions (Porter, 2005; van Staveren, 2002). To illustrate this point, the Women's Environment and Development Organization (WEDO) (2002) reported that only 2.2 per cent of the governors of the IMF were women, and occupied only 2 of the 24 seats on the Board of Directors. Women at the World Bank comprised 5.5 per cent of governors but occupied none of the 24 seats on the Board of Directors. Similarly, in 2006, Cable News Network (CNN) reported that there was a rise in the number of female CEOs in Fortune Global 500 companies being up from just 19 in 2005 to only 20 in 2006 (CNN, 2007).

The historical and gendered nature of this structured inequality of wealth accumulation is explored by directing attention not only to the historical foundations of the ideological, economic and socio-cultural constraints imposed upon women, but also their legal manifestation in terms of legitimating private property as taken further in Chapter 3. In many countries such as England, in parallel with the rise of capitalism, married women ceased to exist as independent legal agents and were subsumed under their husband's legal identity with subsequent constraints on control and management of property. The corollary of this was in effect to bar women from entering into contracts and credit relations, which together with associated ideological barriers, further constrained women's financial activity until at least the 1970s. This then had significant implications for the gendered accumulation of wealth and poverty.

Gender and global political economy

It is within the field of IR studies and, more particularly, GPE where this analysis has been situated, and gender is the tool of analysis.

Critical feminism is used as a method of critique to expose the intimate connections between global financial processes and the deepening and stretching of specific social relations across the world. This has enabled areas of society previous considered potentially unprofitable by financial institutions and ancillary networks now to be recognised as new spaces for accumulation. Such an analysis involves rendering visible, and therefore disclosing, 'deep social relations of power' (Youngs, 1999) which have remained invisible through mainstream IR and GPE scholarship. Feminism shares with the more radical strains of the IPE tradition a dissatisfaction with mainstream IR and its emphasis on ahistorical accounts of high politics, the lack of theorising about relations between the domestic and the international/global and the unsustainable separation of politics and economics. Consequently IR and GPE have failed to deal with women in the political economic system as a whole and the ways in which power and powerlessness are distributed and legitimated (Grant & Newland, 1991; Peterson, 1992; Tickner, 1992; Whitworth, 2000). In this way, women continue to be marginalised and left within the private/domestic domain by, for instance, epitomising particularised versions of 'truth', 'rationality' and 'objectivity'. These have become embedded in the foundations of knowledge, which is constructed upon the binary logic of Western science, with its claim that truth and objective knowledge is justified on the grounds that a clear separation can take place between fact and value, subject and object. This is in part a consequence of the shift in social ontology which took place at the time of the emergence of capitalism and its associated market system and which is discussed in Chapter 2. Of particular relevance here is Sandra Harding's argument that peculiarly masculine ideals have influenced the formation of science (Harding, 1986). If applied to economics and its relationship to finance and financial markets (i.e., reason versus emotion and social commitment, objectivity versus subjectivity, the abstract and the general versus the concrete and particular) striking parallels emerge with similarly distorting outcomes within the theory and practice of global finance.

It is particularly important to note that in undertaking this project from a critical feminist approach, I see belief systems and ideologies themselves as part of social reality, but not simply a subjective part. In terms of dominant ideologies then, this book takes as its starting point Connell's understanding of a masculinist hegemonic ideology (1995: 77). In relation to global finance, the role of critical feminist analysis will be:

Identifying deceptions, distortions and systematic denials in theories which implicitly and explicitly assume that women and their activities are either beside the point or subsumed under men's activities. (Pirages & Sylvester, 1990: 236)

By using gender as an analytical device, it is intended that further insight can be gained into the overwhelming gender-based power structures within the 'industry' of global finance and its historical, social and cultural basis. This entails exploring the ways in which understandings of gender relations have simultaneously a local and global context. It is the case that all observable aspects of gender subordination take place in specific locations, but this does not mean the cause of that subordination is only at the local. An illustration of this is the use of specific forms of micro-credit schemes implemented to alleviate poverty at the site of the local as explored in Chapter 7. However, such micro-credit schemes cannot be separated from the promotion and policy implementation of poverty alleviation strategies imposed in many cases from the global context, not only in terms of institutions of governance, but also under the discipline of global financial markets. A further example is given in terms of the connections between circuits of credit drawing upon the poorest levels of societies, which in themselves have gendered relations, through the strategies of credit and catalogue companies, which themselves are integral components of financial alliances or networks associated with global sources of finance. Firms within these alliances use sophisticated data-collection systems which enable strategic targeting on specific groups in society at the local level and now have global coverage. Making these connections between the local and the global allows us to explore and uncover the ways in which ideas inform different global activities and the impact that these ideas have on practice.

These connections between the local and the global within GPE literature, not surprisingly because of its preoccupation with the three dominant approaches (neo-realism, liberalism and Marxism), tend not to consider the domestic/household level as being of much relevance and so ignore or indeed dismiss these connections. Mainstream Western understanding of the study of the IPE has become a legitimate – and thus legitimising – method of analysing the management of a progressively interdependent world economy, with an increasing recognition of the involvement of influential actors outside the state rather than an exploration or questioning of the structures within the system itself. Within such an approach, a particular set of theoretical ideas, grounded in a specific historical and social context relating to economic and political institutions, serves the same expectations as mainstream IR. That is, there is a basic perception that states are socially created institutions which have evolved from specific human interactions whereas markets have more 'natural' and essentialist foundations. Further, free markets have been seen as the most desirable approach to national and international economic relations, which have been addressed almost exclusively through '...the lens of neo-classical economics' (Murphy & Tooze, 1991: 37). Although it must be said that text books relating to the study of the GPE are beginning to include discussions of alternative theories such as constructivism and/or feminism (such as O'Brien & Williams, 2004; Ravenhill, 2008) and significant contributions by feminists to the debate are published (such as Griffin, 2007; Marchand & Runyan, 2000; Waylen, 2006), overwhelmingly the focus is on the relationship between states and markets. More often than not such a focus is with a view to policy prescriptions with particular reference to matters of trade, money, finance and on occasions, investments, institutions and governance. Underhill underlines this by stating that the most recent expression of the complex relationship between power and wealth (i.e., the political and economic domains) is the link between political authority on the one hand, and the system of production and distribution on the other, that is the market economy. In this context Underhill undertakes a gender neutral approach whereas it is argued here that as women have been excluded from formal financial markets and marginalised to the informal, this has important implications for wealth creation and distribution, as well as security and social reproduction (Stubbs & Underhill, 2000: 18). Not only is the state identified in dominant literature as a unified actor, but 'Its personification as key actor symbolically assign agency to it, and this is supported by the ideas of legitimate internal and external power' (Youngs, 2000a: 46).

By applying a 'common-sense'[3] status and depoliticising notions of the state, Youngs continues 'it removes any need to think of the state as a political space within which power struggles take place and thus to map those struggles including within and across public/private divides' (2000a: 45). Therefore in terms of the concerns of mainstream IPE/GPE – that is the relationship between the state and the (formal) economy and its functions – it is not surprising that gender is not an issue. Whereas the realist and neo-realist approaches focus on the state, a liberal approach tends to see the individuals, firms and households as the basic units of analysis with the motivating force in the economy based on competitive interaction between individuals who are assumed to maximise their satisfaction through the social institution of the market (Gill & Law, 1988: 42). Although many of the debates within GPE question the liberal economic view that a free, open financial system ultimately guarantees allocative efficiency through the economic system, this is usually related back to questions of production in relation to '...money made easy from the trading of money' (Cerny, 1993: xi), rather than concerns relating to the inequitable distribution of wealth within societies.

Changes in the world economy have been seen to be closely related to major shifts in the nature and structure of the international monetary and financial system and in this respect, financial institutions have been an important focus in IPE. Stubbs and Underhill set out the propositions that, first, it is important to consider the relationship between the political and economic domains in the contemporary IPE since 'when the two domains are separated our understanding of the world around us, important errors of analysis and policy are likely to result' (Stubbs & Underhill, 2000: 5). Second, economic structures are not the result of the spontaneous interaction of individual economic agents in that the structures of the market and the larger political economy are inherently contestable. And last, there is an intimate connection between domestic and international levels of analysis. In other words, the international domain reflects the specific social forces of the most powerful states as this balance becomes projected into the international system (2000: 5–6). Gender is rarely recognised as a structural component of 'specific social forces'.

While there are valuable contributions to the study of IPE/GPE from many, including critical theorists, until the gender content of the ideological nature of traditions within the social sciences is

examined, only incomplete and partial understandings of inequitable outcomes of particular activities, or particular historical, social
and economic conditions can be achieved. As Peterson asserts

> Gender is conventionally invisible because the *longue durée* of
> masculinism obscure the power required to institutionalise,
> internalise and reproduce gender hierarchy and its associated
> oppressions. In this sense, gender is hard to see because it is so
> taken for granted. (1997: 199)

The implication here is that the evolution of dominant Western
(male) theoretical constructions and the separation of the relations
between specific understandings of the 'political', the 'economic'
and the 'social' is historically situated and has a direct bearing on
the paucity of contemporary IPE/GPE literature (as opposed to work
coming from development or geography for instance) taking poverty, inequality, gender and the subordination of women as substantive issues of concern: power of specific institutions (state, market,
class) still take prime position. There is an apparent gender neutrality
across the discipline which obfuscates the gendered roots of political economy, resulting in a lack of intellectual curiosity in terms of
women's limited access and control over resources, including financial ones. This limited access and control on gendered terms have
resulted in a negative impact upon women in terms of increased risk
in the volatile global financial system and the restrictive nature of
exploitative financial and credit systems proffered to women, not
least in partial recompense for the withdrawal or shifts in welfare
strategies and increasing levels of poverty in relation to wealth.

Gender and global finance

In the past few years there has been a limited but welcome appearance of literature in relation to gender and global finance (as opposed
to specific elements such as micro-credit schemes etc.), emanating in
particular from feminist economists such as Elson (2001) and van
Staveren (2002) with other more general contributions from Bakker
(2000), Cook et al. (2000), Marchand and Runyan (2000) and Youngs
(2000a, 2000b). Elson (1992, 1993, 1994, 1995, 1999) has produced
excellent, varied and prolific work more particularly on the global

economy and development, and a more recent work focused more specifically on global finance (2001). The understandings of the basis for inequality in this work tend to be given in terms of explanations of public and private, and the 'naturalisation' of the role of women and the household. These equate with the three biases in the economy set out by Elson and Çagatay 'which is increasingly dominated by financial markets' (2000: 1853) and that these biases – deflation, 'male breadwinner' and commodification – prevent the formulation of gender-equitable, people-centred macro-economic policies. Elson's other work is similarly concerned with the integration of what are considered by states and international institutions as 'no alternative', sound and prudent macro-economic policies in an economy increasingly dominated by financial markets (1994, 1995). Throughout her work there are important critiques of macro-economic policies which focus on market-based criteria which '[are] blind to the ways in which macro economic [gendered] outcomes are a product of macro economic policies which are implemented within *historically and socially specific institutions'*[4] (2000: 1860). Although financial markets and institutions are implicitly, and on occasions explicitly, incorporated within her critique of macro-economic policies, a more focused critique of gender and finance is undertaken in Elson's 'International Financial Architecture: A view from the kitchen' (2001), where the effects upon women's lives of financial crises are clearly set out, with particular concern for poor women living in the South. The historically and socially specific institutions which form a significant underpinning of her writing remain unexplored – it is this challenge with which the following chapters seek to engage.

Further work of global finance and gender is undertaken by van Staveren, whose exploratory work on gender relations and finance at the meso- and macro-levels (2002) acts as an overview of the range of areas within which inequalities are reproduced by financial markets and other associated institutions. Van Staveren suggests four types of gendered relationships which occur in the financial sphere: underrepresentation of women in global finance; increased gender gaps which occur; prevailing gender structures which encourage instability in global finance markets and gender discrimination which leads to inefficient resource allocations in global markets. A further welcome sign of recognition of the importance of gender in terms of analysis within GPE and the financial order comes from T. Porter. However, to some extent, his chapter on gender and global finance reflects those general issues raised by van Staveren, such as the underrepresentation of women in financial decision-making and limitations in relation to access to credit, although it also includes a pertinent (and very timely) section on gender and risk taking (2005: 155–174). Further more general work pertaining to global finance has been undertaken by Bakker (2000), who explores some of the potential links between gender and the new agents of structural and strategic power in a period of intensified globalisation. She has argued that the building of the pyramid – the New International Financial Architecture (NIFA) – has been a process of human agency which has created new social forms in an era of intensified globalisation. The architects of this pyramid – mostly men – and its material and distributional consequences can all be assessed through the lens of gender. Such an assessment, Bakker argues, indicates that the new financial architecture is reinforcing previous inequalities between North and South. Bakker's paper makes a significant contribution to the gender implications of heightened capital mobility, translated into more freedom from social costs for capital, with the management of individual economic risk and risk management (in terms of healthcare, unemployment, pensions) becoming privatised. Such work as has been outlined here makes a valuable contribution to a so far largely unanalysed research area, that is gender and global finance. In so doing, these contributions add to earlier work within other disciplines, such as geography, urban planning and development studies, which have been until now at the forefront of taking gender seriously in terms of the impact of financial markets leading to inequitable gendered outcomes.

Nevertheless, however limited this may be, there appears to be more of an awareness in much of the literature outside the central core of GPE in terms of explorations into changing patterns of financial strategies on a global scale and its gendered effect on employment and cultural practices. There is still even less research in terms of changes in the dynamics of the GPE in the past 20 years or so, which has resulted in the complex and competitive relationships between banks, commercial (including retail) and production sectors merging, innovating and evolving. It is very difficult at times to specify which institutions constitute financial institutions, where and what 'banking' is and when it becomes an integral aspect of something else. Such problematic definitions of what constitutes the institutions or boundaries of global finance, or where the 'local' becomes 'global' are indications of the incessant and fast-flowing dynamics of finance.

Chapter overview

Following this initial discussion, Chapter 2 reflects on the period of historical change – the transition from feudalism to capitalism in England. As part of this process, a new social ontology arose, the construction and historical context of which had profound consequences for the ways in which knowledge was constructed and the world understood in political, economic and social terms. The gendered nature of much of its underpinnings also had had profound consequences for the ways in which women became invisible as economic agents, particularly in relation to direct financial activity. Through the abstract construction of the public/political and private/economic spheres where men gained wealth and status, a further domain – the private of the household – was the presumed domain of women. It was with this construction, which accompanied the separation of production out of the household to the external male realm of the economic, that over time finances also became separated and a thing apart from the household and family. This chapter argues that it is necessary to make visible the early connections between this new social ontology, changes in property forms and the emergence of financial markets in England since modern finance and credit is based on commoditised property forms. The necessity for finance to become mobile in order to transcend borders is analysed from a gendered perspective, so exposing shifts in women's access to financial resources. Not only were the foundations of modern systems of finance, banking and credit male-based institutions, but the same gendered processes which aided their formation further exiled women to activities on the margins of the newly formed market economy. It will be seen that this was both a material and ideological process which had direct but differentiated implications for men and women.

Chapter 3 takes the analysis of the shift in property rights from more communal understandings to private individualised property to a deeper level with a discussion of the ideological and material processes by which women lost rights to property. This analysis of the shift in access to property, and more particularly financial resources, is achieved through a careful exploration of the emergence of liberal and liberal economic theories of property rights and the relationship with gender. These transformations within the private/economic sphere of the male were crucial to the development of capitalism in Britain during the seventeenth and eighteenth centuries, in that by separating property from its social relations – of which gender was a significant element – it could be transformed into liquid and mobile capital allowing new forms of credit and finance to be raised for investment in commercial and industrial enterprises. Traditional rights, which were intended to safeguard the security of women and future generations, were replaced by financial 'securities' thus not only commodifying aspects of personal security but allowing liquid assets to be raised on now-private property which then could be used, for instance, in the process of industrialisation. This chapter then sets out how these processes were paralleled with the changing assumptions about the 'natural' roles of women within the household and social reproduction, with production being redefined so as to exclude women's traditional economic activities. The 'economic' was transferred into what was being constructed as the male domain of civil society/the formal market sector. These roles then became institutionalised, embodied in legislative enactments of public policy and judicially sanctioned.

The task of Chapter 4 is to explore in more detail the contention that the transition from pre-modern to modern systems of finance, banking and credit has a gendered history such that those institutions became increasingly masculinised. After a brief overview of the historical context of the emergence of 'modern' financial institutions, a gendered analysis of the shifting constructs of the value, content and use of credit is undertaken as new innovations in finance sought to overcome the obstacles to investment. This involved a masculinised institutional-legal-economic order which saw Common law conditions of *femme coverte* imposing severe constraints of women controlling property and entering into contractual relations, including those of credit. Ultimately such processes provided ideological and material obstacles which severely constrained the access of women to traditional forms of financial security, whilst allowing specific groups of men to utilise the emerging new forms of mobile capital, in pursuit of capital accumulation. The ideological, political/juridical and economic processes are outlined indicating the context within which women increasingly became marginalised from direct control of property and financial resources exposing the processes which saw the increasing exclusion – and thus visibility – of women in the early formation of financial markets.

After outlining the historical emergence of financial markets, Chapter 5 analyses the financial and economic practices in transition at the domestic level in order to indicate that shifts within the organisation of the state, production and market cannot be limited to or separated from changes within the community, society and more particularly the household. It sets out more specifically the changing nature of credit from one embedded within society to a commodified form, leading to a further marginalisation of women from formal finance and credit markets. With the emergence of 'modern' financial institutions, specific and gendered belief systems became associated with competitive financial and banking activities driven by risk and speculation. In turn, this gendered division of formal, orderly and disorderly privileged productive lending over consumption in terms of social reproduction. To illustrate this contention, this chapter makes visible the extensive informal activities of women in disorderly credit markets. Lastly, the discussion draws out the indicative processes through which a particularised masculine hegemonic ideology became firmly embedded within the (financial) market ideal and expanded firstly with establishment of a specific culture of banking within the City of London, which then expanded through colonisation and international trade and investment, leading gendered structures of finance to become internationalised. To paraphrase Marchand and Runyan (2000: 9) by undertaking a gender analysis of the historical foundations of modern financial markets, it allows for the introduction of people or subjectivity into an otherwise abstract discussion about processes, structures, markets and states.

After this examination of the background to the gendering of financial markets, Chapter 6 moves forward to give an overview of the internationalisation and globalisation of financial markets which, together with state welfare strategies after 1945, further embedded gendered inequalities. In terms of 'developing' countries, welfare is discussed in terms of development policies and their gendered impact, which shifted over time. In terms of understandings of welfare in developed countries, although elsewhere it has been argued that the emergence of the welfare state saw the rewriting of social relations in capitalism, the script of gender relations remained very largely unaffected by continuing perceptions of the 'nature' of women and their inability to deal rationally.

With the increased freedom and mobility of financial markets after the 1970s and associated restructuring of states and firms, with consequences for the provision of welfare, implicit in the discussion is the ideological move towards an income maintenance system which combined an increased emphasis on individual moral responsibility and that gained credence at both the national and international level. As part of this liberal economic discourse, 'social exclusion' – with its associated and seemingly integral condition of 'financial exclusion' – at the local level became seen at a global level as a condition which required rectification. As a result of the spread of neo-liberal economic practices after 1980s, welfare increasingly became commodified and sold to the consumer as 'financial products' including pensions, with such commodification often being subject to the vagaries of stock markets and thus leading to increased insecurities. As this chapter argues, since in nearly every country of the world there are gendered structures of inequality, social and financial 'inclusion', many scholars have argued this has rarely lead to empowerment or equitable access to political, economic and social resources for women. Indeed the underlying premise of this chapter may suggest that since fundamental social transformation would appear the only proposition which would enable a more equitable society in terms of gender, rather than drawing women into gendered markets, such a strategy of promoting social inclusion and empowerment would seem counter-intuitive.

Last, Chapter 7 maps global patterns and processes in relation to the targeting in terms of finance and credit of the poorest sectors of society. It seeks to give a more detailed account of the ways in which women are being drawn into deepening circuits of credit. It is not that credit in itself is not a resource worth having – indeed it has stated earlier that it can be an essential resource both in terms of production and social reproduction. However, it is argued that financial actors are treating women as an emerging market for finance, credit and financial services often at extortionate rates of interest when more often than not these loans are required for social welfare purposes.

This chapter illustrates the way in which women with inadequate incomes are targeted by financial organisations through the use of surveillance and sorting techniques for maximising knowledge and asserting influence over savers and consumers. It evaluates the increasing use and sharing of relational databases and the blurring of boundaries of financial and other businesses. In this respect, market strategists utilise general and gendered characteristics associated with risk which are then incorporated into targeting strategies so as to penetrate areas previously considered unprofitable – and here the focus is on women. This chapter agues that there is an asymmetrical process which may bring benefits to an increasing number of individuals within specific sector of society, but in so doing feeds off specific groups drawing them into increased levels of debt, vulnerability and risk. Such processes of drawing poor women into credit relations on market terms are further discussed as a parallel process in terms of micro-credit schemes in the South. Again here it is argued that many of these micro-credit schemes are drawing women into circuits of credit through a deepening of financial market relations thus exposing them to increased risk and insecurity. This is of central importance – particularly when considering the present financial crisis which continues to unfold – when considering credit as a means of supporting activities associated with social reproduction and social development, and the deepening levels of risk and insecurity across the world brought on by financialisation.

2
Period of Change: Historical Context

The eighteenth and nineteenth centuries marked a period of rapid structural change as political revolutions swept across Europe, interacting with forces that saw the emergence of a particular form of market economy. Previously existing patterns of social relations were tested, dislocated or transformed, exacerbating the forces of uncertainty and social change. Within England, the mercantilist policies of an earlier period receded with the growth of a market society and the emergence of a strong and reorganised liberal state. Rationalisations for such a market economy and the reorganised liberal state were enabled and strengthened by a new social ontology, premised on masculinity, which sought to explain the formation of the emerging order. Through these ideas and the social movements with which they were associated, 'Nature, people and the means of exchange were redefined through political action so that they became part of a new social ontology of Polanyi's fictitious commodities of land, labour and capital' (Gill, 1997: 12). As Gill states, these fictions became real in so far as they were treated and thought of '... as if they were factors of production, a process that was extended geographically and socially as the new global market order was constructed' (1997: 12). The emergence of 'formal' or 'modern' financial markets was crucial to this process.

This chapter sets out a starting point for analysis of these structures by exploring how this history developed during a period of formidable change. This is partially carried out by relating it to shifts in the definition of, and potential agency for, forms of property and rights in the early development of capitalism. Since these early changes in property rights, together with other processes, were fundamental to the dynamics behind the emergence of (modern) financial markets, it is essential to examine the gendered nature of these beginnings and to evaluate the extent to which financial structures reflected, built upon and reproduced the assumptions and practices of their historical foundations. These gendered origins subsequently became embedded within the very norms of financial markets so as to be reproduced on an international, then global, scale with related subordinating consequences for women and certain groups of men in diverse territorial and cultural locations.

Organisation and reorganisation of gender relations: the 'new' social ontology

Peterson has argued that gender is conventionally invisible 'because the *longue durée* of masculinism obscures the power required to institutionalise, internalise and reproduce gender hierarchy and its associated oppressions' (1997: 199). In this respect, the gendered nature of the transformation which enabled the emergence of a market society affected key institutions such as the forms of state, market, civil society and households. This shift in society also required a new social ontology, which also drew on and reconstituted key ideas from earlier philosophers, such as Aristotle and Plato (Coole, 1986, 1993; Squires, 1999). The resulting (male) assumptions and understandings of the 'universe', comprising practices, institutions and structures of social production/reproduction, were given significance through systems of meaning and shared ideologies, more often than not supported by binary logic. Claims relating to, for instance, the separation of the public and the private, the political and economic, state and society and rationality versus the emotions, alongside the development of concrete social specialisations, were central to the rationalisations behind this shift to this new social ontology and have been the subject of much feminist critique. Peterson, for instance, directs attention to the ways in which gender, as an analytic category, infused foundational dichotomies so that 'the concepts that structure our thought...and the practices that structure our options and activities...becomes a structural, pervasive feature of how we "order" social life' (2000: 12). This account reflects the analysis of other feminist scholars who have long argued that the new social ontology which emerged had embedded within it notions of power, subordination and exploitation that reflected and supported specific gendered practices (Coole, 1986, 1993; Forget, 1997; Okin, 1979; Pateman, 1988, 1998). As Coole so eloquently states,

> Freedom, equality, justice, consent, emancipation, solidarity, power, oppression ... are all terms whose significance lies embedded in centuries of theorizing about politics and the Good Life. It is difficult to imagine any theory concerned with social change that would not make use of these terms. ... Political theory cannot be divorced from the institutions that manifest the power of which it speaks and which it legitimises or criticizes. Insofar as feminists challenge these institutions, they must also therefore challenge and understand the theoretical assumptions on which they rest. (1986: 130)

In this respect, although subject to some debate, the gradual shift in ideology differed in several ways to the early modern gender system, which was based on different normative and political/economic values to those which followed the era of the Enlightenment and the French Revolution. In very general terms, until the eighteenth century, the household was understood to be the basic social and economic unit with productive roles assigned to both men and women. Although there was a gender hierarchy, productivity was seen as an activity of the household with both men and women responsible for its sustainability (Gray, 2000: 7). Progressively, however, the 'private' of the household became to be understood in ideological terms as the 'private' (social) reproductive sphere of women, whereas the 'productive' commercial and economic sphere was consigned to the private of 'civil society' – the domain of men. Despite the ensuing rendering of women as invisible economic agents, women's activities and roles were given recognition by many philosophers and political economists during the eighteenth and nineteenth centuries, but with very limited effect and in very specific ways. Adam Smith, Ricardo, utilitarians such as Bentham, Malthus, John Stuart Mill and French philosophers such as Jean-Baptiste Say contributed influentially to the history of ideas, and discussion of women's economic role and status were a constituent of this discourse (Dimand et al., 2004: 229–240; Forget, 1997). Underlying speculative arguments by

Adam Smith[5] on the potential evolution of the economic status of women was the conjecture that with the growth of commerce, trade and manufacturing, reliance on physical strength would diminish the importance of physical differences, making it possible for women's social and economic position to be improved. (A. Smith, 1976 cited by Nyland, 1993). Further, Smith's ideas on the possibilities of women's economic advancement were reflected by Jeremy Bentham's insistence that women's utility was equal to that of men (Lurie, 1974 cited by Dimand et al., 2004: 237) and indeed, John Stuart Mill's championing of political women's rights is well documented (Fenton, 2005; Mill, 1970). Nonetheless although women's *legal* rights may have been notionally supported, as Dimand et al. point out, ultimately,

> The core treatises and primers on political economy by classical economists – even those by John Stuart Mill and the Fawcetts... – typically neglected women's economic roles, whether inside or outside the household. When the subject did arise, it was often half-concealed ... (2004: 237)

If women were 'half-concealed' then the position and visibility of men in civil society and commerce was reinforced and supported by this new social ontology, which by its very composition differentiated the nature, role and position of men in economic life.

This general and increasing invisibility of women in the formalisation of the market system reflects feminist arguments that the transition from feudalism to capitalism and the separation of production from (social) reproductive activities, is central to understanding the continuing subordination of women. This transition was accompanied by an ideological structure which progressively 'naturalised' the place and role of women. This process of the 'naturalisation' of women's place was, perhaps, most visible during the nineteenth century, when the vision of women's domestic role in society reached the peak of its most stereotypical image as reflected in popular literature, art and treatises at that time. It has to be emphasised here that such an image may not have been the substantive reality for most women, but it was the middle-class ideological model to which most women were encouraged to aspire, such stereotyping providing a severe structural constraint on other possibilities of being. Conversely, the cultural and other forces which sought to legitimise the place and role of men in the economic realm, and more specifically their role and position in financial markets, were similarly extremely powerful in terms of identity formation. Previous acceptance of the place of productive activities within the overall remit of (social) reproduction was displaced and relocated outside the domestic sphere as the forces of industrial capitalism constructed a new and masculinised 'economic' productive sphere. The same seemingly unstoppable dynamic was also an integral part of the process which increasingly excluded women from the activities and institutions of formal financial markets and raised the status of men as they actively pursued financial and banking activities in pursuit of profit. This conceptual and substantive relocation of men and women and the naturalisation of these ideological structures legitimised and supported the shift in social ontology, and became part of the reasoning for the exclusion of women from formal financial institutions.

Here we can see ideology in terms of a Gramscian hegemonic process which has a set of common-sense assumptions that legitimates the existing distribution of power. This structure of power is then seen to be 'natural'. This can be further qualified by stating that historically it also bestowed on men the power over women's financial and other resources in the quest for accumulation and power. Connell has defined the role of such gendered ideological legitimation admirably:

> The concept of 'hegemony', deriving from Antonio Gramsci's analysis of class relations refers to the cultural dynamic by which a group claims and sustains a leading position in social life. At any given time, one form of masculinity rather than others is culturally exalted. Hegemonic masculinity can be defined as the configuration of gender practice which embodies the currently accepted answer to the problem of legitimacy of patriarchy, which guarantees (or is taken to guarantee) the dominant position of men and the subordinate position of women.
>
> Nevertheless, hegemony is likely to be established only if there is some correspondence between cultural ideal and institutional power, collective if not individual. So, the top levels of business, the military and government provide a fairly convincing corporate display of masculinity, still very little shaken by feminist women

or dissenting men. It is the successful claim to authority, more than direct violence, that is the mark of hegemony... (Connell, 1995: 77)

In terms of this definition, by the nineteenth century the relationship between the 'cultural ideal' of a specific form of economic hegemonic masculinity was firmly embedded in the institutional power of formal financial markets and the very foundations of what was to become the 'modern financial system'. The establishment of this masculinised hegemony, together with private property relations so central to understandings of modern market relations, gradually took on a global scale with the expansion of financial markets. Accordingly women's traditional ties to earlier and different communal and traditional forms of property were displaced wherever these new property forms were imposed. This chapter then, explores the ways in which the ideological underpinnings, supported by the new social ontology, merged, reflected and on occasions conflicted with, but very largely supported, the gendered nature of the emerging modern financial system. The key assumptions of individualism, competition, instrumental rationality and distribution through the market all depended upon a specific understandings of 'the rational economic man' and were crucial to understandings of the workings of formal financial markets. These markets were at the outset male institutions in terms of membership, values and norms and remain outstandingly so. This understanding of ordered, efficient 'male' markets was the very antithesis of perceptions of women's role in productive activities as the separation from the household became more pronounced, so that economically productive women tended to be situated in what became known as informal and 'disorderly' relations of economic activity, including those of credit and finance. This increasingly aided the process of their exclusion from the more formal financial institutions. The consequences of this discourse as it was reflected in practice, in terms of the impact of the organisation and distribution of finance and banking upon women's lives in differentiated localities, was considerable in terms of both material constraints and potential agency. However, the myriad of ways in which women – and men – exercise agency under the most oppressive circumstances should never be underestimated.

Transition from feudalism to capitalism: gendered trajectories

The skewed or partial analysis within IR and GPE work on the transition from feudalism to capitalism means that it consistently omits reference to the relations between men and women. As a consequence, this has resulted in a distorted history since it has been assumed that important historical turning points for men have had the same meanings and trajectories for women. This has been the case with the 'transition' or 'transformation' from feudalism to capitalism, in which significantly different paths for men and for women emerged, embedding highly differentiated access to, and distribution of, political, economic and social resources. Although in most, but not all, previous communities, inequalities in terms of diverse and complex hierarchies between men and women existed, with the emergence of capitalism the content of such inequalities shifted and formed the basis of a more general material and ideological subordination of women. In other words, the organisation and reorganisation of social forces which took place with the emergence of a market society, gender relations – together with class and ethnicity – were crucially significant in the structuring of 'space and place, spaces and places' (Massey, 1994: 191). Such reorganisation covered both ideological and material shifts in terms of gender relations within the private sphere, as well as the norms, values and underlying rules of emerging 'modern' financial markets which encompassed the increasing monetisation and commodification of socio-economic relations so central to aspects of the economic *longue durée* of modern capitalism.

Generally, two debates exist within political circles centred around the emergence of capitalism as a vehicle which either created and continues to create opportunities and thus empowers women, or as a process which further fuelled or constructed specific social inequalities, including those of a gendered nature. In this respect, opportunities within liberalism which, as part of the new social ontology seeking to explain and promote the creation of a market society, are seen as *economic* opportunities with *political* equality lying within the realm of universal suffrage and associated civil liberties. Inequalities associated with the private sphere have remained, at best, irrelevant as being unrelated to the 'political' sphere. Here 'political' as it has been interpreted by conventional conceptions of politics is at odds with feminist assertions that 'the personal is political'. Whereas conventional conceptions of the political are located within the institutional arena of government, feminists have, in various ways, sought to reconstruct the political so that power is extended to cover all social relations (Squires, 1999: 23–25).

Within liberal dialogue, historically women's place within society suggests an improvement after capitalism's emergence. Indeed, as has been argued elsewhere it is difficult to imagine feminism as having no relation to certain principles of liberalism which conceived of individuals as free and equal beings, emancipated from the ascribed hierarchical bonds of traditional society (Dailey, 1993: 83). This continues to be reflected in political discourses today, in which women's empowerment in terms of their relationship with the market, whether through economic growth as a whole or more specifically women's personal relationship to formal economic activity including access to credit, is prioritised.[6] The second debate is whether the process of creating a specific form of market economy necessitated in part the subordination of women. In this view, the expansion of capitalism has constrained the empowerment of women and so this is a constituent element of the expansion of capitalism (Anderson & Zinsser, 1990; Clarke, 1919; Erickson, 1993; Mendelson & Crawford, 1998; Staves, 1990). However, such work has largely been concerned with the domestic (as in national or local) only, so the implications for the international/global continue to be ignored and remain outside the concerns of IR and IPE. Although feudalism can be applied to other societies and systems of governance it has largely been used to denote a type of society and political system which was dominant through the Middle Ages in large parts of Western and Central Europe. Yet understandings of the 'transition' or 'transformation' from feudalism to capitalism have made invisible changes which embedded highly differentiated and gendered access to, and distribution of, political, economic and social resources. The nature of these changes in the domestic sphere had – and continues to have – crucial implications for all aspects of GPE.

In exploring this important historical period, much of the focus within IR and GPE in both Marxist and non-Marxist literature, has been on the formation of state-market relations and/or the formation of social classes and social interests without reference to the domestic sphere. For instance, Sweezey (1976: 1) – in attributing the emergence of capitalism over older systems of production to economic, rather than political, causes – focuses on '...the superior efficiency of more highly specialised production, the greater gains to be made by producing for the market rather than for immediate use' (1976: 43–44). The 'greater gains', in this instance, were the increased potential for capital accumulation via a market economy which became increasingly the domain of men, whereas producing for 'immediate use' across the world has been more often than not seen as the domain of women (and children). Similarly Schwartz (2000) focuses on emerging mercantilist states, the limitations of agricultural production for producing economic growth and the often violent marketisation of the previously self-sufficient micro-economies linking them together with the global economy. What is silent in such explorations of the emergence of capitalism has been the increasing invisibility through marginalisation of women in these micro-economies, as part of this process. With the merging of micro-economies over time to form part of the construction of the 'formal' economy, opportunities for wealth creation – and thus power and privilege – accrued to specific groups and classes of men. Certainly the formation of social classes was central to these explanations in terms of opportunities for wealth creation, but so too was the increasing marginalisation or exclusion of women as a specific group (as opposed to class) from activities within the 'formal' economy.[7] Historically, aspects of such marginalisation were a contingent consequence of specific and existing patriarchal relations, but also a specific historical element of processes of accumulation. Any relations women did have with the emerging 'formal' market economy in this period of transition – and here the focus is on the emerging credit and financial markets – were generally class-based with access directed and controlled through and by particular groups of men. In this respect, although numerous historians and social scientists have explored the process of transition from feudalism to capitalism, and have sought to identify the elements of the social order which led to its demise and/or those aspects which were subversive of capitalism (for instance, Hilton, 1990; Teschke, 1998; Wallerstein, 1980), such work remains oblivious to gender as a potentially subversive entity.

A direct association between particular forms of emerging credit and financial institutions and the increased marginalisation of women can be illustrated through, for instance, shifts in forms of property and abstract notions of public and private spheres which, in turn, were closely associated with the separation of production/ business and finance from the sphere of the household and (social) reproduction. A twofold gendered process was involved in terms of first the gradual separation of household finances from those associated with production/business investment, and second the use of women's property and associated social and kinship networks – by men – as a means of enlarging the financial pool available for potential investment. The gradual reorganisation of this socio-economic aspect of industrialisation and associated commercial activity was closely related to the formation of notions of the separation of formal and 'ordered' male-dominated markets, as opposed to 'informal' and disorderly markets which were heavily inhabited by women. In this respect, formal/ordered and informal/disorderly markets should join the foundational dichotomies in Western political thought, such as the public and private, which are recognised here and by feminists more generally as being profoundly problematic not least in the promotion of thinking that is

static ... stunted ... encourages inadequate analyses ... privilege the first term at the expense of the second ... their deployment [thus] implicitly or explicitly valorizes the attributes of the first term. Because foundational dichotomies – culture-nature, reason-emotion, subject-object, mind-body, public-private – are gendered, action that relies on dichotomies privileges that which is associated with masculinity over that which is associated with feminity. (Peterson, 2000: 11)

With profound consequences for the way in which IR and IPE have been theorised, Peterson argues, political scientists have constituted their field of study by focusing on the public spheres of politics and power, 'this has relegated women and femininity to a depoliticized realm of "private life" and familial relations' (2000: 11). Peterson also states that both political scientists and feminists 'struggle with the question of how economics fits into this binary framework'. If the social is removed from the field of economics (and thus finance), then much will remain hidden and this is indeed the case. Yet often the 'struggle' within this binary in economics (re)surfaces and we see the implicit vilification of supposedly 'feminine' attributes within the workings of market. It is not surprising, then, that from representations of female disorder in the popular culture of early modern England (Wiltenburger, 1993) to discussion of legislative control of women's work at the beginning of the twentieth century (Breckinridge, 1906), the notion of 'disorderly' has been associated with the 'nature' of women. Breckinridge argued that it was evidence that '... the presence of women in certain places or at certain times creates a situation probably immoral or disorderly, within which the state, in the interests of propriety, may interfere' (1906), and so it was that he argued for the prohibition of women from working in the mines and other forms of employment at night. That this was an idea current at the time is supported by Bohstedt (1988) who states that the early modern European women were regarded as the very embodiment of disorder. Wiltenburger puts such arguments into context by arguing, convincingly, that the prevalence of representations of female disorder said less about women's actual disorderliness than it did about the fear of their power and 'unruliness' (1993: 627–629). We might also argue that women's economic activities and their traditional entitlements to resources were perceived to be subversive of the needs of the new commercial class of men, the state and powerful institutions in embracing the requirements of the expansion of markets necessitated by the rise of this particular form of capitalism. As will be discussed in more detail in Chapter 3, both ideologically and materially, groups of women who were economically productive were increasingly marginalised to 'informal' and 'disorderly' economic relationships, with women's productive economic activity – once accepted as integral to domestic production – either ceasing or being increasingly constrained. This, together with the increasing (male) professionalisation and specialisation of productive/commercial/financial activities in the formal sphere, became ever-more institutionalised further marginalising women's economic activities.

The binary 'logic' of the public and the private

As previously stated, earlier, in pre-capitalist systems, the household was perceived as synonymous with the economy. Feudal societies were bound together closely by familial, social and economic relationships where social relations were collectively practised in that, for instance, the entire community would be involved in planting, cultivating or harvesting. Indeed, in many parts of the world this rhythm to community life continues. Villages possessed institutions of self-rule to enforce customs and settle disputes. Marriage was an economic partnership of production and reproduction among the aristocracy as well as within peasant communities so from the earliest times productivity was conceived as an activity of the household under the custody of both sexes (Braudel, 1979: 18). This is not to say there was any form of gender equality, since there were strict notions of hierarchy in both sexual and social terms in that within each social level, men enjoyed privileges denied to women by way of political, legal and personal domination over their daughters and wives.

Within the system of unfree labour, women, children and slaves played – and were perceived to play – varying but essential economic roles (Finley, 1981: 72). The management of the household entailed choices in relation to cropping, breeding, security and '...in the customary relations between men and women, old and young, the teaching of the children, and the administration of justice in disputed matters' (Strange, 1988: 19). Even during the time of Aristotle

> ...the business of household management is concerned more with human beings than with inanimate property: that it is concerned more with the good condition of human beings than with a good condition of property (which is what we call wealth); and finally that it is concerned more with the goodness of free members of the household than with that of slaves. (Aristotle cited by Ryan, 1987: 112)

With this in mind it can be understood that economically, in feudal/pre-industrial and early modern societies most women were active either as members of the household or on their own account. Both men and women had rights to communal resources, including land. In feudal societies and particularly for working women within (and outside) the household, participation in economic productivity afforded them generally direct access to resources – even if on inequitable terms. As Peterson states kin societies did not distinguish between 'political', 'economic' and familial/reproductive activities or segregate them spatially, but '... it was Western state formation [that] constituted such distinctions in processes that simultaneously con- stituted gendered dichotomies' (1997: 188). The substantive concern here is that, this being generally so, in that feudal, pre-industrial and early modern societies, participation and visibility in economic productivity afforded women certain rights of access to communal and kinship resources, what were the dynamics which led to the apparent – and naturalisation of the – systematic exclusion of women from such resources and opportunities, and so to benefits that may have resulted with the emergence of financial markets.

Kinship is a significant aspect of feudal relations which feminists, such as Peterson, argue have had particular ramifications for the subordinate place of women in society today. Changes which took place in feudal structures in relation to kinship relations, according to IR and GPE, are considered of importance only when discussing the rise of political authority and centralisation of the modern state, which necessarily rested on the destruction of the system of kinship relations. The transition from pre-capitalist (kinship, communal) to capitalist (private) forms of property was not as complete or as uni- versal as it is often characterised. There was a mixture of new and old forms, with women more generally being left, both ideologically and substantively, with the pre-existing social relations. That is not to say that specific groups of women were not substantially involved in, for instance, early factory work or agricultural labour, but there an increasing division emerged as to a differentiation of the economic aims to which such endeavours were direct. A significant part of the non-market feudal system excluded the notion of commerce, was not based on competitive ideals and did not strive for accumulation but rested on economic interdependence within the household and thus between men and women (and children). In such relations there was no differentiation between production and social reproduction. With shifts in the spatial and conceptual relocation of productive and commercial activity with the rise of capitalism, the early modern gender system based on very different normative economic values was replaced with those emerging, in part, after the Enlightenment (Gray, 2000: 7). And, indeed, such a gendered differentiation con- tinues in very large part today.[8] Although ideas concerning the role and place of women – and thus men – and the conceptualisation of the public and the private were already circulating before the eighteenth century, the shift in social ontology became hegemonic and consequently further influenced change. And in relation to the gendered nature of the shift in social ontology, as Gray states so clearly, 'Silence about a particular group can denote a potent power relationship between that group and those who own the tools of scholarship and thus control the parameters of discussion' (2000: 12). The implication of this statement is very clear in terms of the silence in the IR and IPE/GPE community with regard to the invisibility of gendered processes, not least in relation to the absence of gender consideration in analyses of global finance.[9]

Exclusion from the emerging financial markets was reflected and compounded by legal, ideological and social constraints as set out in Chapters 3 and 4. Most crucially, the legal status of married women prevented them from unilaterally participating in the civil legal system and as a result, from the legal 'unity' of husband and wife it followed that a married woman could not sue or be sued unless her husband was also a party to the suit, and most crucially in terms of market activity *could not sign contracts* unless her husband joined her (Shanley, 1989: 8). Dower rights regarding real property changed to reflect economic changes in England with The Dower Act of 1833 ultimately proving to favour men's property rights. Dower was the outcome of the ecclesiastical practice of exacting from the husband at marriage a promise to endow on his wife on his death a portion of his estate to be inherited by his widow for life. This inheritance did not represent a return of property that had been brought by women into marriage but the statute of 1833 impaired the inviolability of dower by empowering husbands to cut off by deed or will their wives from dower (Blackstone). As Staves notes, 'Its enactment allowed legal intellectuals to feel that they had corrected an error but preserved for individual women no socially enforced rights; an individual woman got nothing except what her own husband privately elected to bestow' (1990: 49).

Since property was a crucial component of raising security and credit in the emerging financial markets, and with the civil legal system adjusting to support the law of contracts essential to economic activity, women were heavily constrained – at the very least – by the judicial system from participating in 'formal' market activity. Further there was an acceptance of male dominance: throughout the literature reviewed it was men who emerged as the early bankers: there was not one reference to women being active in formal financial markets until the late nineteenth century when a gendered division of labour emerged within the banking and financial sectors. An illustration of this is found in Pressnell, in examining the origins of early banking sets out industrialists, financial intermediaries (scriveners), and remitters of funds between London and the country. He states,

> It must ... be emphasized that these are groups of business activities and not just of business *men*; any one embryo banker might engage in two or all three types of activity, but *his* identification with a particular type is a recognition that the activity was the most powerful influence in *his* progress towards banking. (1956: 12; italics mine)

Or, for instance, in a later period, Cameron and Bovykin states that the centre of wealth in Victorian Britain was London:

> ... and in particular it was the City that produced plutocrats, not just those who have become household names such as the Rothschilds, Barings, Rallis, Sassoons, Gibbs and Montefiores, but generally totally unknown *men*[10] like the Morrisons, merchant bankers and financiers and High McCalmont, stockbroker and foreign merchant. (1991: 41)

It is difficult to argue that 'men' here refers to the ubiquitous use of the claimed generic 'man/men', since histories of banks such as Barings (Zeiler, 1929), Couts (Healey, 1992); Rothschilds (Morton, 1964) and Lloyds (Cockerell, 1984) clearly set out the male lineage of bankers and financiers, with women only appearing in terms of marriage partners, and more often than not in terms of fortuitous marriages into other families of influential bankers and financiers. Indeed a century or so after the events described, Paul Ferris in *Gentleman of Fortune: The World's Merchant and Investment* only mentions women on three occasions. The first is in relation to the 1980s when he relates, '[male bankers] recur in gossip columns with beautiful women in tow (they are not supposed to be women themselves, and although I know that women investment bankers exist in senior positions, I didn't come across any)' (1985: 26). When discussing Japan's investment bank, Nomura, he states 'there are no ... professionals among the female staff.... It's company policy'

(1985: 150) and in relation to the London banker (again in the 1980s) 'A new generation of younger men – not women, needless to say – has been taking over at merchants banks' (1985: 193).

However, despite the overwhelmingly male presence in terms of banking and financial institutions, Eriksson has argued that the specific gender structure of English property law was part of the reason why a capitalist economy developed early in England. Such an argument is based on the twofold (and potentially contradictory) notion that under this system – coverture – married women were deprived of a legal status and stripped of most types of property, so were even more restricted than married women in the rest of Europe (2005: 17). These 'incapacities' necessitated complex legal manoeuvres which Erikson suggests led to the emergence and widespread use of complex financial instruments to alleviate the inequitable outcomes as much as possible. Her second point focuses on unmarried women retaining their legal personality with the result that 'the legal and therefore financial freedom of unmarried English women increased the proportion of the population able to engage in financial markets by fifty per cent' (2005: 2–3). This latter assumption is problematic, not least since the status of legal personality was only one of the obstacles to women engaging directly in financial markets, and such an understanding that the gendered nature of English property law provided an impetus to capitalism at this time does not address the other constraints set out in the following chapters, which saw women being marginalised from the institutions of modern financial markets. Indeed, it can be argued that the gendered nature of English property law provided an impetus to capitalism at this time but approached from a very different standpoint in terms of freeing up capital for investment and this is what this book sets out to demonstrate. Certainly some women did speculate and invest in the emerging financial markets and other women – in particular widows – did *provide* resources for the expansion of capitalism, but on very specific terms and in very particular conditions (Davidoff & Hall, 1987; Holderness, 1975; Laurence, 1994/1996).

There is a need, of course, to qualify 'pre-modern' markets and the subsequent 'market economy'. Further, the period of transition was long and uneven both in terms of space and place and, as stated above, the trajectories for men and for women of different classes varied considerably. Both before and after the evolution of the present dominant market system, there have been a diverse range of economic systems. Local and regional systems coexisted and were culturally distinct yet contained within them a wide array of market and exchange relationships and indeed diverse gender relations. The wider historical debate including Adam Smith's statement that people have an inherent 'propensity to truck, barter and exchange' [1776] (1991) has provided the basic understanding of markets from which contemporary neo-classical theorists proceed to argue that capitalism's emergence was both natural and spontaneous (Stanfield, 1986) and so progressive. According to Polanyi (1968: 62), the appearance of capitalism was particularly revolutionary because 'markets rule people' whilst in pre-modern societies 'people rule markets'. Moreover,

> No society could, naturally, live for any length of time unless it possessed an economy of some sort; but previously to our time no economy has ever existed that, even in principle, was controlled by markets. In spite of the chorus of academic incantations so persistent in the nineteenth century, gain and profit made on exchange never before played an important part in human economy. (Polanyi, 1944: 43)

Products might be bought and sold in markets based on the understanding that the price negotiated was one in which neither party's economic status was altered, in that a 'just price' did not disrupt the status, poverty or wealth of either the buyer or seller. This is rather different from a modern market system where the price is frequently the result of impersonal and competitive forces of supply and demand. Within such a system, 'Justice is not an issue' (O'Hara, 1999: 696). In other words, earlier systems were not driven by market forces but were social – not political or economic in the terms understood today. According to Polanyi (1944), economic activities were embedded in their respective social structures of that time and not part of a separate and autonomous economic sphere: markets and exchange were embedded within each society's cultural norms, which, of course, included those of gender. Neither pre-modern markets nor the contemporary system can be said to be spontaneous, since they were socially constructed, arising from institutional – to include cultural – processes. Here the institution of the market and of property as a means of exchanging ownership of expected value is crucial to understanding the gendered nature of the emerging modern market system since it required a system of authority to sanction the exchange of ownership. Only a state can confer the legal situation labelled 'ownership' and historically, the institutions dictating the form of this ownership acted as a gendered constraint.

Changes from kinship property to a system of private property, that is a shift from entitlement to resources to individual (male) rights to them, and a separation of the social, political and economic relations of the household and the state involved specific gendered processes. The slow but progressive shift in property forms at this time was accompanied by an evolving liberal dialogue in terms of freedoms and rights – freedoms and rights which were interpreted as excluding women. These evolving 'rights' were also fundamental to the evolution and functioning of modern financial markets, since the emergence and widespread use of complex financial instruments at this time was dependent upon these new forms of property relations, and were part of a simultaneous reorganisation of space and place involving the construction of the conceptual distinction between the public and private spheres. The reconstructed economic realm, isolated from the social sphere of the household and household reproduction to a separate sphere of the public world and civil society, had fundamental significance for the repositioning of women in terms of both their 'place' and 'nature'.

From a liberal standpoint, the relation between public and private is often expressed as a relation between the state and 'civil society', the latter being the realm of voluntary associations in which people come together in pursuit of their own political economic interests (World Bank, 2000: 5). The most complete and complex version of this representation is seen to be the market as portrayed in neoclassical economics (drawing rather selectively upon Adam Smith), whereas for Thomas Hobbes, sovereign individuals came together in order to acquire security in their everyday domestic life, that is for the avoidance of war or defence against external threats (Jennings, 1993). In particular, Adam Smith's influential view of the market as the means by which 'welfare' is produced via the 'hidden hand' is explained as the result of a large number of individuals coming together on the basis of private interests which they each rationally pursue through calculations of supply and demand, profit and utility, reckoned in the common denominator of price. Should this 'natural' sphere of economic relations be interfered with, more particularly by state intervention, disaster would ensue, resulting in loss of liberty and economic inefficiency. This shift can be illustrated by a brief reference to earlier understandings of the place of the household and its relationship to state and society. Whereas in Greek and Roman civilisations the public sphere was to be defended from the private household on which it depended, liberalism reversed this in that the private was the source of all ethical value and defined man's liberty and true self. Only such people were deemed sufficiently able to know their own interests and pursue them rationally, so as Jennings states, they (men) might enter the sphere of civil society as voters, as public opinion (including intelligentsia), as economic agents in their own right with power of disposal over money and property (1993). This understanding is in opposition to women as consumers (de Grazia, 1996), who were increasingly confined ideologically and materially to the sphere of the household, and who were considered as spending money earned by the head of the household. Hence the sphere which was private (civil society) was empowering for men but was a prohibited world for women and subordinate males who were increasingly confined to the household, not only through substantive changes in the means of production, but also by the accompanying embedding of dominant ideological structures. In this respect, Ruskin's well-known treatise 'Of Queen's Gardens' (1865), on the domestic and civic duties of Victorian women, mythical and idealised as these may be, is seen as the most articulate advocacy of nineteenth-century England's sharply differentiated gender roles. (Austin, 1987; Lloyd, 1995).

Exclusion from the newly constructed economic sphere had – and continues to have – direct material causes and consequences in relation to the distribution of resources by separating previous property forms from their social ties. Being confined to the private sphere of the household meant that power and independence, status and equality became a particularly male preserve which was directly related to having money and/or property. Ideological claims such as the perceived nature and associated role of women were solely related to social reproduction in the private sphere of the family and, as intimated earlier, were in direct opposition to the role and nature of men as actors in civil society. Such oppositions in turn reinforced the distinction between private/household and the sphere of the private/civil society, and were also bound up with a wide range of social distinctions and dichotomies. For instance, privacy is linked with

> The domestic, intimate and familial world, emotion rather than reason, affection rather than competition, nurture rather than manufacture, substantive values rather than instrumental reason, personal rather than monetary of material bonds. (Jennings, 1993: 83)

Although of course this is not a reflection of the real life of many groups and classes of women, it is clear that such social distinctions and dichotomies were a further reinforcement of the conceptual and material separation of production and finance, particularly in terms of its relationship to property, distancing it from its social ties, into the sphere of 'the economy' and civil society. Massey has argued that the limitation on women's mobility, in terms of identity and space, has been in some cultural contexts a crucial means of subordination. One of the most evident aspects of this joint control of spatiality and identity in the West is related to the culturally specific distinction between public and private so 'The attempt to confine women to the domestic sphere was both a specifically spatial control, and through that, a social control of identity' (1994: 178). In this respect, the possibility of women being economically active by having access to an independent income was itself a source of anxiety in that

> ... it is clear that the fact of escape from the spatial confines of the home is in itself a threat. ... And it was a threat in (at least) two ways: that it might subvert the willingness of women to perform their domestic roles and that it gave them entry into another, public, world – a life not defined by family and husband. (Massey 1994: 179–180)

This argument relating to the confinement to the domestic space poses interesting questions, not least in relation to the perhaps more autonomous position of women in productive economic roles, including as part of a household unit with a more equitable access to resources. But yet again, having access to an independent income does not in and of itself necessarily lead to the empowerment of women as can be seen with the contemporary discourse regarding micro-credit programmes (discussed in Chapter 7).

As implied above, Western culture in its construction of the relationship between masculinity and femininity and its fixedness assigns greater value to that which is associated with masculinity and lesser value to femininity. Since the terms are not independent of each other but form unequal, hierarchical relations, gendered conceptions of power produce gendered effects. In this respect, access and control to resources is a power relation and in the context of financial markets, access to finance and credit through formal markets continues to be a gendered power relation. Indeed the very perceptions of 'male' qualities based upon dichotomies such as rational/emotional, aggressive/passive, competitive/cooperative and detached/caring, risk-taking/risk averse have been seen as the essential characteristics of those who seek gain in contemporary financial markets – at least until recently! This construction of the male as rational economic agent and head of the household is partly counterposed with the construction of the female consumer as suggested earlier. Whilst the male, head of the household, infers productive activity within the private economic sphere, the role of consumer has been seen as a female pursuit but still placed within the confines of the private/family. This will be further developed in relation to financial and credit markets later but it is of note that the socially constructed characteristics upon which the female consumer is drawn are those which have circulated from the earliest times, and still on occasions are used to define the relationship of women to money and finance, that is, the frivolous, wasteful 'natural' tendencies of women. For instance, historically, Aristotle criticised Spartan women for their degeneracy, linking various elements in the decline of Sparta after 479 BC to their conspicuous prosperity. Pomeroy relates how King Ageis attempted to restore Lycugian discipline but reforms failed 'due to refusal of women to give up ease and luxury' and Athens anticipated the Roman tendency to connect vigour of the state with the virtue of the women, and political weaknesses with moral degeneracy, particularly women' (Pomeroy, 1975: 34–40). Centuries later Bailey cites a male critic who dismissed an anonymous female author's attack on coverture (*The hardships of the English laws in relation to wives*, 1735) by accusing her of transforming married women's legal exemptions from 'severe Pains and Penalties' into 'insults grievances and affronts'. He further explained that English wives did not merit more egalitarian property rights as in Roman civil law, 'because their inconstancy and extravagance required that they be protect[ed] from themselves' (published in 1736 in The Weekly Miscellany *and* the Gentleman's Magazine cited in Bailey, 2002: 352–353). Consumption, as Peiss (1998) has argued, is coded as a female pursuit '...frivolous and even wasteful, a form of leisure rather than productive work', but such constructions of a consumer identity obscures women's important contributions to economic and political life. Expressions such as 'Mrs Consumer' and 'born to shop' (Mail Online, 2007) suggest that women appear only on the receiving end of consumer culture but as Peiss contends, far from being a natural of inevitable phenomenon, this feminized image '...was rooted in a specific historical development' (1998). Here as elsewhere, woman's identity and her relegation to the private sphere of the household have been underpinned by wide acceptance of biological determinism. This has been a major barrier to establishing that unequal hierarchical relationships between men and women have been caused by social – and therefore historical – factors. As Mies has argued, one of the main problems is that not only the analysis, but

> ...also the tools of the analysis, the basic concepts and definitions, are affected – or rather infected – by biological determinism...such as the concepts of nature, of labour, of the sexual division of labour, of the family and of *productivity*.[11] (1999: 44)

As women's household and child care work progressively became seen as an extension of their physiology, particularly from the seventeenth century, the notion of the need to 'protect' women and children became increasingly vocal. In particular, the 'protection' of women was most notably extended to the aristocracy and emerging middle classes during the eighteenth and nineteenth centuries. Staves contends that it was only when the household could afford to dispense with women's economic input that ideological notions of 'protection' came into play (1990: 208). With shared ideologies of the role, nature and place of women, it is not surprising to see that as late as 1908 in the Supreme Court of the United States, the Justices, in stressing the special health needs of women and their dependent status' in Muller versus Oregon (in relation to limiting working hours for women in factories and laundries) justified disparate treatment under the law. 'The justices did not see women as equal competitors with men in the market place and thus accepted the necessity for protective legislation' (Ely, 1992: 104). Here 'protection' can also be seen as an euphemism for subordination and part of the labelling of women as irresponsible and lacking the necessary rationality to deal with matters of finance and enter the economic realm of men. However, as will be discussed later, women throughout the centuries have proved to be more than capable businesswomen in their own right, often working alongside their husbands in business or taking over responsibility when men were absent, not least during times of conflict.

These conceptual distinctions of the private world of the family/household from the public (state/politics), and more particularly with regard to finance the private (civil society/economics/the market) as constructed during the seventeenth and eighteenth centuries, were central to the material reorganisation of production and commerce, and so to finance and credit relations with the emergence of capitalism. Weber contended that there were a number of institutional forms which were inimical to 'the modern independence of capitalist enterprises', to a conduct detached from considerations other than the rational pursuit of profit. This is a crucial point to be understood in determining the gendered nature of finance:

> The modern rational organization of the capitalist enterprise would not have been possible without two other important factors in its development: the separation of business from the household, which completely dominates modern economic life, and closely connected with it, rational book-keeping. (M. Weber cited in Giddens, 1971: 21–22)

It is implicit in the phrase 'the modern independence of capitalist enterprises' that specific property relations are central to 'independence' as are social values which may be inimical to 'considerations *other than the rational pursuit of profit*'.[12] It is such social values inimical to capitalism, that is the rational pursuit of profit, which can be argued to be those most often associated with women, and which have been (in Mies's terms) infected by biological determinism. These social values, which previously may have been associated with men and women in relation to the reproduction of the household in the pre-modern era, become potentially subversive to capitalism in its early years. Such potential subversion then takes on a distinctly gendered aura which relates intimately to the changing nature of the distribution of shared resources from within the household for largely subsistence and reproductive purposes to that of the increasingly formalised extraction of financial resources (in terms of profit) out of the domestic sphere into that of the private/economic of civil society. Here there is a conjectural argument to be made, that in order for the expansion of capitalism to take place, those social values inimical to capitalism needed to be displaced from the economic sphere of profit accumulation (and men) to the sphere of social reproduction and subsistence (that is, women). Two different sets of values arose, one relating to the masculinised 'efficient' workings of formal markets and the other to values increasingly seen as essential to social reproduction and subsistence activities – and so inherently feminine.

It requires individualisation and alienation from earlier understandings of kinship and household to a form a household of 'the family' where specific roles are designated on a gendered basis. Although the unit of production was small and productivity low in the in pre-capitalist household all household members worked at productive tasks, although differentiated by age and sex (Anderson & Zinsser, 1990). Although the tasks may have been defined by gender, the household as an entity could be seen as an economic unit. The separation of business from the household during the rise of industrial capitalism, which required the spatial separation of the social reproduction and subsistence activities of the household, together with the feminised values required to support that order, from the productive business of making profit, the 'economic' (profit-making) became externalised and prioritised. This process not only increasingly saw the marginalisation of women from the sphere of more formal economic activity (Anderson & Zinsser, 1989; Clark, 1919; Wiesner-Hanks, 1998) but also necessitated the separation of household finances from those secured and confined via rational bookkeeping to the very largely male domain of the emerging economy. In other words, whereas the pre-capitalist household unit was perceived as a productive economic unit, with the emergence of industrial capitalism 'economic' activities were reconsigned to an external sphere and necessarily reconceptualised, leaving the household/family as only the site where reproductive/domestic activities took place. The growth of the market economy outside the household became increasingly formalised in such a way that a more limited meaning of the term 'economic' developed to encompass the production and exchange of commodities. This then became the domain of finance and financial activities, separated from the private feminised domain of the household by the device of rational bookkeeping. Nicholson contends that this ideal notion of the private nature of the household/family and woman's role within it, cannot be described as merely ideology since the lives of many middle-class women did conform to that idea, and when and where married women among the working class did not conform, it was the ideal of perceptions of married women's labour (1986: 127). In this respect, Maclean argues that subordinated behaviour should not necessarily be taken as evidence in itself of a belief in subordination on the part of the subordinated:

> ...although clearly, and as a matter of social reproduction, large-scale subordination might be expected to operate, as an outcome, more efficiently and smoothly to the extent that the members of the subordinated group do, as a matter of fact, hold to a belief in subordination. (1988: 58)

Although Nicholson focuses on contemporary understandings of the distinctiveness of family, state and economy as being mistaken, she asserts that these spheres of society, if understood as historical creations, are illuminating, since

> ...the point is not that industrialization and market forces had no effect on preindustrial values and practices; it is rather that the story is poorly understood as one where the causal arrow moves in only one direction. That...a nineteenth-century woman would become a prostitute to support the rest of her family is a story not only about the commercialisation of sex, but also about the persistence of familial loyalties in new contexts. This methodological

point becomes a political point in our own day as preindustrial values and practices of kinship and gender continue to affect market relations in the context of a political ideology which denies that possibility. According to this ideology, with the establishment of true equality of educational opportunity and the abolition of old prejudices about women's capabilities, the criteria of merit and effort alone determine women's participation in the economy. (1986: 127)

As the overwhelming majority of research indicates today (Oxfam, 2009; UNIFEM, 2005; World Bank, 2008b) despite educational opportunities and the disappearance of many, but alas not all, of the old prejudices in some societies, on the criteria of merit and effort alone women's participation in the economy is far from being on an equal basis to that of men. This then supports the argument that the transition from feudalism to capitalism was only partial – at least until the mid-twentieth century – in that there was a gendered character to this transition which has seen different gendered trajectories in the expansion of new relations on a now almost global scale. It is here that the 'level' playing field of liberalism can be seen to be decidedly less so for some in relation to others. Although liberalism is theoretically wide-ranging, economic liberalism has generally been associated with capitalism (Gill & Law, 1988: 41). Public goods – international security, monetary stability and an open international economy with relatively free and predictable ability to move goods, services and capital – are seen as desirable, supporting a vision of an international economic order which rests on the argument that economic relations through the market have the character of a positive-sum game. Within this vision, there will be potential for increased global economic welfare, although any increase may be unequally distributed. Politically, liberalism focuses on the relationship between the individual and the state where it aims to limit both the power and the functions of the state by upholding individual rights and the rule of law, leaving large areas of private life outside the direct control of the state. Economically, liberalism focuses on the freedom of agents to own property, make contracts and trade under a common framework of law and regulation. In both spheres, social arrangements are seen as forms of mutual advantage through the coordination of a set of individual rights, law-based political order and the institutions of a market economy (Hardin, 1999). It is a universal doctrine in that it holds that all human beings, by virtue of a common capacity for autonomous rational action, are capable of enjoying similar liberties: it is a doctrine of equality in that it postulates 'a common humanity in virtue of a shared rational capacity' (Freeden, 1996: 159). However, where liberalism sees the emergence of 'the market' in terms of universal welfare and efficient allocation of scarce resources, it is blind to the implications of the historical reconstruction and separation of the public (state), the private (civil society) and private (household) as being intimately related to the maldistribution of resources, including financial ones, on a gendered basis.

The discussion so far has indicated that the emergence of the market was part of a gendered process, and is not compatible with the assumptions of neo-classical economics and liberalism which assert that an ahistorical level playing field exists upon which a harmonious market system operates, directed by an 'invisible hand', within which households, firms and individuals exercise free choice. It is also the point where a deeper consideration of property forms and the implications for gender needs to be undertaken in order that the present gendered structure of global finance can be exposed, by relating it to changes in the definition of forms of property and rights in the early development of capitalism.

3
Property and Gender: Irrational Women and Rational Men

Marxist theorists refer to feudalism and the type of society and economy characterised by serfdom, as generally succeeding the early economic systems based on slavery:

> The means of production and of exchange ... were generated in feudal society. At a certain stage in the development of these means of production and exchange.... The feudal relations of property became no longer compatible with the already developed productive forces; they became so many fetters. (Marx & Engels, 1958)

Marx contended that concepts such as property were not universal in that what is meant by property varied between societies as well as within any particular society at any particular historical period. Sayer supports this view of historical specificity in that

> In previous forms of society, neither individuals as owners nor their property had their modern exclusivity or simplicity. Property did not even appear as a simple relation of persons and things. Who owned what, or even what it meant to be an owner, were by no means clear cut; the very terms at issue are anachronistic. (1987)

Sayer's observation, although not intended as an explanation of gendered access to resources, does contain within it the notion that although men still had an advantage over women, women were by no means excluded from ownership or access to property. However, a closer exploration of property will expose the gendered underpinnings of the property and rights discourse.

Property, an integral aspect of both domestic-group organisation and the economic and political spheres of social life, is a contested social relation since it embraces ideological constructions of the value, content and use of property, as well as the socio-cultural context within which these constructions operate. Various understandings of political economy have assigned different priorities to property and its distribution in that it can be seen as a factor or means of production, and so central to the ways in which production and distribution of resources are organised; it can also be understood as a central goal of much economic activity in the accumulation of property in terms of natural resources and the products which are then transformed into commodities. Like other sources of power, property has been distributed in different ways at various moments of social history. In what ever manner a society distributes property, those who control and have access to that object wield power over those who are propertyless, so it can be seen that through the medium of property rights, individuals construct social relations in the allocation and securing of resources (Burch, 1998: 12). In terms of encompassing ideological constructions of the value, content and use of property, private property – to include finance and credit – can be said to constitute an ideological constraint upon women, over and above the explicitly ideological political theories of Hobbes, John Locke and Mills. In this respect, relations involved in the concept of 'property' can be seen to be '... not primarily as a relation between people and things, but between people and people and thus it is a social relation' (Whitehead, 1984: 128). However, by constructing private property as a 'thing' outside of social relations, and therefore natural, these social relations are rendered invisible and so gendered relations are reproduced.

Further, property is a contested social relation since property forms do not have universal applicability and will vary both between societies and within any particular society over time. This diversity at times is compatible with the dominant hegemonic form of property relations so long as it does not disturb the basic structural (hegemonic) conditions, and at other times is subversive to it. An example of this may be that identified by Wallerstein in his contention that the tension for capitalism involved in the move from kinship social relations to those of production and reproduction, existed within the household, and more specifically, in the shift from households to 'the family' (Wallerstein, 1992). For instance, the tension is the supposed separation of alienated and commodified relations outside the household, in the economic realm of the market/civil society, whilst within the household a different set of relations is expected to exist based on altruism, a responsibility of care and nurturing and shared resources involved in the social and general reproduction of the household. (Wallerstein, 1992: 7). This reinforces the tendency not only to a gendered division of labour – one based on altruism and one on profit – but also to a dismissal of the idea of any social or altruistic relations within market transactions. It then follows that any attempt at disruption of existing property relations can be seen only as a political matter which involves conflicts of interests so that ultimately patterns in changes in property entitlement or ownership affects society generally.

The roots of such an understanding can be seen in the emergence of property rights, understood as rules governing resources and social relations, which became dominant from the seventeenth century onwards, and which forms the foundations and conceptual frameworks of the modern world and international system. Specific understandings of these rights in the seventeenth century, more particularly within England, led to the division of the concept of property into landed and mobile forms and was instrumental in creating the conceptual foundation for a state system (real, territorial property) and capitalism (mobile, intangible property) (Burch, 1998: viii). This process of commodification of property forms can be understood as a gendered process, which cut across class, leading to a maldistribution and gendered control of financial resources, the impact of which has continuing consequences on the organisation and distribution of finance and credit upon women's lives in differentiated localities within the global political economy.

The changes in 'property' from feudal to capitalist forms of organisation, including those in relation to finance and credit, required the subordination of certain social relations so in this process, women lost kinship/traditional claims to property but continued to be transmitters of property, wealth and status (Laurence, 1994/1996: 18) and, as some feminists claim, were treated as property themselves (Peterson, 1997;[13] Pettman, 1996). The focus here is on the changes from property forms associated with social relations to those of ownership/alienation of property – private property rights – so that the gendered process of that alienated property forms and rights passed into male ownership or control. Such changes enabled those male individuals with the means to access unencumbered (capital) assets, status and political resources. This form of ownership of property enabled an extra dynamic to investment potential and the requirements for capital expansion. For example, reinvestment of profits would be secured to the individual entity, such as an individual or firm, who invested, but furthermore, these changes in property rights fuelled innovation in financial products and mechanisms, including sophisticated forms of credit, providing valuable funds for the urbanisation of industrial society as well as investment overseas.

In this respect, Western concepts of property are highly specific and associated with the development of capitalism, which assigned the right of the individual to utilise resources through 'private ownership'. This understanding of private property has given rise to political and economic assertions within the liberal tradition which became internationalised and promoted on a world scale mediated not only by states and firms but by international institutions such as the IMF, World Bank and World Trade Organisation (WTO). This is in opposition to earlier forms of property, including land, which were seen as socially essential in terms of use as well as in terms of productive value (exchange) and closely associated with consumption rather than for reinvestment and accumulation.

In the early seventeenth century, patriarchy was the dominant world-view with all places in society assigned in terms of the natural order of things. By the end of this same century, a new understanding of human nature and of social and political organisation was emerging whereby contract and individual choice supplanted birth and divine designation as crucial factors in social and political orders (Butler, 1991: 71). A foundational principle of liberalism is taken from Locke's argument that personal liberty is dependent upon private property, which must be secured under the rule of law. Writing at a time of political and religious upheaval, Locke sought to analyse the nature of government and justify the events leading to the Glorious Revolution of 1688, asserting that legitimate government was based on a compact between people and their rulers. Of particular importance was the theory of property rights, where private property existed under natural law before the creation of political authority. Property ownership was consequently identified with the preservation of political liberty. Once acquired by *him*, however, the rights belonged entirely to *him* although tempered in its execution by every *man's* God-given right to the minimum necessary for existence (Locke in Tully, 1993). This is in opposition to classical conceptions of property, which saw the ownership of land and arms as the condition of citizenship and political participation:[14]

> To own property was to occupy a distinctive, virtuous political-moral sphere, the polity and only in the *oikos* did property suggest production and exchange as well as identify subordinate gender, classes, and status ... (Burch, 1998: 27)

Locke's definition of property hinges on the addition of personal labour, making ownership an intimate act of creation perceived as personal liberty, which assigned the right of the individual use through 'private ownership' and embodied, according to Macpherson:

> ... individual (or corporate) right to exclude others from the use, or benefit of something [and] ... a right in or to material things rather than right to a revenue. (1978: 86)

so that there is

> ... firstly the legal separation of subject and object, and secondly the legal separation of subject from subject in his or her capacity to have control over the disposal of a thing which has been designated his or her property. (Whitehead, 1984: 123)

It is in this process where the gendered nature of shifting property relations becomes apparent, in that in the eighteenth and nineteenth centuries it was men who increasingly had the right by law and 'custom' to exclude others (in particular women) from the use, or benefit of something, even the property of women themselves. Accordingly in liberal thought, in order that values of freedom and individualism can be achieved, people must be understood to have property in themselves, that is ownership in themselves, which enables them to exclude others from the use of their abilities and labour as well as in the goods they acquire in a free economic market. A 'thing', then, becomes 'property' only within a specific social and historical context, and ownership of which by the individual (as opposed to communal property) is then subscribed by law. Mary Murray encapsulates the gendered nature of this process by stating

> Feudal property was transformed into individualistic ownership. Property became a right to objects or commodities, material things. In capitalist societies property involves rights of legal individuals to exclude others. Give the long historical patriarchal structuring of property relations…it is unsurprising that the individualistic nature of capitalist relations has often involved the assertion of the rights of men over those women…. Both the ideology of the male breadwinner and women's exclusion from citizenship added weight to the subordination of women as daughters and wives. (1995: 128)

The implications of these understandings of the nature of property forms are central to the redistribution of resources, not only within the household, but in respect of relations with the state. Locke in particular was focusing on the theoretical state of nature, the rule of law and political sovereignty, and reflected the historical, social and gendered context from which he emerged. As such, he was part of a much wider movement in Europe, critical of mercantilism and providing fertile ground from which future political and economic theorists would draw, not least scholars of IR.

An illustration of the historical, social and gendered context of Locke's writing can be seen where although he suggests that a wife can own property in her own right, and even envisages the possibility of divorce, in his treatment of marriage he stresses that wives should be subject to men. He states 'generally the laws of mankind and customs of nations have ordered it so and there is, I grant, a foundation in nature for it', in that the will of the husband prevails in nature because he is 'the abler and stronger' (cited by Pateman, 1988: 52–53). As Pateman argues, on the one hand according to Locke, women are naturally subject to men, and on the other they are expected to enter into a marriage which secures their subordination. This, she states, is where the full theoretical significance of the separation of what Locke calls paternal power from political power becomes apparent, since it was during the genesis of civil society that the sphere of natural subjection was separated out as non-political (1988: 93). However, what Pateman and other feminist political theorists (such as Coole, 1986, 1993; Okin, 1979) tend to understate or not make clear is the crucial importance of this sphere of natural subjection in terms of its separation from the economic. This is important in many ways, but not least in terms of Locke's focus on self-interest as an overriding element of human nature, and as a result a central force in social organisation. This was reinforced by Smith's critique of mercantilism in that he proposed that self-interest could be utilised in a natural manner, serving everyone's needs. Needless to say, self-interest as an overriding element of human nature has been critiqued extensively both within feminist research and within critical theory more generally as not serving everyone's needs (Folbre & Hartman, 1988; Sequino et al., 1996).

The basis of liberal theory of property rights, then, was based on the assumption that a communal property or a 'no-ownership' system would give way to private property if there was an effective means of replacing less efficient forms of ownership with more efficient ones. Since efficiency was perceived to be maximised when resources were in the hands of those who would pay most for them, it is a theory based on classical liberal economic suppositions that the institution of property emerged in response to the need for clear signalling in market relations and so of satisfying wants, in terms of desires, rather than needs in terms of necessities. In other words, it is concerned more with efficient allocation of resources, than the just and equitable social allocation of resources in relation to reproduction and as a result has been critiqued by feminist economists for its overwhelming reliance on mathematical models of individual choice, to the exclusion of other approaches. In this respect, these models '... reflect masculinist biases rooted in Cartesian divisions between rationality and embodiment' which should be concerned not 'merely with goods and services traded in the market but with all necessities and conveniences that sustain and improve life' (Nelson, 1993: 14). The underlying assumption in classical and neoclassical theory is that scarcity requires choice, all choices entail an opportunity cost and that in this process, people are 'rational' decision-makers who make choices based on their own self-interest.

Here 'efficiency' is seen to be the prime gain or value. However, as stated by May and Sell

> Although efficiency may be valued in economic transactions it is only one, and not necessarily the most important aspect to the emergence of property as a social institution. In abstract terms, we may explain property rights in terms of gains from co-ordination and cooperation. However, in the actual history of social relations particular property institutions emerged from much more diverse circumstances, including the exercise of economic power, the impact of technological change, *and shifts in ideas about who could own what.*[15] (May & Sell, 2001: 471)

In this should be included shifts in ideas about *who* could control what and why, since women may have been legally entitled to *own* property, particularly in its newly emergent forms, but control of such property lay elsewhere. Ownership here is as characterised by A. M. Honoré

> ...the right to possess, the right to use, the right to manage, the right to the income of the thing, the right to the capital, the right to security, the rights or incidents of transmissibility and absence of term, the prohibition of harmful use, liability to execution and the incident of residuality. (as cited in Ryan, 1987: 54)

Within classical liberal economic theory, the assertion and 'naturalisation' of the individualisation of these rights in effect bestowed these individual rights of ownership and control of property upon men, and so privileged these over women's entitlement, which was very largely embodied within tradition, culture and common law. In this context, these rights need to be distinguished from entitlement in that the latter does not necessarily assume overriding ownership. It can therefore be associated with, for instance, various members of a kinship or communal group's entitlement to those shared resources required for the material reproduction of human life. In other words, a necessary part of the expansionary dynamics of the emergence, then expansion, of capitalism required a transformation from an entitlement to resources – including financial – for use in the material production of life for a community or household, to those of proprietary rights for men. Whereas liberal theory presupposed and confirmed the 'natural' right of (private) property and related it to notions of liberty and the individual, in pre-capitalist or other forms of society, property as a resource was generally perceived as kinship property – a communal resource and provider of needs – not as private property with 'rights' of ownership and individualised rights of exchange. These individualised rights of exchange then became naturalised as outlined by Ryan, in that

> Grotius in the seventeenth-century and Robert Nozick in the twentieth ... hold that the 'natural right to property' implies that when we acquire something over which others have no right of ownership we get an outright freehold in it. (1987: 65)

Ryan then directs us to the modern conception of 'fully fledged' property, which ultimately leads to a perception of a natural right to make free use of whatever is *legitimately* possessed or acquired, which is not infringed by the competition of others, whatever the impact on welfare. *Legitimate* possession here is, however, not only a matter of history as Ryan suggests but also a matter of gender. However, the legitimation of the inequitable distribution of resources on a gendered basis is not raised in this otherwise comprehensive book on property. In his stated objective of exploring connections between property and freedom, Ryan does not raise the seemingly obvious question of the naturalisation of the exclusion of women from the historical right and consequences of lack of direct access to private ownership of resources, including land, and those concerned with finance and banking, and the ownership of the means of production. Historically, the legitimation of rights to property – or indeed the legitimation of dispossession of entitlement to property (alienation) as a necessary part of that development – was not only a process relating to class formation, modes of production and division of labour, but also one of gendered assumptions and practices which dispossessed many women of their direct entitlement to resources for use as an integral activity of community relations. In other words, acquisitions of rights ('the right to possess, the right to use, the right to manage ...' as Honoré characterised above), as legitimated by wider political, legal and ideological social forces over time, took precedence over women's traditional kinship claims. This legitimation of rights to private property can be seen as a necessary part of the development and theoretical separation of state and market, politics and economics, public and private, private/economic sphere and private/women-household and the family sphere, production and reproduction and the division of labour. It was promoted as part of the process of the 'efficient' distribution of resources within the theoretically separated economic/private sphere of male activity and so became naturalised as something separate and apart from the political.

Although the roots of natural rights theory go back before Locke, his writings on perceptions of personal liberty being dependent upon private property, secured under the rule of law, are deeply implicated in the emergence and 'economic' conclusion of the ideology of the free market. Pateman's interpretation of Locke brings to the fore the gendered ideological underpinnings of early liberalism. His support of the patriarchal structuring of property relations is apparent in that he specifies that women were not to count as individuals who have a say in the social contract, since married women cannot own their own persons. Therefore, by this account they cannot acquire property by 'mixing their labour' with unowned resources. Consequently, Pateman argues, sexual difference is political difference, the difference between freedom and subjection (1988: 6). Coole cites Locke's explanation that where 'the hand is used to the plough and the spade, the head is seldom elevated to sublime notions' but must content itself with 'plain propositions, and a short reasoning about things familiar to their minds', and 'more nearly allied to their daily experience', suggesting that this is even more true of 'the other sex' (1986: 86). Coole maintains that by this the marriage contract, which excluded most women from command over the family property, simultaneously excluded them from the means and signs of substantial rationality. Therefore women would be destined to be ruled not because they are naturally irrational, but because their status and 'natural' role in the family were inimical to the development of reason (1986: 86–88).

Yet, as Coole and others have argued, as far as liberalism is concerned, market relations first appeared in a society where there was a rough economic equality – or perhaps better expressed as rough economic status – between the sexes and this could have provided the basis in the seventeenth century for a theory of sexual equality (1986: 132). Instead liberal theorists proffered new justifications for women's exclusion from political and economic life, which of course included *direct* access to the new forms of resources such as finance and credit. These justifications in turn reinforced women's poor economic opportunities by legitimising and advocating their dependence on male breadwinners. Locke's definition of property depending upon the addition of personal labour so that ownership becomes 'an act of creation' is contentious since women are then excluded both in theoretical and concrete terms from personal liberty as it is defined in relation to private property. Further, reproduction is excluded from 'acts of creation'. In order that values of freedom and individualism necessary to the formation of private property and so the free market system might be achieved, it required the exclusion of others from the use of their abilities and labour. The assumption of values of freedom and individualism within liberal ideology may be relevant to production for the market under conditions of individualised rights of exchange and capital accumulation, but it precludes more inclusive types of ownership/property/resources as, for instance, prevailing within social groups such as household or kinship, and more particularly within the more general experiences of women in the roles they undertake or which are imposed upon them. This had important implications for access to credit by women at a time when innovation in credit mechanisms was being honed to the requirements of the market, rather than the traditional needs of the reproduction of the household. When material requirements for life are inequitably distributed and that distribution is based on gender, women not only lose entitlements to property for use as a sustainable resource, but when these rights to property can be transformed into wealth-producing resources outside the household, women lose access to this process too. When wealth is transformed into power – political, economic and/or social – and women have inequitable access to wealth, then with or without formal political rights, women lose equitable access to political, economic and social processes.

The gendered impact of shifts in property forms

Susan Staves, in her work on changes in the law and married women's separate property during the seventeenth, eighteenth and nineteenth centuries in England, states '...when large social structures change, provisions for women change to fit the new structures' (Staves, 1990: 208). Assumptions and practices for women in this period adapted to the new requirements of state formation, wealth creation and accumulation. In parallel with critiques of realism where the 'national' interest is perceived to mask and legitimise the interests of particular interest groups, so Stave argues that assertions of 'the public interest' served no unitary whole but sought to mask the diversity of interests, including class and gender, in order to legitimise the interests of particular groups (1990: 208). This can also be related to Massey's observation that the question at issue in times of disruption '...is their [capitalism and patriarchy] mutual accommodation and the kinds of synthesis which result' (Massey, 994: 181). Perceptions of 'public interest' in the eighteenth century included having a system of property law that ensured title to property, the public interest in promoting the alienability of land, and the public interest in promoting families and good behaviour (Brewer, 1995: 181–182). (This notion of good behaviour had direct implications for accessing credit, particularly in the early modern period, as set out on pages 101–103). From a liberal approach, changes from medieval minimal alienability to modern notions of maximised alienability were seen as representing progress, a consequence of which would be a general increase in wealth and so an 'inevitable' improvement in the condition of women. However, although there may have been a general increase in wealth through new forms of finance and banking, women as a whole were further excluded from direct access to and control of these new resources in that the commodification of financial property, as with other types of property, was not only conducted by and for the benefit of particular groups of men in banking and finance, but by men – husbands, fathers and brothers – on behalf of women.

This gradual exclusion of women from financial activity was also facilitated by the emergence of a 'new male heroic image', which had profound effects on the lives of women, first in the towns and, by the nineteenth century, all across Europe (Anderson & Zinsser, 1989). To function as the provider, the man of the family was given new responsibilities, including being responsible for the protection of the lives of women, and to meet those responsibilities, men of the towns advocated attitudes and supported laws to protect their means of livelihood. 'Protection' in most instances meant limitations and regulations that affected women far more than men, with gendered restrictions underpinned by '...the age-old assumption of female incompetence and its traditional corollary, the need for male guardianship' (1989: 394). Anderson and Zinsser concluded that in the world of emerging commercial capitalism, women of the towns '...would in law and practice be protected and provided for by men, but at an awesome price: the loss of their potential and actual autonomy' (1989: 394). Jennings also reflects this loss by arguing

> The romantic language of chivalrous 'protection' of the wife under coverture in common law, the presumed 'partnership' in owning (though not in managing) marital assets under the law of community property gives an illusion of beneficent treatment of wives while leaving decisions about their actual economic welfare firmly in the hands of their husbands. While many husbands no doubt have acted in ways that ensure a rough equality of material welfare, many other couples have no doubt found the argument 'I earned it so I get to choose how to spend it' influential in decision making. (1993: 6)[16]

Although there may be an apparent ambiguity in 'the age-old assumption of female incompetence' in Anderson's statement above, tending towards patriarchal attitudes being a constant throughout history, here the claim is related to the possession by men of new forms of property which were necessarily alienated from communal access, for instance within the household. It was a process by which alienated property and its ability to be commodified and converted into liquid capital for investment increasingly became regarded as a resource for profit, as opposed to a resource for need. In other words, it is a separation in very large part between the needs of the household/family/ women and the needs of the market/individual/man. One aspect of this 'mutual accommodation' (of capitalism and patriarchy) was the increasing dominance of specific forms of private property which took on individualised rights of male ownership, as illustrated by a gendered evaluation of the statement by Weber regarding the necessary changes required for capitalism. These included '...separation of business from the household, which completely dominates modern economic life, and closely with it rational book-keeping' (Weber cited in Giddens, 1971: 21–22). Generally within IR literature, it is usually argued that changes in property forms constrained and/or dispossessed many groups or classes in society whilst empowering others, but rarely if ever is it argued that it was women as a category that in every class lost direct access to forms of authority over financial resources during this period. Weber's statement is particularly relevant in suggesting that the advent of modern rational organisation enabled business and finance to be separated both conceptually and materially from the household (Giddens, 1971: 21–22). It was through the mechanism of rational bookkeeping that certain sources of finance were separated from their social – and consequently gendered – ties. Further, increasing legal, ideological and socio-cultural constraints on women meant that although investment and commercial activity led to increased prosperity for in particular mostly male groups and classes over time, it also directly impacted on the security of social reproduction within the household. Shifts in legal constraints meant that married women became increasingly constrained in access to formal credit and financial resources whereas previously such resources had been very largely accessed and mediated through social relations of community or kinship. In other words, in order for capitalism to become established and expand it required the transformation of previous assumptions and practices, which crucially included those associated with property forms, integral to which were general social – and thus gendered – relations of access and control. The separation of business and finance became objectified as being separate and apart from the social ties of the household and increasingly under the 'protective' mantle of male control. Together with increasing state endorsement – not least through growing bureaucratisation of the male as head of the household – together with the common law constraint of *femme coverte* and the reconceptualisation of public and private, perceptions of the role and place of women increasingly excluded them from emerging financial and credit markets.

It can therefore be seen that whereas changes in England and Europe's economies during this period of transition led to increased opportunities for many men, particularly with the development of the commercial capitalist town, women experienced new kinds of disability and vulnerability. As Anderson and Zinsser's research indicates, at first women in towns continued to enjoyed access to craft associations and participation in new professions and new commercial enterprises but gradually these opportunities were closed to them. Anderson and Zinsser state that privileged women in the merchant and banking elite lost legal privileges in that in the changed economic circumstances, a woman's expected marriage became part of a family's business considerations. As part of raising credit and finance, marriage might mean a financial alliance, access to a craft, the dowry and a widow's portion a gain or loss in the account books (Anderson & Zinsser, 1989: 392–393). Capital and property became the subject of royal law and even wealthy women, whether married or widowed, lost the ability to act independently except in the most constrained situations. Although the common law concept of coverture made the wife a dependent of the husband (at least until the Married Women's Property Acts of the 1880s, see page 92), communal property, in theory, recognised the wife as a partner in the marriage. This was closely related to the wife being recognised before the eighteenth century as a partner in the productive activities carried on within the marriage. Adoption of communal property principles may then be taken as recognition of the value of household production, at least when comparing contributions to the marriage between husband and wives, but the power to manage the communal property was still vested in the husband (Babcock, 1975: 604–613). The married couple was the 'simple community of work, the elementary unit' in pre-industrial households with the contribution of each spouse seen as vital for the creation and survival of the family: 'Each partner brought to the union either material resource or the ability to help support each other' (Tilley & Scott, 1978: 43). However, during the transition to a capitalist economy, the norms and traditional rights of women's were increasingly questioned.

Irrational women and rational men

'Women as clogs to progress was the an eighteenth-century lawyer's characterisation of women's common law right to dower (cited in Staves, 1990: 203) and reflects the perception at that time that earlier common law rights were obstacles to alienability, thus interfering with the process of capital accumulation through commercial and financial ventures. Investment as a means of nurturing economic growth had been hampered by the lack of financial mechanisms to facilitate savings being diverted, from either hoarding or direct consumption, into productive investment. Economic development depended on the creation of an economic surplus as well as a transfer of such surplus from savers to producers (Braudel, 1982: 164). The emergence of private property in this process and its relationship to enabling the value of seemingly immobile capital assets to become mobile required the elimination of 'clogs' or 'the legal separation of subject and object' which in this case involved the removal of the personal rights of women – such as dower rights of life-security in tenure – to resources which were then replaced with annuities and other investments (perhaps the beginning of a market in financial services). In other words, traditional rights to material security in property for use were replaced with annuities and other investments – monetary and financial forms of 'security' – where women received limited income, as in interest on capital whereas the capital asset (initially land) remained with the husband or guardian (Staves, 1990: 32). This development was part of the changes in, and expectations of, finance and monetary forms which took place during the transition from feudalism to agrarianism then industrial capitalism. Whereas in the seventeenth century land ownership was the more exclusive form of wealth, closely associated with status and political power, at the end of the century and the beginning of the eighteenth century, new forms of wealth were emerging, including the development of the mortgage market and the invention of government funds. In particular, mortgages and government funds were considered 'safe' investments for women, yet dowry in land was considered a more valuable and secure form of security for a woman than a dowry in capital. With the transition from land to capital dowries, power over money was given to the husband – through common law mechanisms such as *femme coverte* – and it was then incorporated with his own and effectively limited a woman's control of her wealth (Anderson & Zinsser, 1989: 3). One minor exception to this related to widows but even then there were limits. For instance, the Dower Act of 1833 regularised the process whereby new commodities, such as stock and bank annuities, replaced land as major ingredients of wealth, not least limiting widows' rights to land but giving them equivalents in new forms of wealth. This change was viewed as an erosion of women's property rights as widows were entitled only to an equitable jointure in their husband's estate. Yet through their repositioned status as *femme sole,* widows were prevented from amassing great amounts of wealth, although they did regain legal power over the property they brought to the marriage (Staves, 1990: 216).

These transformations in property relations within the private/economic sphere of the male were crucial to the development of capitalism in Britain during the eighteenth century, enabling liquid mobile capital and credit to be raised for investment in commercial and industrial enterprises. Indeed, Staves makes the point that sharp distinctions were made between the interest of the 'family' (understood as economic interests) and the interests of women who were taken to be individuals competing against the family interest, rather than integral and necessary parts of the family (Staves, 1990). Traditional rights, which were intended to safeguard the security of women and future generations, were replaced by financial 'securities', thus not only commodifying aspects of personal security but allowing liquid assets to be raised on now-private property which then could be used, for instance, in the process of industrialisation. These processes were paralleled with the changing assumptions about the position of women based on what were constructed to be women's 'natural' roles within the household and social reproduction. Production was then redefined so as to exclude women's traditional economic activities from being transferred into what was being constructed as the male domain of civil society/the formal market sector. These roles became institutionalised, embodied in legislative enactments of public policy and judicially sanctioned. However, the traditional combination of women's productive and economic activities for many continued to take place in what was becoming to be known as informal and disorderly markets, including networks of credit and finance.

By themselves, transformation of forms of property might suggest advantages in the replacement of women's entitlement to land with entitlements to other and newer forms of financial property, since shifts from medieval minimal alienability to that of modern maximised alienability are presented as progressive and advantageous to all. But such commodification processes, aligned with the increasing acceptance of liberal political and economic ideology, of efficiency and free choice, are laden with gendered significance, not least replacing more secure forms of well-being with those more vulnerable to risk and loss. As Nelson argued so concisely, in general models of free individual choice are not adequate to analyse

behaviour fraught with issues of dependence, interdependence, tradition and power (1993: 6). Women, with perhaps the exception of
widows, did not have individual choice in that they did not have
direct access to or control of these new financial securities and property, more generally since with the rise of the formal economy, transactions were increasingly mediated by and between men. Even single
women with property who had some degree of control faced significant social and ideological barriers to direct participation in financial activities. More generally, women as a group were subsequently
left in highly dependent relationships and involved in a web of inter-
dependency as carers and providers of last resort – a role which for a
significant proportion of the women in the world today, continues.

In terms of the previous analysis, any assumption of a liberal 'level
playing field' becomes deeply suspect or impossible to uphold since
the inequitable distribution of assets on a gendered, and indeed class,
basis has since become replicated on a worldwide basis through the
incorporation of certain values and assumptions embedded within
the market economy and, more particularly here, global finance.
Capitalism and liberal ideology have the ability to dominate and disrupt traditional or customary methods or systems of resource allocation, including financial, in different localities which may have
offered a more emancipatory choice for women and indeed men.
This gaping chasm in the overwhelming maldistribution of or access
to property for women as a result of structural changes, more particularly in the seventeenth and eighteenth centuries, has been overlooked by most political theorists. An example here is Ryan whose
lack of curiosity regarding theory and this maldistribution of access
to and control of property for women is underlined in the following quote, which also emphasises the surely unintended (by Ryan)
nature of the process by which women became dispossessed. In this
respect Ryan reflects the gendered nature of much of the property
and rights discourse. In setting out his understanding as to why liberal theory disregards questions of initial distribution, he states

> As explanation, all that [economic theory of property rights]
> says is that the way property rights have developed and *the way
> they have been transferred from one man to another* is at any rate
> frequently best explained by the need to make the most effi-
> cient use of resources. It is, so to speak, not the theory's business

if some people have very few resources and some people not. (Ryan, 1987: 112)[17]

Indeed Stave's comments explicitly echo the above in that the inventors of new legal rules between 1660 and 1833

> ...were motivated more by desires to facilitate the transmission of significant property from male to male and to ensure a level of basic protection for women and young children than they were by an interest in increasing the autonomy of married women. (1990: 221)

As such this is surely a defect of liberal history in that any legal changes allowing married women to become 'autonomous' owners of property did not notably empower married women. The very rules that conferred ownership on women gave them a kind of ownership different from that suggested in a legal property regime in that women were entitled to the right to profit from capital, but not control over capital or the power to alienate capital. For example, Davidoff and Hall cite evidence in the nineteenth century of the increasing use of annuities, either for life or fixed periods with conditions attached as a reasonably (but not always) secure income. The majority of recipients were women, but

> ...the type of annuity was a type of income even more carefully controlled by the donor and his representatives, since unlike the trust, the recipient did not have a claim on the capital but solely on the income. (1987: 212)

In other words, the characteristics of ownership as cited by Honoré in that the acquisition of property may be said to limit the freedom of non-owners '*inter alia*, other personas are not at liberty to use, consume, alter or otherwise deal with whatever it is without the owner's leave' (Ryan, 1987: 78–79) were considerably restricted.

From an analysis of the evolution of private property rights, it is clear this was a gendered as well as class process. Women lost autonomy when their entitlement to resources under kinship relations was handed over to the individual male head of the household in the form of private property to control, manage or invest. Alienation of

property changes the social relationship and individualises ownership. Women in this context lost authority and shared expectations
of control. Liberal theory, on the other hand, perceives the acquisition of property rights as creating freedom, enhancing individual autonomy and as a liberating force from natural constraints of
various kinds. This has supplied the basis for the modern defence
of property '...as an aid to pluralism and dispersion of power and
political liberty' (Ryan, 1987: 79). Marx contrasted the freely acting
individual of capitalism with 'identical' rights in relation to other
individuals, with the feudal person embedded in his social relations
and a particular set of social statuses. Within Marxist approaches, the
changing relationship between property forms and political authority can be understood to be directly related to economic organisation. So it can also be argued that the acquisition of rights to private
property limited, constrained and subordinated the freedom of non-
owners, and in every group of non-owners, gender considerations
limited the options even further. The state is centrally implicated,
in that historically liberal theory dictates that it is the state's duty to
protect the law of contract and private property rights. This process
and those related to it can be said to have removed women from direct rights to financial property and the full benefits which may have
accrued to them since the relegation of women historically to the
private domain of the household, under the 'protection' of the male
head of the household in effect was one of the ways in which women
were excluded from direct involvement in formal financial markets.
As Staves has stated, society seemed to have succumbed '...to a bourgeois illusion that there can be a clear separation on the one hand
of the public and economic sphere, and the other, private domestic
sphere...advocated by 18th century advocates of domesticity' (1990:
221–223). This distancing of women from the emerging financial
markets is again reflected by Davidoff and Hall:

> The same forces which favoured the rise of the private company
> and ultimately the business corporation, the development of
> public accountability and more formal financial procedures also
> shifted the world of women even further from the power of the
> active market. (1987: 279)

4
Emergence of Gendered Credit and Financial Institutions

In terms of global processes, Marchand has stated, '...spaces and practices associated with so-called masculine values, not only maybe more accessible to certain types of men, but are likely to project a certain image of power and to be associated with the exercise of power' (2000: 219). Not only are the spaces and practices associated with global finance heavily embedded by so-called masculine values, but financial markets are seen as a particularly powerful dynamic in the global economy. Most, if not all, understandings of the rise of systems of finance and banking have emerged from a masculinised approach, where the state and state formation, and/or modes of production, provide the central focal point of analysis (for instance, Braudel, 1979, 1982; Brenner, 1977; Landes, 1969). These narratives and analyses, although varying in their explanations of causal consequences, set out how from the earliest centuries of long-distance trade, nodes of power were connected by centres of financial activity stretching across cultures and civilisations. For instance, the earlier period of the Holy Roman Empire was seen as an attempt to create a politically unified Christian empire which was counterbalanced by the system of social and economic relations which developed within it. Feudalism arose out of the coalescence of a ruler giving his subordinates grants and rights of land in repayment for gold and in exchange for military services. Lands were not granted outright but awarded as a contract between lord and vassal, and as such there was a social world of overlapping claims and powers in that the estates were exploited economically by the vassal lord who in turn utilised and exploited the labour of a dependent peasantry tied to the land.

Authority and power were transparent in these narratives, the political and economic a fused entity, and society was bound by ties of reciprocal obligation, not divine right, with rival centres of power emerging that had very different systems of rules such as the towns and cities which fell outside the feudal system. These centres developed different social and political structures dominated by trade and manufacture and were connected by centres of financial activity. Consequently banks arose out of the business of dealing in foreign money necessitated by the activities of traders who frequented the great medieval continental fairs (Braudel, 1979, 1982; Landes, 1969; Pierenne, 1937). With the expansion of European trade in the Middle Ages, the first 'international' (perhaps better described as 'inter-city state') banks emerged in Florence as a result of Florentine merchants financing wool workers who imported wool from Spain, England and Africa. As a consequence, agents of the Florentine bankers, the Bardi and Peruzzi, moved to London where they lent money to finance the kings' wars (Sampson, 1981). For Landes it was the rise of trade which dissolved the subsistence economy of the medieval manor and generated the cities and towns which provided the political and economic cultural nodes of a new society. This view, which can perhaps be related to a 'natural and harmonious' rise of a market economy, focuses on entrepreneurs – 'the men of commerce' (1969: 14) – in banking and industry who, Landes states, provided the increased resources that financed the ambitions of rulers and statesmen.

Finance and credit were then, and continue to be, integral constituents of trading activities but also, historically, were an integral aspect of the consolidation and rise of the modern state, with national debt, mortgaged estates, credit for commerce and loans for industry defining much of the early histories of credit (Dickson, 1967; Germain, 1997; Holderness, 1975, 1976). New financial innovations were required in order to expand resources for private loans for trade and governments or armies, and was one element in the rise of modern banking. Sampson further states that financial activity and transactions, particularly on a large scale, were shaped not only by efforts to surmount the practical problems which emerged from distance trade but also from the social – ethical and religious – principles in which its participants were enmeshed (1981: 30). Overall, for Sampson, the two prime aspects of the emergence of the modern banking system were the provision of loans for trade, governments or armies, and (citing Ricardo, 1871/1971) the distinctive function of the banker, which was the ability to use other people's money (1981: 30–31). However, practical problems associated with the supply of finance and credit arising at that time, crucially included traditional practices of a social and ethical kind, not least those relating to traditional property forms. Such practices constrained new types of investment by forming barriers to the 'to the use of other people's money' – not least in women being seen as 'clogs' to progress.

The lending of bank deposits formed a significant aspect of the basis of the contemporary network of formal credit transactions and can be traced back to goldsmiths entrusted with the gold of others. The practice of lending this gold depended upon exceptional trust and on stable currencies which were fortified by the rise of national banks such as the Bank of England, which came into existence in 1694 when a group of merchants agreed to lend £1.2 million to King William III in return for the monopoly of bank notes and the right to receive deposits. It continued to finance governments through its bonds, and so the national debt was created. Consequently

> The regime of 'economic nationalism' was fundamentally concerned with favourable balance of trade within well ordered commerce, with great privileged merchanting combinations, colonial expansion, rapidly expanding businesses, extension of markets, new sources of supply, new trade routes, sea power, increasing public expenditure and the sinews of economic warfare. It was under such economic conditions that banking emerged in England. (Richards, 1958: 202–203)

Yet this brief very general overview of the rise of modern banking and finance is partial at best since not only was the regime of economic nationalism predominantly a male activity, but the advancing of individual liberties which accompanied the social changes at this time – and particularly citizens' property rights as discussed earlier – was a gendered process. This institutional order, which was deemed to 'promote social stability, and advance individual liberties – particularly citizens' property rights' (Burch, 1998), was one which saw previous subordinations of women utilised and embedded in financial and institutional structures in very definitive ways. The specific emphasis on masculine understandings of the state, power and citizenship has been analysed to great effect elsewhere by many feminists and critical theorists (for instance Grant, 1991; Lerner, 1986; Pateman, 1988; Peterson, 1992). The links between property, political rights and gender subordination are important elements in all these debates, not least in questioning the epistemological considerations of how men have historically dominated women and have had control over how they construct both themselves and others. This has resulted in institutions which socially and politically privilege men over women, affecting the structure of meaning and reality by pervading our categories of knowledge (Hirschman, 1992 cited in Steans, 1998: 53). As such the above serves as an illustration of the overwhelmingly male historical narrative which continues to dominate understandings of the ways in which finance and banking have emerged. What is left invisible in this admittedly brief overview, based on a small but representative selection of the background historical texts on of the emergence of modern financial markets, is that the transition, or restructuring during this period, was highly gendered in its ideology and its material reality. Further financial activity and transactions were shaped not only by efforts to surmount the practical problems which emerged from long-distance trade but also by efforts to free property from its ethical, religious and communal social relations to allow it to become mobile and liquid. The freeing of property from these social relations has been supported by economistic explanations of the workings of financial markets which are defined not only by their subject matter but by a particular world-view based on mathematical models of individual choice and as such reflect gender-related biases (Nelson, 1993: 5). As Dickenson states

> The refusal to acknowledge context – to acknowledge the actual lives of human beings affected by a particular abstract principle – has meant time and time again that women's well-grounded experiential knowledge is subordinated to some one else's protection and abstracted presumptions. (1996: 26)

Markets, being a social construction, thus reflect the shifts in cultural, political and economic structures which arise from society at particular historical junctures. The specific economistic approach adopted with the rise of liberal thought was constructed from a particular world-view, which prioritised individual choice in a competitive market and necessitated new forms of finance for investment that were essentially mobile and liquid property, that is, property released from its social content. Similarly the construction of 'the rational individual' also required the separation of the individual from its social content and so is an abstraction (Jennings, 1993; Nelson, 1993; Waring, 1989) and unrepresentative of humanity as a whole. The social content is here argued to be those ties of communal and familial reciprocity, values which became increasingly seen to be those of a feminised domain. Such values, together with the social ethics of medievalism gave way to a new economic radicalism:

> Ecclesiastic pretensions were pruned with the growth of the City interest; the old religious theories could not withstand the new economic realities; the canonist ethics of money lending broke down with the rise of a monied class in a new world of business enterprise. (Richards, 1958: 212)

This ensured that by the late seventeenth century two features of the market economy were relatively well developed: the doctrine of self-interest was firmly entrenched as a guide to economic behaviour although still questioned, and the institution of private property was recognised and accepted, although not entirely secure, so that the 'victory of the gospel of profit maximization was virtually complete' (Clarkson, 1972: 19). Although some historians have placed the general acceptance of these features in society to a later period, the understanding of widespread acceptance of these 'doctrines' (self-interest and the institution of private property leading to profit maximisation) is not contested since it is based on the assumption of the separation of the public/state and the private/market, and the relegation of other values to that of the private/household as stated earlier.

Although the modern financial system has been explained in terms of commodification and private property, as stated by Reeve '... putting boundaries round the political theory of property poses special difficulties, because property as a social institution is a legal, economic, and political phenomenon' (Reeve, 1986: 10). He argues that the significance of property in these theoretical genres illustrates the division of the social world into discrete political and economic realms as opposed to the pre-modern era when society was seen as an organic whole. It was only in the liberal era that political theory could be maintained as a distinct subject from moral theory, economic theory, legal theory, social theory and philosophy '...private property rests altogether on partitioning' (1986: 10–11). This separation or partitioning has resulted in the construction of political economic theories which have hidden the gendered structures of access and control over financial resources, as an increasingly masculinised and liberal ideology sought to depersonalise and separate the workings of the market from society, and from women in particular.

The consequences of changes in the seventeenth and eighteenth centuries were far reaching for the expansion, power dynamics and impact of modern banking and financial institutions. Emerging financial institutions became generally more concerned with production and business interests than with those activities involved more directly in 'social reproduction' and so displaced more traditional understandings of the role of credit and finance. In terms of financial structures, over time there has been a process of concentration of markets and institutions, which can now be envisaged as a single system. In the process of this shift, the continuation and stability of social reproduction was seen as necessary, but it was increasingly situated in the household/family, within which, integral elements of the (feudal) kinship system continued to be central. Whereas the public (male) 'outside' sphere was characterised by relations of agency, productivity and political power, the 'private' household was characterised by dependency, reproductivity and personal – therefore not political – relations. In this respect, it has been a male account which has emerged, in that although women have always been an integral part of the economy, with the emergence of industrial capitalism women retreated into the background and the invisibility afforded by a specific rendering of the political economy. This invisibility has been even more pronounced when researching the historical presence or relationship of women to and in finance in earlier centuries.

The shifts from feudalism to capitalism, and women's relationship to the economy, were defined by social and economic expectations, which, together with changes in property forms, made it increasingly difficult for women to play a direct part in business and professional activity.[18] Staves and Davidoff and Hall (1987) document the serious consequences of this pattern for those left without support and contrast this with the way in which men were able to grasp the expanding opportunities 'underwritten by women's capital and labour in both home and enterprise' (1990: 224). Staves argues that there was a strong correlation between public ideologies and economic motivation which masked state and economic forces on the family. 'Bourgeois ideology' insisted upon the private sphere of the family and denied state and economic realities had any power in its construction, with the notion of the 'individual' proving very powerful in determining that life and morality consisted of making the 'right' choices (1990: 195–225). Activities inherent in social reproduction required at specific times and in specific circumstances the use of finance and credit, albeit often in primitive forms, which involved activities of a productive kind to help support and sustain the household/family. And here as a general pattern throughout history and in different localities, women in their role as mothers, wives and daughters have been instrumental in the family's sustainability and survival, yet constrained and imperilled by masculinised formal financial and economic structures.

Finance in transition: property, innovation and gendered relations

The expansion of new forms of finance and credit – techniques upon which the expansion of trade and investment rested, both nationally and internationally, during the seventeenth, eighteenth and early nineteenth centuries was integrally bound up with the increasing acceptance of new property forms (Brewer, 1995; Brewer & Staves, 1995; Ely, 1992). During the sixteenth and seventeenth centuries money became of major importance to an increasing number of people, yet at the same time, ready money became extremely scarce. Reasons given for this are linked to the vast growth in the European economy, the rapid rise in population, the emergence of new industries, the intensification of land use and the growth of European internal and external trade (Muldrew, 1998; Parker, 1977). As a consequence of this disruption, in particular to the commercial activities of merchants, innovations in business methods were aimed at attempting to avoid the use of gold and silver. This resulted in the early modern period with an unprecedented expansion in the use of credit techniques such as loans, securities, credit transfers, bank money, paper money, annuities and negotiable obligations (Braudel, 1982; Burch, 1998; Muldrew, 1998). The significance of this development was considerable:

> The establishment of sound financial institutions, of an elastic money supply and of easy and cheap credit were the indispensable preconditions of industrial growth.... It is doubtful whether Europe would have known an 'Industrial Revolution' had a 'Financial Revolution' not preceded it. (Parker, 1977: 531)

This financial revolution rested on the evolution of financial techniques originally developed in the Netherlands, such as the bill of exchange, transferable shares in the permanent capital stock of corporations and perpetual annuities issued by government – which made them free of risk. This unprecedented expansion in the use of credit techniques which supported the expansion of trade and investment both nationally and internationally, was crucially tied to the increasing acceptance of new property forms. (Burch, 1998; Parker, 1977). As Schwartz states 'International money [finance] exists to make non-bilateral, non-barter transactions possible, particularly those that are discontinuous in time and thus impossible without some form of credit' (2000: 161). The commodification of finance and credit forms was therefore an essential dynamic in the expansion of international financial markets as international trade extended its reach with, and as a consequence of, the Industrial Revolution. With purchasing power based on credit increasing more rapidly than the technology of production and organisation, from the mid-sixteenth century to the mid-seventeenth, constant inflation resulted. The cycle of demand grew, as profits made from increased sales of basic commodities were invested in the purchase of more refined goods by wealthier individuals and '...more opportunities arose for men in local manufacturing trades' (Muldrew, 1998: 15). And here, it must be emphasised that generally, with the exception of mostly feminist historians, there has been an assumption that it was opportunities for men that arose at this time. In other words, there has been an unquestioned belief that it was men who were the 'new' force and energy behind industrialisation, just as with 'the entrepreneurs' – 'the new men of commerce' – of Landes (1969: 14).

Muldrew draws on the relationship between the increased practice of competition in the early sixteenth century, which he considers led to the increased supply of people selling their labour in order to survive, social polarisation and problems of disorder, and the way in which credit was structured in the English economy. With increasing consumption and investment in the expansion of production, household debts grew to levels at which financial failure was an increasingly common experience, with more people owing more and in turn being owed more by others. This led to economic instability as the economy expanded, where volatility of supply and demand was still largely determined by success or failure of the season's harvest (1998: 16). Muldrew supports the understanding that before the sixteenth century, production, distribution, sale and consumption were organised around the household, whereas during this later period the scale of marketing expanded over a short time, propelled by increasing demand and competition for the profits generated by higher prices. In this context, he states, until the end of the seventeenth century, English accounts did not distinguish between business and household expenses, underlining Weber's contention. Further, the fact that both household and business expenses were mixed together in household accounts 'is ample testimony to the centrality of this concept' (1998: 158). And 'More important, however, is the fact that wealth was an attribute of the household and family, even though some parts of this wealth were divided among them' (1998: 158).

Throughout this era chronic money shortage threatened the newly established foundations of civil authority but by the 1690s

> ...a distinct, integrated institutional-legal order combined recrafted authority, rule and administrative efficiency with commercial mission to promote social stability, advanced individual [male] liberties (particularly citizens' property rights) and sought to protect the nation from internal and external rebellion. (Burch, 1998: 16–18)

From the beginning of the eighteenth century, landed property and intangible property were contributing towards the distinct but related activities of English state-building in that they were 'unified into a striking single dynamic' (Burch, 1998: 124–125). Early forms

of intangible mobile property included patronage, which was transferred to merchants, with profits, surpluses and interest also being
recognised as forms of property. Braudel states that although these
property forms had been socially significant for decades, by the
late seventeenth century they were transforming well established
social relations, with many new forms of mobile property emerging
(Braudel, 1982: 111–112). These 'well established social relations' must
also include subordinated gender relations, which were implicitly
being developed within, not least, the shifting terrain of property
relations. The relinquishing of the social – and gendered – content
to new forms of financial property in order to achieve mobility can
also be regarded as integral to the formation of this 'striking single
dynamic'. Further, it was crucially related to the associated process
of state-building at this time, which was grounded on the notion of
property as landed and territorial, to which exclusive property rights
were attached:

> Efforts by English rulers to maintain and extend statecraft
> became intimately, inextricably involved with English com-
> mercial ascendancy and hegemony. Commercial success rested
> squarely upon notions of intangible, mobile property. (Burch,
> 1998: 124–125)

Burch states that credit was the most significant form of intangible,
mobile property since credit made production and exchange liquid
and dynamic and strengthened the institutional order and the
fledging state. 'Credit's intangible quality as property was decisive'
(Burch, 1998: 125). This understanding reflected that of Braudel, who
also argued that commercial success rested squarely upon notions
of intangible property and the most significant of these was credit:
'It was credit that fuelled English commercial ascendancy' (Braudel,
1982: 112).

   However, Staves considers that this shift to liquid capital (intangible and mobile) and the middle-class reinterpretation of property
forms were also decisive in enabling dependent women to be supported while keeping their capital in circulation (Staves, 1990: 19).
This explanation relies on new forms of credit and the mobility of
capital being dependent on the reinterpretation of property forms

from their social content and their social relations to women in particular. As set out in detail in Chapter 3, such intangible and mobile property required the disembedding of social relations into a individualised and commodified form since disembedding allowed it to become unattached, unencumbered, alienated and, consequently, mobile. As Staves states, the very rules that conferred ownership on women gave them a kind of ownership different from that of men in that it gave them an entitlement to profit from capital, but not control over the capital itself or the power to alienate capital (1990: 202–204). Women received income only from trusts, annuities, subscriptions and insurance and even where women had a direct financial stake in the family enterprise, their legal status prevented them from active partnership (Davidoff & Hall, 1987: 278). Davidoff and Hall cite evidence of the increased use of annuities during the nineteenth century, either for life or for a fixed period, with conditions attached as a reasonably – but not always – secure income. The majority of recipients were women but '... the type of annuity was of a type of income even more carefully controlled by the donor and his representatives, since unlike the trust, the recipient did not have a claim on the capital but solely on the income' (1987: 212). In this manner, trusts for women were structured with the implicit goal of giving the male trustees (normally relatives) 'access to woman's capital to use in the pursuit of their own economic interests' (1987: 229). Further, during the early eighteenth century, the idea of individual responsibility for wives and children saw the rise in the emergence of life-assurance policies, a by-product of which was once again to produce collateral to raise capital – for men – of which, Davidoff and Hall argue 'In no other economic form does the concept of female and childhood dependence show more clearly than in the concept of life assurance, the epitome of masculine responsibility' (1987: 212–213) and indeed control over finance.

A further impetus to changes in forms of credit arose with the creation of the Bank of England. Muldrew states that by the 1690s, the collection of tax was centralised, which meant that credit, or payment in kind (as in previous centuries) was made virtually impossible since the government needed to find cash to pay wages to the army and to pay for supplies in Europe. The crisis which resulted led to the creation of the Bank of England, which established a form of public paper credit which could attract money from the large cash holdings of merchants seeking safe investment. Further it could also 'tap' into the internal and still largely personal credit networks in London (1998: 559). From this claim, together with other sources (Davidoff & Hall, 1987; Smail, 2003), it can be inferred that the nature of this 'tapping' was related to raising liquid/mobile capital for investment through reinterpretation of property forms. As discussed previously, part of this process of the commodification of resources required changes in women's earlier common law rights, which were perceived to be a 'clog to alienability' and interfered with the process of capital accumulation through commercial and financial ventures (Staves, 1990: 203). Once these clogs were removed, and control and management of women's property were in the hands of men, a further significant source of property for raising resources for investment was made available. Further, this 'tapping' from the resources of women by men for commercial and investment reasons can be related to Smail's statement that the difficulty in raising capital in the increasingly commercial environment of the eighteenth century, and the entry of new firms together with existing firms wanting to expand '...almost always needed external capital from an inheritance, a *marriage*,[19] a partnership, or the deep pockets of a London factor' (Stephen Hillman Ledger, 1769–1812 cited by Smail, 2003: 317). This evidence of the 'tapping' of women's resources for investment purposes is also supported by Davidoff and Hall, who stated that the 'right wife' constituted an important source of personal connections and capital (1987: 275). What is quite explicit here is that the 'right wife' constituted an important source of capital which could be raised for investment or other use by the husband – or indeed guardian. It was the male guardian, husband or indeed father who invested for profit in return for the wife or female dependent receiving an annuity or interest. As a result, these new property forms saw women increasingly lose *direct* access to, and control over, resources and, together with the increasing marginalisation of women from formal economic activity, had major implications in terms of the shift in distribution of resources and security for women and wealth creation. In other words, historically it was the male's ability to utilise the financial resources of women for his own use that allowed a transfer of potential wealth – and thus potential power – from women to men. It was the ability of men to raise finance for investment for profit on their

wives' or other female relations' property which contributed significantly to the credit supply that fuelled English 'commercial ascendancy'. And it was the new forms of credit enabled by the alienation of
property from its social – and gendered – ties that made production
and exchange liquid and dynamic, so being an essential factor in the
dynamics of an expansionist capitalism

> By 1700 policymakers and merchants had constituted a union
> of statecraft and capitalist practices. Actors conceived these as a
> unity but with the unity they also constituted a pair of conceptual
> crosshairs that dominate the modern world-view and practices.
> Thus seventeenth century actors constructed a relatively effi-
> cient institutional-legal-economic order bound by the practices
> and relations of property rights. ... Actors worked to transform far
> flung colonies into empires. (Braudel, 1982: 130)

Indeed, these seventeenth-century actors constructed a relatively efficient and *masculinised* institutional-legal-economic order, which was
bound by the practices and relations of property rights. It is now particularly relevant to return to Connell's (1995) notion of hegemonic
masculinity in relation to the social construction of gender and gender identities in the context of the contemporary global political
economy. In this, Cornell identifies and traces a Western hegemonic
masculinity being articulated in relation to other masculinities
as well as femininities. In accord with feminists' understandings,
Cornell states that it is important to understand that the construction of gender is historical and dynamic, in that periods of transformation are also characterised by changes in the social organisation of
gender. For Connell, the foundation of contemporary capitalism was
laid by the accumulation and concentration of wealth during colonial times (1995: 185–190). He asserts that accumulation of wealth in
the past and the present has been beneficial to men in core countries
because it has bestowed on them power over natural resources and
other people's labour and services. To this we should add that historically it also bestowed upon men the power over women's financial and other resources in the quest for accumulation and power. In
stating that hegemony is likely to be established only if there is some
correspondence between cultural ideal and institutional power (1995:
77), Connell admirably sets out the foundations of the masculine

cultural ideal and institutional power which characterise the practices and assumptions which became entrenched within modern financial markets. The establishment of this masculinised hegemony in financial markets took place over time and space with an integrated process of the imposition of the private property forms necessary to this type of market economy. This also required the transfer of Western assumptions, including notions of the male head of the household who took ownership of private property forms, resulting in the loss of women's traditional rights of access. Such values were supported by an increasingly dominant liberal economic ideology, with its assumptions of individualism, competition and instrumental rationality. The formalising of banking and credit institutions was part of this shift in the change in the content, form and meaning of property which placed access and control of finance and credit securely into the hands (and wallets) of specific groups of men, particularly those men of commerce within the emerging institutions of the formal economy. The custodians of women's resources were then free to invest those assets in the private sphere of the market. In other words, certain groups of women, who were the bearers of assets but who lost customary rights to property/resources, were excluded from direct participation in the market economy and, as part of that process, were excluded directly from any benefits of participating directly in the formal institutions of finance. This process of reconstruction in terms of the content, meaning and value of private property, necessarily involved the reinterpretation of traditional understandings of credit.

Transformations in credit

Germain, in defining finance, uses the term 'credit' because the key question of finance is gaining access to credit. This is accessed through '...a closely knit yet intensely competitive network of institutional agents who control the access of others to the resources which they either own themselves or have access to' (1997: 17). This definition of finance by Germain relies upon an understanding of 'the system whereby credit is created, bought, and sold' (Stopford & Strange, 1991: 40; Strange, 1990: 259), that is credit is defined as a commodity divested of its social relations. However, this is a very specific and market-led definition of credit, far removed from its pre-commodified understanding, and is based on a specific historical and cultural interpretation. In pre-modern understandings, there was an emphasis on a social rationality of trust, as opposed to the emerging, then dominant, understanding of masculinised instrumental rationality based on self-interest. Muldrew argues that before the mid-sixteenth century, only one understanding of credit existed stemming from the Latin credo:

> ... to believe or to trust. To be a creditor in an economic sense still had a strong social and ethical meaning. Most credit was extended between individual emotional agents, and it meant that you were willing to trust someone to pay you in the future. Similarly, to have credit in a community meant that you could be trusted to pay back your debts. (1998: 3)

Such an understanding of emotional agents would later be feminised and exported as part of the 'Western civilisation's' organising principles which established new forms of

> ... group re/production in the form of patriarchal states, 'family' households and the division of labour, new meaning systems (philosophy, objectivity, rationality) and subjectivity (heterosexist) dichotomised, gender, intra-group identities and adversarial intergroup identities. (Petersen, 1997: 187–188)

The separation of credit from its emotional-rational content into a commodified form would be an apt illustration of the separation of property/credit out of social relations with the emergence of capitalism. As the requirements for the expansion of credit facilities for commercial reasons increasingly took on the economic values as underpinned by emerging philosophies such as those of Adam Smith, and the market structures became more complex and dynamic, Germain's understanding of credit became hegemonic. Private property forms underpinned new forms of finance which were the basis of formal market mechanisms. This resulted in pre-capitalist understandings and systems becoming feminised and this then assisted with the marginalisation of economically active women to the fringes of society. Under kinship systems, social relations to property usually secured specific, if unequal, traditional protections for women and children in their access to certain resources; the commodification of property required women to relinquish those securities or rights for other more insecure or indirect forms which overwhelmingly depended upon the mediation of men. This process has taken a variety of forms but in relation to finance, the commodification of resources through financial mechanisms enabled the emergence of a particularly dynamic form of mobile property. This change in understandings of credit, the removal of communal resources from kin and community and the use to which it increasingly was put – that is, capital accumulation – required shifts in the ideological constructs of the value, content and use of property/finance.

If the value, content and use of finance and credit within the household both before and after the emergence of capitalism are considered, they were seen as a function of producing welfare: they are not seen in terms of liberal market values and individual choice but in terms of social security, stability and reproduction of that unit. Even within Marxist interpretations of the changing form of the familial unit/household and fragmentation of kinship ties, that is, the rise of the 'family' as producing and socialising labour, certain other functions and relationships continued (Marx, 1990: 620–621). Within these functions, thrift and good household management have necessarily always been expected and commended, from Aristotle (cited by Ryan, 1987: 112) through to Margaret Thatcher,[20] not least in order to sustain social reproduction. More particularly, with the rise of capitalism and the relegation of women to the private sphere, there appeared to be a split between the perception of values internal and external to the household, as well as different expectations for the use of credit and finance for social reproduction in relation to those for business and commerce, at least until after the 1980s.

As stated earlier, focusing on the household sets out clearly the tensions for capitalism in relation to production and reproduction but not necessarily the distribution of resources within and external to that unit. Returning to Wallerstein's statement that it is within the historical development of household structures that the interests of accumulators of capital as a world class are mediated (1992: 18), his comments can also be interpreted as having relevance for financial allocation and use of such finance/credit when considering the contradiction between the objectives pursued by the accumulators in terms of household structures, and their frequent need to engage in behaviour that undermines those objectives. This is particularly relevant in the growth of initiatives to 'alleviate' poverty today through market-led or 'alternative' micro-credit schemes, which either directly target women or draw them in because of their dire position in global poverty, as will be seen in Chapters 6 and 7. (Ardener & Burman, 1996; Cohen, 2002; Mosley, 1996; Mosley & Hulme, 1998; Weber, 2001). As Wallerstein comments

> The household as an income-pooling unit can be seen as a fortress both of accommodation to and resistance to the patterns of labor-force allocation favoured by accumulators. As more and more responsibility for reproduction of the work force moved away from the 'community' towards the 'household' as constrained by the 'state', the very malleability of the institution ... was also useful in resisting or circumventing the pressures over short runs. Indeed, until the rise of the movements ... household decision-making was perhaps the principal everyday political weapon available to the world's labor force. What have frequently been analysed as atavistic thrusts were often socio-political parries in defense of given use-values or simply efforts to minimize the rate of exploitation the contradiction between the objectives pursued. (1991: 108)

Wallerstein then further discusses capitalism's involvement in increasing (but partial) commodification when

> Despite themselves, and against their own long-run interests, accumulators constantly push to the commodification of everything, and in particular of everyday life.... In the long run, this secular process guarantees the demise of the system. In the meantime, it gets translated into household structures whose internal dynamics have been, and are increasingly, commodified, from the preparation of food, to the cleaning and repair of home appurtenances and clothing, to custodial care, to nursing care to emotional repair. (1991: 108)[21]

To this list should be added sources of credit for social sustainability. Here it should also be noted that 'Home', particularly since the eighteenth and nineteenth centuries, has become a gendered construct. The construction of 'home' as a woman's place has been seen as 'a source of stability, reliability and authenticity' (Massey, 1994: 180), but Massey states that such views, embedded with nostalgia, are coded female:

> Home is where the heart is (if you happen to have the spatial mobility to have left) and where the woman (mother, lover to whom you will one day return) is also. The occasional idealizations of home by the working-class lads … often constructed that view around 'Mum', not as herself a living person engaged in the toils and troubles and pleasure of life, not actively engaged in her own and others' history, but a stable symbolic centre. … In general terms what is clear is that spatial control, whether enforced through the power of convention or symbolism, or through the straight forward threat of violence, can be a fundamental element in the construction of gender in its (highly varied) forms. (1994: 180)

Since institutional structures are not given, but are subject to contradictory attempts to shape them, there have been two primary struggles surrounding the institution of the household which involved frequently opposing interests. Not only is the household an income-pooling unit, but it has its own internal dynamics in respect of the distribution and use of resources within the household. The deepening commodification of 'everything' translated into household structures is heavily implicated in access to and provision of credit and finance both in relation to profit accumulation, investment and to the welfare of the inhabitants in and across households. This is no more aptly illustrated when a 'home' is used as security to raise money, for example, for business purposes. In May 2001, six women appealed to the House of Lords in relation to NatWest Bank seeking possession of 'houses' their husbands had put up as security for their businesses. The question for the House of Lords was what duties does a lender – usually a bank – owe a wife when wives resist possession on the basis that they signed documents creating charges against their 'homes' only because their husbands had subjected them to 'undue influence'. In the ruling by the Court of Appeal three years previously the Court found that if the marriage was secure and the indebtedness has been incurred by the husband's business, there may be no conflict between the interests of the husband and the wife. The only concession was the Court considered it was unwise for the solicitor acting for the bank to also act for the wives (*The Guardian*, 2001). Needless to say, ultimately the House of Lord's found in favour of the banks. Although this issue raises many questions in relation to power and authority both within and outside the household (not least the focus of any decision being in large part reliant on whether the wives had received independent legal advice instead of the true interest of the wives), it is also interesting to note the language used in the proceedings, which could be considered value-laden. It was stated that it was a time of great 'emotional vulnerability' for the women, although one assumes that in fact it was a time when the family was placed in a position of great 'financial vulnerability', having repercussions for the security of the social unit. The banks and their lawyers spoke of 'houses' – that is, property – which are objects, capital assets which were to be used to raise 'security' (that is a commodified financial mechanism) for business/profit accumulation, which was acceptable, as opposed to 'homes', which was the term used by the women and their lawyers. 'Home' is a far more subjective concept; an integral part of one's everyday living experience and closely related to feelings of personal and familial security.

This is an example of the disembedding of social relations from the economy, a concept which has been referred to as the tendency for economic relationships to become dominant over the social relationships of kinship and polity (Stanfield, 1999: 214). This is part of the dichotomy of the separation of politics and economics, which simultaneously dispenses with social and familial relations and continues to dominate mainstream theories of power, with deleterious effects (Peterson, 2000: 14). As Polanyi emphasised with his concept of the disembedded economy, the exchange economy tends to dominate other aspects of culture (Polanyi, 1944) whereas the definite aspect of reciprocal and redistributive transactions are embedded in the fabric of social and political life (Stanfield & Stanfield, 1997: 111–126).

The process of disembedding the economy was accompanied by the increasing sophistication of financial innovations and commercial activities in the seventeenth and eighteenth centuries. The rules of property law continued to be heavily formulated in terms of categories or amounts of property and the ownership of particular categories or amount of property was class-specific. Freehold land was bounded with special protections tending to prevent its loss whilst owners of commercial property inhabited a legal world in which the limited liability company was unknown so there were personal fortunes at risk for liabilities incurred by their business. Middle-class sons were given land and cash and expected to treat both as capital assets, while middle-class daughters were given income from property in trusts which were structured to allow, if required, male trustees access to the women's capital to use in the pursuit of their own interests (Davidoff & Hall, 1987; Staves, 1990). This, then, was a specific instance of changed understandings of the purpose of property, a change from considering property as a stable resource in a fixed form for the purpose of maintaining human life to considering property as a more abstract, unstable asset, easily transformable into whatever its highest economic use might be at a given time. The gradual replacement of women's traditional rights to property (for instance by inheritance) as security for financial forms which provided an income at low interest resulted in increased insecurity and risk. To the extent that the privileged class continued to own land as their preferred form of property, their sisters and wives were given forms of personal property which were more vulnerable to loss (Davidoff & Hall, 1987: 209, 275, 279). Overall, whereas in the seventeenth century land was the more exclusive form of wealth – and so status and political power for men – at the end of the century and the beginning of the eighteenth new forms of financial wealth had emerged to include development of credit mechanisms, the mortgage market and government funds, all of which were considered 'safe' investments by men for women. With regard to middle-class property, mainly in the form of leasehold and copyhold lands, buildings, investments and effects, with the ending of customary rights of dower (recognised by law in 1833), legal control of women's property was assigned permanently over to her husband:

> Under common law, married women of all classes were united under the extensive property disabilities of coverture, the legal status of married women: husband and wife were legally as well as spiritually considered one flesh and one body, but coverture reserved to the husband alone the role as that body's head. All women of all classes therefore took their husband's surname and

consigned into his keeping all their property and chattels, over which they could no longer exert any decisional or administrative powers. No married woman could in her own right contract debts, enter into covenants, alienate her own property, or make a will without her husband's permission. (Kreps, 2002: 86)

This is not to say that in everyday living women did not retain certain possessions or indeed agency in relation to property, but for married women, any control over management of her financial property was undertaken with the agreement of husband. Adoption of community property principles may then be taken as recognition of the value of household production; at least when comparing contributions to the marriage between husbands and wives, but the power to manage the community property was still vested in the husband (Babcock et al., 1975: 604–613; Munnell, 1980: 254). Although Davidoff and Hall comment that doubtless many women used this property 'even becoming the moving force in many a commercial undertaking' (1987: 276–278), the concept of dependence was enshrined within these legal practices providing both a material as well as ideological constraint.

Dependence on male intervention and goodwill, together with legal disabilities, compounded ideological assertions regarding women (such as emotional, irrational, disorderly, extravagant) so they were increasingly seen as poor credit risks. Banks were wary of lending to women, so their sources of capital and credit continued to be mainly kin and friends in the period when men were turning to other institutional sources. This general lack of commercial credibility was an important factor in limiting the scale of women's business operations (Davidoff & Hall, 1987: 278–280), as were the legal and economic limitations imposed upon married women, arising from the legal fiction that a husband and wife were one person. Bailey cites from the anonymous *The laws respecting women of 1877* which explained

By marriage the very being or legal existence of a woman is suspended; or at least it is incorporated and consolidated into that of the husband; under whose wing, protection and cover she performs everything; and she is therefore called in our law a *femme-coverte*. (2002: 351)

Lacking any separate existence under coverture, a wife could not technically enter into economic or financial contracts in her own right and basic purchases on credit had to be enacted in her husband's name. Ideological restrictions further impacted on women's direct financial activity, in that problems of maintaining their own and their family's status relied on not being openly involved in market activities. Although Davidoff and Hall (1987) have stated that it then becomes understandable why women found it difficult to form groups based on mutual interest which also relied on mutual control and manipulation of funds of property – commonplace amongst middle-class men – Lemire (1997, 1998) suggests otherwise, in that historically amongst various groups of women, strong networks of credit relations did (and indeed continue to) exist.

A long campaign by women for property reform gained momentum in 1867 and was closely related to the movement for women's suffrage. The Married Women's Property Bill of 1870 was debated during three sessions before the Act became law in August 1870, but was substantially weaker than originally sought by its proponents. Only some of a wife's property was removed from her husband's control. Lord Penzance's objection to the Bill was echoed by many in that its potential could 'subvert the principle on which the marriage relation had hitherto stood' (cited by Shanley, 1989: 72). As Shanley remarks, his objections revealed 'a remarkable mistrust not only of women's ability to manage property' but of their emotional and sexual infidelity in that a 'married women with liberty to contract might set up business without her husband's consent or even knowledge so leading to possible partnership with men' (Hansard 202 [21 June 1870] cited by Shanley, 1989: 73). A further Act in 1882 saw married women being given complete power to acquire and dispose of all kinds of property as 'if she was a *femme sole* without the intervention of any trustee' (Married Women's Property Act 1882, s.1 cited by Cornish & Clark, 1989: 311). Although the reform of the Married Women's Property Act at this time has been seen as 'the most important of all the legal reforms won by feminists in the nineteenth century' (Halcombe, 1983: 23), Cornish and Clark state

> But the concession of separate private rights to married women, as with the admission of women to universities and professions was more symbolic than real. The wife who remained at home

and depended on her husband for the family's upkeep or whose own earnings were absorbed in the cost of day to day living, would have nothing that she could call her own. Even her savings out of housekeeping provided by the husband in law belonged to him. In this context, the separation achieved by the Married Women's Property legislation was a crude device for an institution that ... was inherently communal ... [and] if the property remained the husband's her only protection against his whim, his dislike or his revenge came in 1938. (Cornish & Clark, 1989: 312)

Shanley considers the language that gave married women control of their property in this Act, and enabled them to make contracts and wills by proclaiming that a married woman's property was to be her 'separate property', circumscribed a married woman's ability to use and be responsible for her property in particular and significant ways. A married woman still did not acquire full contractual capacity, and was only bound personally to her separate property. Further, the 1882 Act did not make a married woman responsible for her torts so to recover damages from a married women for a tort, she still had to be sued through her husband (1989: 126–128). Although the Married women's Property Acts of 1870, 1874 and 1882 began to lend support to giving wives some control over their belongings, the underlying assumption that a wife's body and property were irreversibly vested in her husband continued to provide ideological support to practices which were either resistant to change or indeed provided a buttress to shifting political, economic and social practices. Such ideological support further embedded the roles and place of women, particularly within the family, as 'natural', 'traditional' and so ahistorical. This can be seen in the social, political and economic changes instigated in Britain during and after World War I, when women's work and the wages earned by women were considered as being secondary to those of men, which had significant financial consequences. Further, the concept of wives (and women generally) as chattels – property rather than property-owners – was more particularly evidenced in the sphere of money – and I would stress finance – where women continued to encounter often insurmountable obstacles when they tried to assert ownership, whether of houses or their own incomes. This lack of security – in more than one sense of the word – in turn added to the ideological barriers of obtaining credit or finance for personal or business reasons in their own right (J. Smith, 2001). In Britain, for instance, it was not until the end of the 1970s that women were able to obtain mortgages and loans in their own right and on the basis on their own income, without special conditions which usually required the signature of a male guarantor (J. Smith, 2001: 105). Therefore even 100 years or so after the legal changes, such as the Married Women's Property Acts of 1870, 1874 and 1882, which began the process of allowing women to become autonomous owners of property these had not as liberal theory would implicitly suggest empower married women but may have increased prolonged vulnerability.

It was not only legal restraints which saw obstacles to women's direct involvement in financial activities, but also the dominant ideology was a powerful force in restraining and constraining financial opportunities for women. For instance, Davidoff and Hall considered that few widows had the option of remaining in active business with high incomes, not least since the bankers, solicitors and agents, as well as fellow traders with whom she would have dealt, would have been men with firm ideas of 'proper feminine behaviour' (1987: 315). This was, of course, in contrast to, in particular, middle-class men who with the increasing predominance of ideological individualism which assumed power to determine choices, began to define themselves as competent and fiscally responsible managers and manipulators of new forms of financial property. With the separation of the household economy from the business, there was an assumption that female members of a household were also being excluded from knowledge about the business and the building up of 'the persona competence in business affairs which was part of the masculine persona and not part of the feminine persona' (Davidoff & Hall, 1987: 226). This reinforced notions of a lack of female rationality in relation to citizenship but also that specific rationality required for active property management. For Davidoff and Hall, the same political economic forces which favoured the rise of the private company and ultimately the business corporation, the development of public accountability and the more formal financial procedures also shifted the world of women even further from the power of the active market (1987: 225).

Again it is emphasised here that the gendered belief systems that stereotyped the characteristics of men and women supported, reflected and reproduced the perception of the legitimacy of these dealings, thereby naturalising the domination of men and the subordination of women through the social construction of gender. This historical naturalising of gendered values within financial institutions can be seen in terms of Peterson's assertion that 'this silence on gender tells us ... how "naturalised" masculinism is, how deeply entrenched in the *longue durée* of human history' (1997: 186). Such entrenched masculinism consequently obscures '... the power required to institutionalise, internalise, and reproduce gender hierarchy and its associated oppression' (1997: 195). The substantive expression of this power is well illustrated by Cameron where when he sets out the institutionalisation of a male-dominated banking scene

> London bankers ... became ennobled landowners, while members of the peerage become company directors and their daughters married bankers' sons. Just as the merchant groups behind the chartered trading companies formed in the City at the end of the seventeenth century were absorbed into the leading elements of society over the course of the eighteenth century, so by the 1890s, senior London bankers had become assimilated into the continuing aristocratic elite. Furthermore, by the end of the nineteenth century they had become largely a self-perpetuating caste. These processes had gone furthest with London private bankers, long established merchant bankers and directors of the Bank of England; by 1900 about 87 per cent of this group were sons of bankers. London banking families became landowners, ennobled and involved in politics but over generations did not move away from the bank. For most of these families the bank – whether private, joint-stock or merchant – remained the hub of the family's activities, and where the younger sons could not be accommodated within it, they were often placed within the City, in a discount house, a stockbroking firm of a legal practice. (1991: 41)

This can be illustrated further by considering men's conduct in competitive financial and banking activities driven by risk and speculation in the formative years of the transition from pre-modern systems of finance to the emergence of 'modern' financial institutions. Here it is interesting to note that new forms of masculinity in the 'casino capitalism' of today's (or perhaps yesterday's now) financial markets have seen speculation and willingness to take risk as *male* characteristics – one which was essential to the dynamics of wealth creation. As a result of the huge losses caused by the recent turbulence in banking and associated financial markets, this assumption – at long last – is already undergoing significant questioning.

Credit as a female persona

Three studies (de Goede, 2000; Ingrassia, 1998; Russell, 2000), bring to the fore the ways in which credit was given a female persona in literature in a period of 'fundamental anxieties' (Russell, 2000: 481). This involved 'cultural resistance to speculative finance' (Ingrassia, 1998) in an era of changing social and political order during the early to mid-eighteenth century. In de Goede's work, in which she politicises current understandings of financial crises, she argues that financial discourse and specifically that which located financial crises in the realm of madness and delusion, is founded upon a distinctively masculine conception of agency. Lady Credit (Daniel Defoe's satirical personification of the emergence of credit and paper money) embodies all the irrational inconstant and effeminate aspects that had to be purged from financial discourse before it was able to gain respectability as a rational, disinterested and scientific sphere of action (2000: 58). De Goede further argues that the virtues of strength and activity required of financial man 'to tame temptress credit must be read as the strength to resist her temptations' (2000: 67), which included falling into debt because 'they desire luxurious Extravagancies in eating and drinking...; or in Magnificent Equipages...; or in Drunkenness and Play' (Defoe, 1706: 26 cited by de Goede, 2000: 67), – and asserts that ruin will be the effect of 'Luxury, Gaming, Lewdness, and all sorts of Vices (Defoe, 1706: 27) thus threatening financial man's self-control and his mastery of his passions' (2000: 67).

Russell's work focuses on the political crises of the 1790s, the controversy surrounding Edmund Burke's *Reflections on the Revolution in France*, which led to an increasing emphasis on the role of women as guardians of domestic virtues and, ultimately, the health of the nation. The Faro ladies (1790s aristocratic female gamesters, so named after the traditional gambling card game popular in the eighteenth century), according to Russell, were representative of a form of entrenched 'womanpower', 'the sexual, financial and class power of the aristocratic woman, traditionally seen as threatening by both aristocratic men and middle-class opinion' (2000: 481). Russell moreover agues that by using gambling as a form of independent income, 'the Faro ladies brought to their class privilege the entrepreneurial instincts of the marketplace, thus making them even more of a threat to established codes of feminine behaviour' (2000: 482). Although the gambling male was seen to be anomalous and threatening to the values of the Enlightenment, in that a man might place his family, friends and property at risk, the stakes, Russell argues, were much higher for a woman because the only 'real' property she had to risk was her body. 'The Husband has his Lands to dispose of, the Wife her Person' (Steele, *The Guardian*, 1793 cited by Russell, 2000: 484), making it clear that the meaning of debt for a woman was very different from that for a man since it was her virtue which was at risk. Russell also draws out the relationship in the late eighteenth century between gambling and 'other forms of financial speculation' (2000: 497). The Bank of England came to be identified as the repository of public credit and a symbol of national identity, bringing some control to the national debt. Concerns over these changes also found gendered expression in the representation of public credit 'as an inconstant woman – unpredictable, mercurial, elusive, an object to be tamed by the rational masculine subject' (Russell, 2000: 496–497). Ingrassia also focuses her research on the literature of this period, which saw authors concerned at the increasing centrality of speculative investment and the mechanisms of the new financial markets and, as such, fears about the deterioration of culture. This was in relation to a critique by Alexander Pope, in which he perceived that the decay that speculative schemes wrought stemmed from the 'implicit shift from a world of material goods and property ... to an invisible universe of paper credit, stock schemes and unseen market forces' (Ingrassia, 1998: 24). This deterioration of culture was then projected in the form of a woman:

> The economic man's subordination to potentially emasculating allegorical female figures of disorder – unstable 'goddesses' like credit, Fortune and Luxury [a repetitive gendered theme throughout history] further threatens his cultural performance of masculinity. (1998: 24)

In both de Goede and Russell's work, the figure of the body of woman as credit in its inconstant and unpredictable form is counterpoised with the masculine image of finance as self-regulating and rational. Ingrassia further states that the cultural anxiety about women's possible new financial interests, the perception of the feminisation of culture and the diminished control over (feminised) men had at its base a material context in the pattern of women's investment activity. Such an ideological discourse on the emergence and increasing centrality of transitions in credit and finance in the eighteenth century were predicated on particular social constructions of gender which were illustrative of and a crucial component of the founding structures of modern financial institutions.

Credit in transition: its underlying gendered content

Changes in ethical and moral attitudes to private finance during the early modern period were crucial to the concentration of credit facilities in a restricted number of large commercial centres and, associated with this, the evolution of private property and an international system of multilateral payments (Germain, 1997). Such changes in 'popular attitudes' towards lending money were reflected in shifts from hostility towards moneylenders and their trade and the associated practice of 'usury', to a more 'liberal' attitude towards moneylending and the increasing acceptability of interest (Pierenne, 1937; Richards, 1958; Sampson, 1981). Lending at interest had been seen as morally and ethically untenable in that it was a reflection of the Church's conception of the world where land had been given by God to men in order to enable them to live on Earth with a view to their eternal salvation.

> To take usury for money lent is unjust in itself, because this is to sell what does not exist, and this evidently leads to inequality which is contrary to justice ... [but] It is lawful to borrow for usury from a man who is ready to do so and is a usurer by profession; provided the borrower have a good end in view, such as the relief of his own or another's need. (St Thomas Aquinas cited in Pierenne, 1937: 119)

For instance, good ends might be harvest failure, trade recession and times of conflict. The object of labour in this view was not to grow wealthy but to maintain oneself in the position in which one was born. Pierenne states that to seek riches was to fall into the sin of avarice since '... poverty was of divine origin and ordained by Providence and it was through charity that poverty could be relieved and the rich could seek redemption' (1937: 119–120).

In the period leading up to the emergence of capitalism in England, almost all buying and selling involved credit of one form or another and it was credit that dominated the way in which the market was structured and interpreted. Further

> Every household in the country, from those of paupers to the royal household, was to some degree enmeshed within the increasingly complicated webs of credit and obligation with which transactions were communicated. ... people were involved in tangled webs of economic and social dependency which linked their households to others within communities and beyond. Although society was divided by hierarchical gradua- tions of status, wealth and patriarchy, it was still bound together by contractual credit relations made all over the social scale and this introduced some degree of equality to social exchanges. (Muldrew, 1998: 95–97)

Alas, it is not stated by Muldrew whether 'some degree of equality' to social exchanges with regard to credit included that of gender. To explore whether relations of credit were more or less gendered after the emergence of formal financial and credit markets is extremely problematic since substantiation of this is extremely difficult to unearth. Therefore it has been necessary to draw on evidence of women's economic activity since economic activity necessarily involved forms of credit of one kind or another. With the transform- ation of Europe's economy from subsistence and barter to specialisa- tion, commerce and the use of money, there were initially increased opportunities for enterprising women as well as men in that towns- women enjoyed access to craft associations, participation in new pro- fessions and new commercial enterprises (Anderson & Zinsser, 1989; Laurence, 1994/1996). In parallel with these new economic circum- stances, Anderson and Zinsser also state that women had initially been allowed more legal autonomy but as royal jurisdiction super- seded the customary negotiated charters of towns with their lords, political circumstances changed and capital and property became the subject of royal law and '... even wealthy women lost the ability to act independently except in the most circumscribed situations' (1989: 393–394). Within this new mercantile world of towns, it was men who defined the new functions and roles for themselves and this had adverse consequences for women. Conditions of participation in guilds (codification) restricted women, in that even as the new professions evolved, women found themselves gradually relegated to the least lucrative, least prestigious aspects of work (Anderson & Zinsser, 1989: 394). This shift in the activities and status of women is reflected in work by Laurence (1994/1996) who argues that ancient institutions such as guilds, which had flourished in the Middle Ages and survived through to the seventeenth century, promoted a sense of common good rather than the primacy of the individual's profit. This sense of common good worked to women's advantage in that early medieval guilds allowed full membership to some women, normally the widows of freemen, but with hard times from the mid-sixteenth century and greater competition for trade, women were increasingly excluded from new professions and business (Laurence, 1996: 5). This increasing exclusion of women from the new professions and business at this time is reiterated by Rowbotham (1973: 13). New secular authorities took over what had been the concerns of the church, while towns became the principal source of charity and regulated the acts of giving, which took on a punitive attitude towards destitute and unfortunate women who lived outside the protection and provision of a household (Anderson & Zinsser, 1989).

With the increasing marginalisation of women from the emerging (formal) political economy, it is not surprising that, as stated by Landes – seemingly unaware of the gendered import of his statement – 'within this new society it was seen to be the men of commerce, banking and industry who provided the increase of resources that financed the ambitions of rulers, and statesmen who invented the polity of the nation-state' (1969: 15). However, since economic activity necessarily involved relations of credit, it can be deduced that if women were economically active – and here it is not intended to confine this to 'productive' activities in the formal markets – at some stage it would necessarily have involved them in credit relations of some kind or other. Women's involvement in production and access to early credit resources can be illustrated by their activities in the wool textile industry in the eighteenth century, in that, as stated by Smail, trade credit was a persistent characteristic of the commercial transactions at all stages of production 'and by all the personnel involved in the trade, from journeymen and *spinsters*[22] to wealthy merchants' (2003: 303). Alice Clark's research indicates the more equitable role women played in the family and/or domestic businesses in partnership with men, fathers or husbands. She further states there was no perception of women being economically dependent on family resources since they were an integral part of the economic activity which produced them. There are many references to women of the aristocracy who, for various reasons, managed their husband's estates, activity which included not only the management of accounts, but also the management of debt. One example given by Clark is in relation to the daughter of Judge Fell who not only managed the household accounts but also the accounts of other enterprises '... including a farm, a forge, mines, some interest in shipping and something of the nature of a bank' (1919: 16). Further archival material upon which Clark drew for her research relates to women's names appearing in lists of contractors to the Army and Navy; an Insurance Office established by one Dorothy Petty; and Mary Hall, Barbara Riddell and Barbara Millburn being documented as Hostmen (coal owners) of Newcastle (1919: 31–34).

Fletcher cites work by Peter Earle (1989), which indicated that women in the fourteenth century were commercial brewers in town and countryside, both brewing and selling ale. The key point here is that ale houses were also places where credit could be sought and women were active in this form of loan. However, there was a slow masculinisation of this trade, partially as a result of the '... capitalisation of brewing and the development of a government scheme of regulation of brewing and ale-selling which encouraged local authorities to place responsibility in men rather than women' (Fletcher 1995: 243). By the seventeenth century, women were excluded from brewing but still very active in retailing and the clothing trade which involved credit relations (Lemire, 1997, 1998). In relation to the removal of women from commercial activity, Fletcher draws on ballads of the time which accused alewives of 'fickleness, capacity for dishonesty, dangerous sexuality and the propensity towards evil'

(1995: 243), which threatened the patriarchal order. Fletcher cites
J. M. Bennett as stating

> ...in flirting with customers they undermined the authority of
> their husbands; in handling money, goods and debts they chal-
> lenged the economic power of men; in bargaining with male
> customers they achieved a seemingly unnatural power of men;
> in avoiding effective regulation of their trade they insulted the
> power of male officers and magistrates and, perhaps most import-
> antly, in simply pursuing their trade they often worked independ-
> ently of men. (cited by Fletcher, 1995: 243)

Clark also makes the point that, although declining in the latter part
of the seventeenth century

> ...the capacity of a woman to understand her husband's business
> seldom aroused comment earlier in the [seventeenth] century....
> Further evidence of women's business capacity is found in the fact
> that men generally expected their wives would prove equal to the
> administration of their estates after their death, and thus the wife
> was habitually appointed the executrix. (1919: 39)

This practice partially explains the more privileged position of widows
who on occasions would take over the running of their husband's
businesses on their death (Clark, 1919: 40). Tentative though this
may be as evidence, it is a clear indication that, historically, there
were economically active women involved in relations of credit
which became increasingly difficult for women to access with the
formation of formal credit markets.

By the late sixteenth century, the scale and complexity of credit
relationships and networks were socially and economically crucial
and, as implied above, attracted much cultural attention (de Goede,
2000; Ingrassia, 1998; Russell, 2000). Muldrew narrates the changes
in relationships which were initially personal social relations and
seen in terms of trust but as market competition and disputes became
common, 'society' came to be defined as the cumulative unity of
the millions of interpersonal obligations which were continually
being exchanged and renegotiated. This relates closely to liberal economic assertions of 'the invisible hand' and abstract notions of the

private sphere – the 'harmonious' emergence of the private/market – on the one hand assumed to be a male domain but on the other inhabited by neutral individual economic agents. Muldrew contends that Hobbes's proposition that people would not extend trust unless they were confident that the authority of the law was present ultimately to enforce promises was intimately related to changes in English society created by the development of credit. Market relations and commerce were interpreted in ways which stressed the importance of trust and the maintenance of human obligation in a world where the complexity of bargaining and competing desires was causing many contradictions (Muldrew, 1998: 124–125). Here it is assumed that Muldrew is intending a limited meaning when speaking of 'competing desires and its contradictions' to include 'the maintenance of human obligation' and 'trust' solely in terms of honouring credit sought and received. This is in opposition to modern economic models derived from classical economics which utilises rational choice theory wherein the 'emotional' content in decisions about trust has been minimised to the mechanics of utility and self-interest (Williamson, 1985: 52–67). This is a clear shift from the early modern discourse about the workings of the market, in which 'economic trust was interpreted in terms as emotive as other forms of human interaction such as neighbourliness, friendship and marriage' (Muldrew, 1998: 126). Certainly within this latter understanding, both men and women can be understood to be central to the process whereas in the former, 'the mechanics of utility and self-interest' as in 'the rational economic man' can be recognised as heavily gendered (Jennings, 1993; Nelson, 1993; Waring, 1989).

Within Muldrew's research on credit and obligation, there is no explicit consideration of gender whereas Lemire's studies (1997, 1998) indicate that there is a long history of women's roles being multifaceted, combining social and economic priorities. Reciprocal cordial behaviour set many of the parameters for early modern credit relations at this level and in the eighteenth century, and in spite of legal prohibitions, married women acted as guarantors for other women, borrowed and lent money in their own right and pawned goods on their own account (1997: 37). It must therefore be assumed that Muldrew either considered the area of credit in that period to be a wholly male commercial environment ('In the sixteenth century the natural sociability of men ... was increasingly seen to consist primarily of individual interpersonal communication, especially of bargaining and contract' [1998: 123–124]) or he implicitly utilises the liberal perception of the neutral individual, so often critiqued by both feminists and critical theorists (Brown, 1988; Jennings, 1993). Yet potential gender considerations are deeply embedded within his otherwise interesting and illuminating research. To illustrate this, Muldrew asserts that because households were the basic economic unit, reputation had definite competitive economic implications and for this reason making a distinction between economically rational transactions and other social transactions (such as courtship, sex, patronage or parenthood) to Muldrew, does not make sense. Consequently 'What we choose to call "economic" must be treated very carefully' (1998: 149) – again, the cry of many a feminist and critical theorist. Work such as Muldrew's even seeking to be sensitive to 'the economic', implicitly appears to accept the separation of activities into political cultural/social and economic domains. In so doing he is compounding 'the assumed separation of polity and economy [which] has taken different forms, but some form of separation has been causally necessary to reproduce modernity, particularly the naturalness of capitalist social relations' (Maclean, 1988: 181). This requires qualifying: by stating 'particularly the naturalness of gendered capitalist social relations', it is the reproduction of gendered capitalist social relations within financial structures which is being activated by the naturalisation of a masculinised dominant ideology which includes notions of the functions and workings of the market. As intimated above, the implications of specific understandings of early modern forms of credit were tightly bound to a system of judgements about trustworthiness. The virtue of a household and its members gave it credit so that it could be trusted – and so was profitable in terms firstly of reproduction, then increasingly in terms of accumulation. The way in which households sought to construct and maintain their credit and to justify the credit of other households in the community had a tremendous effect on the way social relations were formed and mediated (Muldrew, 1998: 194). Further, the assumption of the aim of a household to be 'profitable' does not take in other aspects of credit, particularly amongst the lower social ranks, as an indispensable aid to survival.

Returning to Staves's contention that perceptions of 'public interest' in the eighteenth century included the public interest in promoting families and good behaviour (Staves, 1994: 181–182), this too can be seen to be related to issues of credit. Muldrew notes that in the seventeenth and eighteenth centuries there was a need for households to acquire a reputation for trustworthiness so that credit could be obtained. Such requirements appear to be heavily gendered, not least in terms of terminology, in that

> Contemporary definitions of the morality of the household and its members, of order and *disorder*, of needs and luxury, of husbandry and prodigality, licence and *virtue, chastity and wantonness*, all were concerned with the cultural formation of the household as an economically reliable unit, whose motivation was both competitive and communal at one and the same time. (1998: 150)[23]

'Disorder', 'virtue', 'chastity' and 'wantonness' are all highly gendered terms, yet Muldrew does not comment on the gendered nature of credit relations. As such, otherwise illuminating research continues to reproduce – or at the very least leaves unquestioned – the deeply embedded gendered relations of power within the foundations of the financial and credit system. Connections between ideological perceptions of the role and position of women in society at that time and access to credit can be recognised in what were the deeply entrenched moral and honourable properties essential to the construction of the 'virtuous' – and so creditworthy – household. Poovey states that when considering the debates surrounding the Matrimonial Causes Bill of 1857, there were two important issues: the first was the paradoxical fact that in Britain, when a woman became a wife, she became 'nonexistent' in the eyes of the law and the possibilities that this position would be questioned and even changed. This indicates the reluctance of lawmakers to examine their assumptions about women, the relationship between the sexes and the gender bias of British law. Second, and importantly, an acknowledgment of marital unhappiness would inevitably expose the limitations of the domestic ideal, and threatened to reveal the artificiality of separate spheres 'which was the foundation for the middle class's image of itself and its economic consolidation' (1988: 51–52). The relevance of this is that Poovey goes on to state that partly because of the rudimentary nature of the British banking system and credit arrangements, and partly because of the flexibility and fluidity of middle-class property, 'the personal reputation of a middle-class man became critical to his ability to obtain credit. For both symbolic and material reasons, the domestic ideal was crucial to establishing this reputation...' (Poovey, 1988: 52). This can also be related to the previous discussion on ideological constructions of virtue and credit (de Goede, 2000; Russell, 2000). However, feminist literature, in particular within IR when discussing the increased focus on women's virtue and morality during this period, tends to link such constructions to the need to control women's sexuality in terms of women as transmitters of property (Peterson, 1997; Pettman, 1996), rather than associations with access to finance and credit.

Muldrew's discussion of the social and political implications of the development of trusts and covenants also fails to unearth the gendered content, although stating that these were bound by inequitable relations

> Just as the culture of credit led to a process of social differentiation on the basis of moral judgement, the equality of bargaining and contract was equally stressed in order to provide the moral basis for the practice of competitive virtue. All ideally had the potential to achieve credit and this was reflected in the institutional framework of the law and local courts in which even the poor had equal access while at the same time they were being excluded from the cultural networks and estimations conferred by wealth and credit.... The intensification of the market thus made the social order more fragile.... As a result while the expansion of the market led to a relative swellings of the ranks of the poor, because of credit it also led to the expansion of a contractual legal culture in which responsible members of the households who engaged in economic exchange were given a great deal of moral autonomy in their economic agency.... The powerful justificatory force of contract did nothing to address the increasingly inequality of accumulation but it did give the poor equality of access to rights. (Muldrew, 1998: 316–318)[24]

This gender-free analysis, not least in relation to contractual relations, is in contrast to that provided by Poovey, who draws out the inequitable gendered relations of these trusts and argues that although common law was considered sufficient protection for the majority of English women, men wealthy enough to afford additional protection for their daughters and property could engage another kind of law. She illustrates this by setting out the precedent made in the early nineteenth century in the Court of Chancery, when it was decided a married woman may possess property (both land and chattels) separate from her husband whereby a man would settle property upon a woman (usually his daughter) in the form of a trust. An agent appointed to oversee this trust was usually a male relative or husband who could raise money upon the property, sell or rent the title and make contracts upon the property. These trusts generated income from women's property that was protected from liability, but were also an important source of the liquid capital 'so essential to the success of middle-class men so while equity could give the married woman the right to own property, this relation was both indirect and limited' (1988: 71). This also reinforces the argument that in this period, women's resources were being utilised substantially as sources of liquid and mobile capital for investment.

What is also missing from Muldrew's consideration of the process of social differentiation is its increasingly gendered nature, since 'all' did not, progressively, include women, and 'responsible members of the household' can only be understood in terms of the (male) head of the household as far as those involved in the emerging formal financial and credit networks. Indeed, it was the 'institutional framework of the law' which had increasingly seen the transformation of women's traditional rights to security (such as access to communal resources) to a more narrowly defined set of less secure rights in its increasing consolidation of rights to private property. Again, other historical research also reinforces this process in terms of how changes in property forms were instituted and embedded through the law so that trusts for women were structured with an eye to giving the male trustees access to the woman's capital to use in the pursuit of the men's own economic interests (Davidoff & Hall, 1987: 229; Poovey, 1988). Further, Davidoff and Hall relate that women were considered poor credit risks, given their legal disabilities and dependence on male intervention and goodwill. It was more common, therefore, for a woman to inherit or raise a lump sum rather than establish a viable credit chain to support an ongoing enterprise but even so perceptions of women's general lack of commercial credibility were an important factor in limiting the scale of women's business operations (Davidoff & Hall,1987: 278–280). This downgrading of women as economic agents in their own right has been succinctly described in relation to commodity and labour – although this is just as applicable to finance and credit – by Delphy and Leonard:

> The actors in these [commodity and labour] arenas have been men by definition: the quality of being a full economic subject, of having full access to the market, is something which distinguishes men (as a gender and age group) from women, children and the elderly. It has been an important element in what constitutes men as men. (1992: 34)

5

From Formal Financial Institutions and Orderly Men to Informal Markets and Disorderly Women

It has been generally understood that from the point of view of women engaging actively in banking and finance (lending, borrowing and working) the professionalisation and specialisation of banking and finance served to exclude women almost entirely until the late nineteenth century (Dickson, 1967; Kwolek-Folland, 1994; McDowell, 1997), when a sexual division of labour appeared within the ranks of finance and banking. As has been set out in the preceding chapters, the earlier exclusion from 'formal' economic activity was supported by shifting social expectations, legal restraints and changing property forms which made it increasingly difficult for women to play a direct part in financial, business and professional activity in the emerging formal markets. Indeed it was the formalisation of markets, and the abstract separation of formal from informal, which in part served to make invisible and so marginalise women's productive and financial activities.

Clark's work on women in the Elizabethan era indicated substantial economic activity by women who owned and managed businesses requiring a considerable amount of capital. She stated that they acted as pawnbrokers and moneylenders as well as often being connected with the shipping trade and contracts. Some were engaged in business with their husbands such as Collet, wife to Thomas Price, both of whom were fined for shipping '200 dozen old shoes' with the intention to transport them 'beyond the seas contrary to a Statute...on account of their poverty' (Analytical Index to Rembrancia cited by Clark (1919: 29). A Joseph Holroyd employed a woman as his shipping agent in 1706 (cited from Letter Bks of Joseph Holroyd [Cloth Factor] by Clark 1919: 30) or on their own account such as Dorothy Petty who established an insurance office, an account of which was written in 1710 'The said Dorothy had such Success in her Undertaking, that more Claims were paid, and more Stamps us'd for Policies and Certificates in her Office than in all other the like Offices in London besides; which good fortune was chiefly owing to the Fairness and Justice of her Proceedings in the said Busines' (cited from the Case of Dorothy Petty, 1710 by Clark, 1919: 34). However, as Clark goes on to state, although able business women might be found in every class in English society throughout the seventeenth century, 'but their contact with affairs became less habitual as the century wore away' (1919: 37). Clark argues that it was only after the Restoration that a change in attitude towards women in business occurred (1919: 39).[25] It was changes during the seventeenth century which

> ... abrogated customs in favour of common law and in effect eliminated women from what was the equivalent to a share in the custody and interpretation of law, which henceforward remained exclusively in the hands of men.

This, led to a succession of laws which in order to secure complete liberty to individual men,

> destroyed the collective idea of the family, and deprived married women and children of the property rights which customs had hitherto secured to them. From this time also the administration of the law becomes increasingly perfunctory in enforcing the fulfilment of men's responsibilities to their wives and children. (Clark, 1919: 237)

During the early modern period, although an unmarried woman or widow had the right to dispose of her own property as she saw fit (*femme sole*), a married woman theoretically lost the right to make any contract without the agreement of her husband (*femme coverte*). However, it was possible to appeal to an appropriate governing body to lift this restriction. Further, records indicate that women could receive formal legal approval and many married women at that time were carrying out business independently, although the law still allowed anyone to deny them a loan (Wiesner-Hanks, 1998: 209).[26] As Finn's work indicates, since forms of resistance are forever present, married women as consumers were not averse to utilising devices in order to evade the strictures of coverture (Finn, 1996: 703–704).

The quasi-construction of 'occupational' identities such as spinsters, wives and widows, ensured that 'housewifery' became the 'natural' female skill and became central to the organisation of the private sphere of the household/family (Lemire, 1997). Skills, occupations and activities (including the acquisition of credit for household use in times of need), which previously were seen as an integral part of the communal household security, were increasingly separated into either formal (male) economic and commercial activities (Lemire, 1997: 112–114) or those which became increasingly feminised and marginalized to informal and 'disorderly' domains. Lemire recounts how throughout the early modern period, women embarked on temporary, full-time or part-time business that they combined with commitments to home and family. She cites evidence of sophisticated systems of barter and cash sales and that in the specific neighbourhood researched, dockyard workers' wages could be years in arrears and alternative sources of currency were invaluable (Lemire, 1997: 114). Indeed, women's involvement in barter systems still has a vital role to play in many societies, particularly in times of crisis (Powell, 2003).

Protestantism has been seen as a powerful reinforcement for the prevalent social order, in that in court and ecclesiastical probate records women were almost never identified by occupation. At the same time for the purpose of government, the state was embedding understandings of the social and gender order which reduced the complexities of men's working lifestyles to a single occupational commitment which excluded women. 'Heads of households' was a role utilised as a fiscal entity since 'heads of households were the only interest in their role as fiscal and legal entities' (Fletcher, 1995: 225). Whereas men's occupations were noted as 'gentlemen, yeomen, husbandmen and labourers' and 'shoemakers, tailors, wheelwriters and masons' (1995: 225), women's occupational identity was given as their gendered role: spinsters, wives and widows. (1995: 225) Before the mid-sixteenth century, both the husband and wife were named in apprenticeship indentures. After that time, the name of the wife was omitted:

> For the purposes of government, the state was successfully inculcating a way of looking at social and gender order which reduced the complexities of men's working lifestyles to a straightforward and usually single occupational commitment and left women out altogether. What officeholders were interested in … was heads of households: the active and representative person, male if possible, with whom the state conducted its dealings. (Fletcher, 1995: 225)

Such exclusion of women from records of economic activity enhanced the perception of women's absence from commercial activity and so ultimately, reinforced their exclusion from the private sphere of the market. This also illustrates the way in which the state was intimately involved in the construction and embedding of gender differences, not only through classification and the recording of data itself, but the associated practices which furthered the reproduction and deepening of gendered institutions.

This process of classification cut across pre-capitalist multiple occupational subsistence identities of both men and women by assuming – or prioritising – a single work identity (Mendelson & Crawford, 1998: 32). Mendelson and Crawford contend that civil, criminal and ecclesiastical law all began with the axiom that the two sexes were different in their essential nature, and unequal in moral as well as intellectual capacity (1996: 37–38). Even though the gender inequality of patriarchal relations was initially carried over from the theological into the modern economic domain, 'this inequality soon manifested itself as irrational in relation to the claim that economic individuals were structurally equivalent in the market place.' (Poovey, 1995: 15). The law was increasingly one of the fundamental constraints on the personal civil and property rights of women but cannot be seen to be as separate from the political and social/religious/cultural historical context from which it evolved. Adam Smith's narrow view of the theories of value (1667/1991) began to influence or support and reproduce the organisation of production and labour on gendered lines, a process which continues to have particular relevance to the global political economy today when a sexual division of labour exists on a world scale. This sexual division of labour continues to cross the boundaries between formal markets and feminised informal markets (Bakker, 1994; Elias, 2005; Fussell, 2000; Kofman & Youngs, 1996; Sen & Grown, 1987). This gendered division of formal and informal, orderly and disorderly, markets in finance and production has specific implications since by privileging the formal over the informal, and the orderly over disorderly, not only has it excluded or marginalised women from wealth-creating financial activity, but it has privileged productive lending over consumption in terms of social reproduction.

Productive versus consumption: formal versus informal markets

Scholars of IR and GPE when considering the rise of the modern economy, tend to dismiss consumption lending or small-scale credit systems as not worthy of analysis. Indeed, within GPE, study of international or global finance is seen to be entirely located in the sphere of wholesale lending and borrowing (Germain, 1997; Helleiner, 1994, 1995; Strange, 1986, 1988, 1998, 1998). Yet the overwhelmingly masculinised financial markets of today cannot be separated either historically or substantively from small(er)-scale investment which has also existed within, on the margins of or outside formal financial markets. Understandings of the dichotomy of formal/informal markets have been shaped as a result of changes in property forms which have converted secure communal property into commodified individualised property forms to be traded in pursuit of capital accumulation in the private sphere of the (male) market. Small-scale financial processes have been – and continue to be – relegated to the margins of debate on a local/'grassroots' or domestic/internal level, and more specifically with regard to processes of economic development. In this way women's involvement in the economy via informal credit networks remained (and remains) obscured. And yet, as Lemire argues, the 'disorder' that women engendered in the market during the early modern period (and after) was '...a fruitful disorder which added to the vigour of the economy as a whole' (1997: 120), not least in that it provided some limited access, control and agency for women in relation to credit as a resource.

The form of finance and credit which became dominant, however, was that distributed through market-led financial institutions, which leads us back to the definition of finance 'the system whereby credit is created, bought, and sold' (Germain, 1997: 17; Stopford & Strange, 1991: 40; Strange, 1990: 259). Such credit is defined as a commodity divested of its social relations, far removed from its pre-commodified understanding, and is based on a specific historical and cultural interpretation. This limited women's access to resources (particularly those of married women) since they were by law unable to borrow credit (except in very specific circumstances) from the newly emerged formal networks of credit within the private sector of the economy, which were shaped, controlled and utilised by particular groups of men, re-enforced through institutions bounded by ideological and legal norms and exported or replicated on a global scale.

Lemire (1997, 1998) explores the differential opportunities for women and the changing nature of their commerce within the formalised trade in old clothes during the period of transition. The market-place, ideally, was reserved for sanctioned dealers who were controlled and regulated. When intrusion into the market became apparent, both town guilds and city fathers fought against the infringement of their privileges. Lemire states that two elements in particular wrought women's condemnation: the commercial production or refurbishment of goods by unregulated labour in households rather than approved workshops, and the hawking of goods to consumers by itinerants. In both cases, 'disorder' and 'irregularity' were the points of contention. Chief amongst the abuses listed by the author of *The Trade of England Revised* was the proliferation of retailers, hawkers and pedlars; for example '...the Women in London, in Exeter, and in Manchester, who do not only Profer [*sic*] Commodities at the Shops and Ware houses, but also in Inns to Country chapmen' (cited by Lemire, 1997: 99). It was covert home-based production which was particularly seen as an affront to the social order.

Indeed, as previously stated, disorder itself held a particular association with the female sex and this has often been utilised as an explanation for their exclusion or limited activity within public life and claims to citizenship (Elstain, 1981; Pateman, 1988). Carolyn Merchant states that the scientific revolution during the seventeenth and eighteenth centuries influenced this perception of women as disorderly. With the change in world-views, the world began to be visualised as a machine rather than a living organism with a mechanism for everything previously seen to be natural. The new-found knowledge caused the power relations that linked women to nature to become characterised in the same manner: 'Disorderly women, like chaotic nature, needed to be controlled' (1980: 127), and so it was necessary for women to be restrained so as to regain or retain order. Women were seen as disorderly, wild, weak, gullible and unable to control themselves. Therefore 'women needed to be kept in their place' (1980: 132). The nature of women was understood to be essentially unstable and liable to outbreaks against the natural order unless carefully restrained (1980: 127).[27] Hartsock similarly argues that orderly domestic politics have been defined '... in opposition to dangerous, disorderly, and irrational forces... consistently conceptualised as female' (1983: 283). Legal status and societal methods attempted to limit women's opportunities and in this respect, Poovey states that British law included three discrete, overlapping and sometimes competing systems of law. Statute law took the form of protective legislation in the nineteenth century implicitly embodying the assumption that women were by nature passive, whereas case law, as articulated in court-room procedures and judicial decisions concerning rape, vagrancy and prostitution, implied that female sexuality was an aggressive force requiring regulation and control (1988).

As regards trade, then, it is not surprising to find that women were frequently depicted as less trustworthy than males and invariably more susceptible to ethical transgressions that would hurt unsuspecting customers. The theological and cultural attributes assigned to women in Western Europe militated against tolerance or acceptance of their economic activities outside established structures of production and distribution, and these attitudes were particularly evident in times of crisis. The view that an independent woman in the market place was an affront on many levels contributed to the dichotomisation and reconstruction of formal and informal sectors, with women progressively ideologically and materially marginalised and so excluded from formal economic activity. The outcome was that women's access to resources in terms of finance and credit was further constrained.

However, credit was an indispensable aid to men in formal markets, and to women of all social ranks, both within informal market activity and for those who were disproportionately responsible for household functions including the management of small-scale household credit. Locating the arenas within which women secured credit assists in making visible the interrelationship of the household with the market, and is a further illustration of the ways in which gender operates at various levels valorising certain social institutions, in terms of financial actors, practices and processes. Market exchanges were never a homogenous trade of cash for goods, and pawnbroking proliferated both formally and informally in neighbourhoods (W. C. Jordan, 1993; Lemire, 1997). Although costs of pawning and borrowing impacted upon household budgets of the lower social ranks, such credit was perceived as indispensable since the options available were limited, as they are for many women today. Lemire drew on surviving ledgers of South London businesses containing evidence of more than 440 credit transactions from the last third of the seventeenth century to reveal complex systems of credit and a community of reciprocal guarantors making loans available to residents. This is considered to be a typical cross section of labouring and trading city people who relied for their survival on combined social and economic connections within their neighbourhood, the most striking feature of which is the large number of women with no designated occupation. Although a woman's occupational status fluctuated with life cycle changes more dramatically than did a man's, Lemire contends that it is important to recognise the functions they had within their community. 'Whatever their training or trade, female creditors such as those found in the Pope ledgers, played a pivotal role in the organisation of credit in their households and throughout their neighbourhoods' (Lemire, 1998: 117). The argument here is that there is clear surviving evidence of cooperation and reciprocity amongst the borrowers of this South London community, elements which persisted in parallel, necessarily for women, with their increasing exclusion from sources of credit with the development of capitalism at this time. Muldrew (1998) reflects similarly on the 'moral tenets' embedded in many market activities which he considers to have functioned in combination with the personal ambition of Smithian self-interests. However, this vision is limited since in his comment that relations of obligation and dependence between credit and debtor forged commercial bonds that were tempered by sociability, he does not explicitly recognise any gendered aspect to this process. Women's access to (formal) resources was clearly more limited and thus women continued to seek other avenues for credit, including those with relations of reciprocity.

There were very different patterns of credit relations during this period, as indeed there are in some societies and communities today. Although kinship, community and business ties were essential ingredients in securing credit, research has indicated that male borrowers showed an almost equivalent selection of male and female partners, women on the other hand formed a higher proportion of alliances with other women. (Lemire, 1998: 120). Lemire states that not only did networks of female sociability contribute to part of this pattern – directly contradicting Davidoff and Hall's assertion that women lacked social networks – but additionally the complex commercial links at the periphery of mainstream markets should be recognised where women were disproportionately represented (1998: 121). The prevalence of women at the margins of market places and as street peddlers is also confirmed by the increase in regulation which banned women's trade throughout the medieval and early modern period. Women were confined physically to the margins of some later medieval markets and their patterns of informal trade were castigated by the terms 'regrater' or 'forstaller' (Wright, 1985). It was at this interconnection between the street-corner enterprise and informal, predominantly female, trade where women were active in securing small loans and short-term credit. It is here in very large part that the transformations in women's commercial functions, as the business of credit became more regulated during the course of the eighteenth century, that the further marginalisation of women from sources of formal credit took place (Lemire, 1987). The evidence suggests that neighbourhood women employed their knowledge of character and local commerce to fulfil supplementary credit functions, acting as petty pawnbrokers themselves in arranging loans, and acting as agents for lenders within their communities. Lemire recounts how in late sixteenth-century Leicester, city fathers condemned such activities by several enterprising women by describing them as 'evil persons'. These individuals were designated as 'Brogers or pledge women' and seen by officials as meddlers in the market place, interfering with mercantile conventions. These pledge women disrupted Leicester's commercial harmony and the City Corporation barred the women from any future transactions, and the trade of these townswomen was formally reassigned. However, as stated by Lemire, the commercial affront they suffered cannot obscure their initiative and the significance of their standing as providers of credit. (Lemire, 1997: 266). However, there was a further aspect to the marginalisation of women. Tebbutt, in discussing the survival activities of poor elderly women, states that the contradictions of the hidden society to which they belonged were well expressed in the credit expedients women often had to use (with echoes of the stereotyping of 'feckless' mothers today):

> Their own organization of credit (despite the collective efforts when neighbours arranged credit facilities between themselves) tended to be shadowy and extremely ambiguous, as in the case of street money lending. ... working-class women were condemned as morally inadequate for failing to measure up to middle-class standards and since poor management was invariably represented as the root cause of indebtedness, the very act of resorting to credit did in fact become the fulfilment of a damning sexual stereotype. (1983: 36)

Wright's research into Tudor and Stuart Salisbury confirms the role of women in pawnbroking during the seventeenth century, citing widows in particular '... amongst whom were a good number of alehousekeepers and innkeepers' (a traditional source of small loans), who were in a position to act as pawnbrokers:

> The network of individuals mentioned in the case of buying or pawning goods consisted entirely of poor women, for whom such an informal system was possibly the only means of obtaining 'new' clothes or household goods. (1985: 111)

W. C. Jordan also demonstrates that women in pre-industrial times played an integral part in the economy, by both being a source of labour and participating in lending and borrowing, particularly of the small loans that were needed by poor people or people temporarily unable to pay for a particular event, such as a christening party or wedding feast.[28] Women moneylenders made small consumption loans which, W. C. Jordan states, were just as varied as 'those upper class Christian women and men' who lent money to various groups of people. Of note, again, were the pawnbrokers and alewives and here

W. C. Jordan indicates that this was not just local to England but cites evidence, too, of activities in medieval France, Germany, Denmark, Italy and Russia (1993: 20). His findings concur with Lemire's understanding that women did not seem to have benefited in terms of status or great wealth from their roles as moneylenders but neither were they perceived as having a subversive effect on the overall hierarchies of medieval society as they would be in later centuries. The non-threatening character of this particular form of 'female empowerment' at that time has been ascribed to the idea that women were concerned with the very smallest loans – 'the "domestic" part of the market' (as indeed they are today in many developing and developed countries) – whereas men's loans were categorised as business loans, and thus imparted to men 'something of the emerging... prestige of businessmen' (W. C. Jordan, 1993: 23). Further, women borrowed significantly less than men and, again 'Nor should it be surprising that an enormous number of transactions involved woman to woman exchange' (1993: 25). This suggests that strong social networks supported by kinship, friendship and respect existed within the world of lending and borrowing, which included male as well as female borrowers and lenders, and sometimes women and men involved together in credit transactions. However, such transactions and such actors did not cross over to the emerging formal financial markets.

Further evidence of credit activity by women in the informal sector is given again by W. C. Jordan (1993) who cites research by Majorie McIntosh (1988 cited in Jones, 1993: 32) where women from immigrant Flemish communities, a response to the growing commercialisation of the London economy, borrowed from English women whereas professional moneylenders were involved in making larger loans to the sector of the expanding economy involved with the cloth industry. In this 'volatile' economy

> ...where more masculine credit networks accentuating class and ethnic differences became prominent, the older pattern of small domestic consumption – women to women loans – across ethnic lines persisted in sustaining vulnerable immigrant households. (Jordan, 1993: 30)

W. C. Jordan notes that in the later medieval period

the informality [of small-scale lending and borrowing] under-
mined all legalistic attempts to prevent adult women, married or
otherwise under the judicial 'cover' of a male, from making contractual obligations without their husbands' or other appropriate
men's consent. (1993: 50)

In the late seventeenth century, there was a similar pattern, in that
whatever the legal constraints of coverture, married women of labouring and artisan status took initiatives in securing loans, through direct loans, pawns and other assorted alliances in credit arrangements.
Seen as part of their domestic responsibility, balancing the needs of
the household and apportioning resources in as thrifty a manner as
possible, the predominance of women in all loan transactions under-
scores their pivotal function in the sphere of small-scale credit not
least by the exclusion from the emerging formal sector. It is also clear
evidence of continuing agency in a period of increasing constraint
for women in the gendered structuring of emerging formal financial
markets.

Widows, spinsters and married women have been documented in
local studies as making important contributions to capital formation. Holderness states that 'the most prominent economic function
of the widow in English rural society between 1500 and 1900 was
moneylending' (1976: 105). Mutual support and cooperation were
important vital components in the lives of working-class women,
although the collective aspects were most apparent in the poorest
neighbourhoods. The losing battle against poverty and indebtedness, however, placed mutual support in a state of continual conflict with the individualist pressures of a cash economy. In the
nineteenth century women acted collectively in organising various types of savings clubs, including rotating credit associations,
but these were considered risky undertakings. (Tebbutt, 1983: 50).
William Booth is cited as observing that in one deprived area of
London 'every street has its lender, often a woman' underlining
the 'over-riding characteristic of moneylending at this level, that
it was a dominantly female occupation' (cited in 1997: 51). Again,
of 1,380 moneylenders registered in Liverpool in 1924, 1,000 were
women.[29] Tebbut also states that as late as 1924, moneylending was
deeply entrenched in the poorest areas of Britain, but indeed it is
still firmly entrenched throughout the poorest societies across the

world and indeed is now, progressively, becoming big business. However, although women were major providers of small-scale credit, active in pawnbroking and (credit-related) second-hand sales in the eighteenth century, Holderness's wide-ranging research into banking and credit reveals they played very little part in the wider commercial world (1975: 131).

The implications for this wide-ranging financial activity by women throughout the period of transition from feudalism to capitalism and beyond, drawn from research in Britain and Europe, within what became termed as 'disorderly' informal finance and credit activities, directs attention to the gendered structures of financial markets. On the one hand, such feminised spheres of informal credit and financial activities sought to underpin the everyday lives and activities in social reproduction, whereas the increasingly masculinised material and ideological constructs of formal financial markets were the domain in which wealth and power accrued to specific groups of white Western males. It is concluded that networks involving women (and some men) frequently responded in distinctly different ways to social and economic pressures from those involving just men and this is where different interpretations of the value implicit within understandings of forms of credit given or received defines the formal from the informal, the masculinised 'Credit [as] a resource which people, firms, and governments have access to at the discretion of others, and at a cost established by others' (Germain, 1997: 17) as opposed to those largely 'feminised' informal and disorderly ('reciprocal' or 'mutual obligation') sources of finance and credit.

The City of London, colonialism and the internationalisation of masculine financial markets

Throughout this exploration of finance and credit, the relationship between the emergence of modern financial institutions, the rise of industrial capitalism in Europe and the requirement for mobile forms of finance, has been crucially and intimately related to long-distance trade. The expansion of the activities of finance and banking was a crucial dynamic in the expansion of capitalism at this specific time, reproducing itself on a global scale with the development and internationalisation, then globalisation of financial markets. It required the shift to private property forms which enabled capital to become liquid and mobile and has been a gendered process. It has involved complex and changing relationships between banking, commerce, industry, institutions, development and what has been described more recently as 'unstoppable' technological forces.

The foundations of modern financial markets and the network of supporting institutions such as trade and commerce more generally emerged in a particular historical and social environment which repositioned the place of women from one that might have allowed more equitable control over and access to financial and other resources to one of exclusion from direct activity in formal markets. Subsequently the gendered structures within which financial markets operated became the foundations upon which men were awarded opportunities to accumulate wealth and power and from which the majority of women were excluded. This temporally and spatially differentiated process was advanced by and through the internationalisation of financial markets.

The Industrial Revolution and Britain's rise to world trade dominance led to the emergence of London, and in particular the City of London, as a centre of international finance – the foremost financial centre in the nineteenth century (Germain, 1997: 45–46). The reach of trade finance was not an essentially new phenomenon, in that from a long historical perspective forms of international financial markets had existed for many centuries (Edelstein, 1982; Helleiner, 1995). However, it is the surge in international expansion of trade and finance which marked a significant shift in innovation and dynamics in these early modern markets. Edelstein states that from the early seventeenth century, joint-stock trading and colonising companies, interloping merchants and wealthy agrarians invested long-term funds for overseas warehouses, shipping, port facilities, slaves and plantations. In the longer term, overseas accumulation was tied to the success of British arms in foreign wars and the extension of the European and North American market for sugar, coffee, cotton and other raw materials. In this context, London was not important as an industrial centre but its port was a dominant centre for trade with traders seeking ancillary financial services. At the same time, these traders generated the capital which was then again invested in international trading ventures (1982: 9).

In explaining the emergence of financial institutions and innovations during this period, McRae and Cairncross discuss the importance of the evolution of quayside and coffee-house auctions of the eighteenth century with the eventual emergence of commodity futures markets and the Baltic Exchange. Through the traders' use of bills of exchange, discounting of bills and provision of credit for international trade, the domestic financial network evolved which, in the years following the Napoleonic Wars, made the City of London the main centre for financing world trade (1991: 3). From the late seventeenth century, British trade with Europe and its overseas colonies expanded, as did participation in international trade more generally. Edelstein explains this success in relation to the growth of Britain's markets abroad, which afford greater specialisation and economies of scale. Further, together with Britain's military successes, technical change augmented and supported overseas markets (1982: 11). These shifts in the momentum and character of trade influenced the size of the market for British borrowers, lenders and financial intermediaries. Ostensibly, the borrowers, lenders and financial intermediaries active in this emerging private sphere of the market were men, although as discussed previously, this participation was often dependent on access to women's property. Domestically, through the development of country banks in the provinces and private London banks (for instance, Barclays originally being a country bank and Coutts a private bank), rich farmers and wealthy Londoners lent the money – or indeed forms of credit – at their disposal to provide emerging industry with working capital. English private bankers combined into powerful joint-stock companies such as Lloyds and Barclays. The male lineage of these well-known banks is set out clearly in various histories of banking. For instance, Sayers's account of the male lineage involved in the foundation and expansion of Lloyds in 'Members of the Taylor Family connected with the Bank' (1957: 28–29) mentions women only in relation to marriage, particularly into other wealthy banking families. Balogh agues that if in this process (combining into joint-stock companies) the private bankers in most cases lost their corporate identity, 'the social prestige and the connections which the families owning these private banking firms enjoyed, in many cases secured them a very powerful voice on the board and management of the bigger institutions'

(1947: 228). Foreign firms, such as Rothschilds, Hope and Co. and Higginson and Co. established themselves in London; some bankers from Europe sort refuge from political insecurity and others were attracted by '... the unrivalled opportunities in trade, banking and finance. ... As England became the most powerful industrial country, London became the financial centre of the world' (Balogh, 1947: 229).

In this expansion, the City of London became a crucial and powerful institution and central to the internationalisation of modern financial markets, a position which continued to be supported by British financial authorities – 'The Bank of England-Treasury-City nexus of British Politics' (Helleiner, 1994: 14). Further, the City and its relations with British financial authorities were the catalyst in the formation of the Euromarkets (Burn, 1999), the emergence of which has been forcefully argued to be a further crucial dynamic in the growth and form of global financial markets and capital accumulation after the 1950s (Burn, 1999). Feis remarks on British foreign investment as resulting from 'the greatest free financial force in the world' and that the London financial market 'derived its strength from great wealth, diversity, experience, world connections – all directed by a sober yet daring energy' (1934/1974: 4). This energy was seen by Feis as clearly a male, civilising and heroic venture in that through many decades the London financial market offered great opportunities for gain 'solicited and directed by able young Englishmen, who in large numbers sought their fortunes in developing the resources of young countries ... and in so doing propelled that outside world into the stream of history along which Europe moved' (1934/1974: 4). It is a male account about male financiers from a specific elite within a specific historical context reflecting class specific, male, white societal values. 'Most men of property held some foreign securities – even though they were of the lords who stuck to the land' (Feis, 1934/1974: 5). 'The movement of British capital to other lands was one of the shaping forces of Great Britain's economic structure and political destiny – steadily turning men's thoughts outward' (1934/1974: 4). Feis outlines the influence of British capital moving through 'huge' commercial banks which 'financed commodity movements through the world, [and] were the greatest source of credit' (1934/1974: 7). Alongside the commercial banks, he lists the banks, public and private, of the British Dominions which set up a presence in London: the Commonwealth Bank of Australia, the Imperial Bank of India, the National Bank of South Africa and the Bank of Montreal (1934/1974). In a further narrative of the internationalisation of finance and, implicitly, the inherent values supporting this process, Bagehot illustrates how 'ideas' from 'Lombard Street' were transported as part of financial institutions to the colonies:

> English colonists do not like the risk of keeping their money and they wish to make interest in it. They carry from home the idea and habit of banking and they take to it as soon as they can in their new world. (1905: 77)

Further impetuses to the growth of financial institutions were the gold standard and colonialism, which encouraged a number of commercial banks to develop overseas branch networks. Jones states that on the eve of World War I, British-based institutions held between a quarter and a third of all bank deposits in countries including Argentina, Australia, Brazil and New Zealand (Jones, 1993: 40 cited in Scholte, 2000: 69). The gendered shift in property forms which took place over this extended period, together with the emergence of new forms of financial products and mechanisms such as annuities and credit as discussed earlier with their implications for the limitation of women's access to financial security, was also a crucial part of this process of 'new financial intermediaries and institutions to achieve mobilisation'. This mobilisation was intrinsically one of spatial mobility in terms of liquid and mobile capital – and territorial mobility, that is international and then global. It is also a narrative of the increasing importance attached to capital accumulation over societal need with the proviso that in the nineteenth century finance provided by the City to the world economy was tied to a real exchange of goods, in the form of trade bills, rather than potentially unproductive bonds as in the 1970s and 1980s (Strange, 1988: 101) to say nothing of the whole gamut of 'toxic' financial products from the late 1990s to the present day.

Explanations for the rate of foreign lending being significantly higher by the third quarter of the nineteenth century, continue to be aired, but among them the most influential was that of Hobson whose articulation of the connection between under-consumption and foreign investment (1914/1963) form a crucial element of Lenin's writings on European imperialism (1915/1939: 216). By the nineteenth century, then, London was operating as the world's leading international financial market and British banks were expanding and developing their activities on what eventually became a global scale with the vast majority of major currencies being controlled by the Gold Standard under the aegis of Pax Britannica (Strange, 2nd edn 2000: 87). In parallel with developments in England, the growth of US transnational activity and manufacturing in the late nineteenth and early twentieth centuries reflected the country's emergence as the world's major industrial nation, but in 1914, the major source of overseas investment was still the United Kingdom (Dicken, 1998: 20). According to Dicken, the geographic spread of UK overseas manufacturing investment was considerably broader than that of US firms or from Europe. It was, however, the dominance of the United States and the dynamics of capitalism during the twentieth century which very largely carried with it the Anglo-Saxon value system inherent in the workings of modern markets and institutions.

The value structures inherent in modern financial institutions have been drawn into policy-making, within which the gendered structural component of male networking arising out of a specific elite or class is implicit in Feis's description of the relations between finance and the British government in the nineteenth and twentieth centuries. He states that the habits and structure of British society

> ...contributed to fostering a natural harmony of action. In the small circles of power, financial power was united with political power, and held mainly the same ideas. Partners of the important issue houses sat in the House of Commons or among the Lords, where they were in easy touch with the Ministry. In clubs, country week-ends, shooting parties, Sir Ernest Cassel, Lord Rothschild or Lord Revelstoke could learn the official mind and reveal their own.... [T]he smallness of England, the concentration in the same circle of those possessing influence or prestige, the responsiveness to group opinion which ruled, the personal honesty and

discretion of English officialdom, the acceptance by the financial world of a high standard of honour – all these combined to make it easier to understand the freedom left to private judgment. (1934/1974: 87)

Unstated, but implicitly, the 'small circles of power' – political and financial – were indubitably male: that is to say 'In clubs...shooting parties', both male activities; 'the concentration of the same circle of those possessing influence or prestige', the male domain of the political and economic sphere; 'English officialdom', the male public/state sphere; and 'group opinion which ruled' were inordinately male preserves with male values arising from a small but elite section of men. These were indeed the male ruling class and it is within this emerging 'modern' international financial system that the gendered structures need to be situated. In *The Money Lenders*, Anthony Sampson (1981), in discussing international bankers in the 1970s and 1980s, states

[it] isn't misleading or sexist to describe senior bankers as *men;* they maintain a male stronghold. Tens of thousands of women have become tellers...and some have excelled at corporate and international finance.... But at the top of commercial banking, women are rare. 'The men are always playing their own macho game' one woman banker explained. 'It's not really the money they want – it's beating their colleagues by making that extra phone call at night'. (1988: 19)

Work by McDowell (1997) and McDowell and Court (1991) also testifies to the overwhelming masculinist culture which has dominated the City and financial markets for centuries. The values and dominant ideology of this culture are closely intertwined with the assumptions and claims embedded within the principles of neo-classical economics which seek to explain, and so reproduce, the workings of the economic institutions of capitalism. Neo-classical economics prioritises certain explanations of the functioning of markets over others, thus naturalising certain gendered characteristics over others.

Rationality (divided into maximising, bounded and organic) and self-interest orientation (opportunism, simple self-interest and obedience) are also set out as important behavioural aspects of 'contractual man' by Williamson (1985: 43–52), and are essential aspects of understanding the workings of 'economic' institutions. This inclusive environment was reinforced by a network of men-only social institutions, as indicated above, requiring formal membership, such as The City Corporation, the Livery Companies, the London Clubs and Freemasons Lodges which were mechanisms of social regulations and ways of extending contact networks. The effect of this homosocial environment was to exclude women from the City's workforce until towards the end of the nineteenth century when 'gentlewomen' of good family were able to apply or be nominated for clerical positions (Leyshon & Thrift, 1997: 310). This sexual division of labour was also mirrored in the expansion of the US financial industries (Kwolek-Folland, 1994: 14–40) from the mid-nineteenth century onwards. As Kwolek-Folland states in her conclusion, financial industries based a holistic, benevolent image of business on the dichotomies of appropriate gender roles but by doing so

> ... they obscured the power relationships inherent in the corporate hierarchy, inviting confusion of the social or biological structures of gender roles with the social and economic mandates of corporate organisation. In this process, patriarchy and managerial capitalism reinforced each other. (1994: 188)

The history of colonialism is well known not only for the conflict wrought within Europe but also with the rise of great trading companies such as the Dutch East India, Hudson Bay and British East India Companies. Since most people in pre-colonial societies gained their living from the land, the alienation of land to settlers and colonial companies by formal decree or of outright right land seizure had a profound impact. Indigenous people were increasingly restricted to the less productive land and the competition for land as it became a commodity contributed in major ways to the restructuring of labour in colonial economies. An illustration of this is Lord Cornwallis's Permanent Settlement of 1783 which was designed to rationalise the collection of taxes through with the support of zamindars for the treasury of the East India Company. This Act granted the zamindars the status of 'land-holders' reflecting Western ideas of landed property and replacing flexible tax with an annual tax of a fixed amount. The legal consequences were quite profound in that the settlement established individual property rights in land thus making it an exchangeable commodity (Allen & Thomas, 2000). Allen states that this is a good example of colonial policy preserving the existing form of rural society but profoundly changing its content and monetization and the appropriation of a surplus through taxes and rent as integration with the international economy contributed to the commercialisation of economic life.

The changes in ownership which necessarily accompanied this form of capitalism had profound effects on peoples in pre-colonial societies. There was a growth in female poverty since colonial rule disfavoured women's traditional access to land, as private ownership of land was imposed as a requirement for export-orientated commodity production. This not only alienated large sections of the population from adequate and stable resources, but often reduced women's access to resources even more (Sen & Grown, 1987: 29–31).

Colonial appreciation of property rights was strongly shaped by the English constitution, with insistence on taxation only by consent. Attachment to property ownership was powerfully reinforced by intellectual currents in England as political and religious upheaval led to political thinkers analysing the nature of government. However, other aspects of the Anglo-Saxon value system were also transferred. As Nancy Wolock states

> The ships that brought the earliest settlers to Jamestown and Plymouth also carried a heavy load of ideology. Along with their chests and trunks, cows and bibles, English colonists imported firm ideas on how society should be ordered and authority distributed in the family, community and church and state. ... They also knew the basic patterns of power, submission and mutual obligation determined the nature of all relations. ... The position of women was a vital part of this social ideology. (1994: 15)

Ideological understandings of the position of women, Wolock argues, transferred from England were defined by her perceived deficiencies and limitations. She had no innate assets 'God and nature made her weaker in wit, will and physical capacity' (1994: 15–16).

Last, returning to women's activities in informal markets, W. C. Jordan's research covered not only England and other European pre-industrial societies but also pre-colonial and colonial societies. In his conclusion entitled 'Persistent concerns' he concludes that pre-industrial forms and networks of credit provided a vital and important place for women not only within Europe but to a certain extent in pre-colonial, colonial and post-colonial Africa and the Caribbean. General patterns emerged of women's role as creditors in the market for consumption, especially distress loans where women to women networks were particularly strong. Particularly in pre-colonial and colonial societies, women were brokers in regional trade, established clientage relationships with their suppliers and provided 'hidden credit' (both productive and consumption) to husbands and other women even under cultural regimes that severely circumscribed their public activity. However, as in early modern England, commercialisation and urbanization cut deeply into their power (1993, 125–126). With undertones of historical parallels with women in Britain and Europe, Jordan considers a further constraint was that the strong prejudices of Europeans against the active role of indigenous women in colonial markets resulted in the absolute refusal of (and one must assume male) European merchants, colonial bankers and post-colonial development specialists to offer credit to these women, effectively reducing them to domestic traders. However,

> Traditional forms and patterns of domestic credit – women in a prominent role as givers and receivers; small, short-term loans at high annualised interest; face to face interaction; flexibility in relation to defaults; pawning; informal credit associations – survive in Third world societies, in immigrant communities in developed countries, and on the fringes of economic life – often inhabited by illegal immigrants and ethnic minorities – in highly industrialised and post-industrial societies. Every sharp economic crisis gives new life to these forms and patterns. Indeed, it is not likely that they will ever entirely disappear. (1993: 126)

This can only give the briefest outline of the some of the processes which accompanied colonialism and trade, but the central point made is the imposition by colonialism of a specific and masculinised hegemonic ideology inherent in financial markets effectively constrained the ability of women to become independent financial agents.

6
Global Financial Markets: 'Add Women and Stir'

Nannerl Keohane once famously stated 'In women's studies, a good piece of conventional wisdom holds that it is simply not enough to "add women and stir"' (Keohane, 1982: 87). In terms of the gendered construction of financial markets, it too has to be said, it is simply not enough to 'add women and stir'. As previous chapters have shown, historically global finance has excluded the majority of women from credit and finance. However in recent years, both in the North and South, women have been targeted as potential recipients of credit. In this respect, it is crucial to understand that 'At its most basic assumption, credit is when you can afford the loan and debt is when you cannot' (Cunningham, cited in Barty-King, 1977: vi). However, particularly for women in the South, proponents of small-scale credit argue that providing credit contributes to poverty alleviation and empowerment. These proponents have included a variety of institutions such as the Organisation for Economic Cooperation and Development (OECD), the United Nations (UN) and United Nations Development Fund for Women (UNIFEM), the Department for International Development, UK,[30] the World Bank and Oxfam. On the other hand it has been argued that the expansion of a highly volatile, crisis-prone global financial system has already added a further dimension of risk and insecurity to the lives of specific groups and societies, within which structures of gendered inequality further impact on existing processes of subordination (Elson, 1995, 2001; Goetz & Gupta, 1996; van Staveren, 2002).

Globalisation is a complex and much-disputed phenomenon, but there is little dissent towards recognising that global processes are uneven and incomplete. In particular it is economic flows, predominantly in relation to the activities of multinational enterprises, which have seen the most dynamic changes in trans-territorial relations. The increased cross-border flows of traded goods and services, foreign direct investment (FDI), foreign portfolio investments and financial instruments have been greatly facilitated by innovations in information and communication technology (ICT). Some characterise globalisation processes, particularly in terms of economic growth, as integral to 'modernisation', 'progress' and 'development' and ultimately promoting global welfare (Bhagwati, 1985; Feenstra et al., 1995). Many have a more negative understanding of the forces of globalisation, as having increasingly destabilising and inequitable effects upon societies and groups worldwide (Burback et al., 1997; Callinicos, 1994). Societal destabilisation as an outcome has been no more apparent than in the contemporary financial crisis, which has threatened to disrupt the whole project of globalisation itself (Jacques, 2009; Mandelson, 2008).

As stated by Gill (2000), the proponents of globalisation – political economists of the neo-classic persuasion often trained in British and North American universities and in multilateral development banks – have taken as an essential premise a possessively individualist concept of human nature. If the first view is correct, that is of globalisation as a progressive force, we would expect to see an increase in women's equitable access to political, economic and socio-cultural resources. The second view would lead us to expect further entrenchment of gendered power imbalances. The IMF has defined the benefits of globalisation purely in liberal economic terms. Economic globalisation is seen as historical process, the result of human innovation and technological progress, so '...leading to the increasing integration of economies around the world, particularly through trade and financial markets' (2008). Interestingly, the IMF's understanding of the term goes on to state

> [globalisation] refers to an extension beyond national borders of the same market forces that have operated for centuries at all levels of human economic activity – village markets, urban industries, or financial centers...markets promote efficiency through competition and the division of labor – the specialization that allows people and economies to focus on what they do best.

> Global markets offer greater opportunity for people to tap into more and larger markets around the world. It means that they can have access to more capital flows, technology, cheaper imports, and larger export markets. (IMF, 2008)

Although this statement goes on to qualify the promises of globalisation and aver that markets do not necessarily ensure that the benefits of increased efficiency are shared by all, it is implicit in its statement that 'all' are countries, and do not relate to specific groups or classes within and across societies. This chapter argues that, indeed, the deepening and extension of the activities of financial markets within the processes of globalisation have built upon previous subordinations and have done so because of the gendered nature of the international organisation of credit and finance.

Indeed research has indicated that in the past 30 years or more, global restructuring has further entrenched gendered power imbalances (Boserup, 1989; Mies, 1999 [6th edn]; Vickers, 1991) and more generally have noted embedded gender inequalities in relation to the global political economy (Bakker, 1994; Marchand & Runyan, 2000). The focus here is in terms of global restructuring as the critical approach undertaken to explore the significant change in the pace and mobility of financial markets since the 1980s. This, together with the related deepening of competitive structures within the world political economy, has resulted in the search for new markets for capital accumulation activities. Whereas historically gendered structures constrained and directed social relations so as to reproduce inequalities in terms of access to resources for women, in the past couple of decades financial markets have increasingly targeted women, and more particularly specific groups of poor women to draw them into circuits of credit – or as Barty-King inferred – into circuits of debt. Having been excluded very largely by the earlier activities of financial markets, women have been increasingly seen as an 'emerging market' for finance and credit within the context of the opportunities of capital to expand and increase its competitive edge. This has been accomplished by the stretching and deepening of activities so as to reach those areas until recently considered unprofitable and so previously outside the remit of processes of accumulation. Access to resources is at the heart of wealth and poverty, which in turn are intimately linked to distribution.

In the previous chapters, it has been argued that the emergence of formal financial markets as 'male' institutions within a male economic domain can be understood in terms of the historical exclusion of women, in large part, located in the initial transition processes from feudalism to capitalism. It has also been suggested that this transformation was not as complete as some would suggest, and that historical trajectories for men have not been the same as for women. Although the drawing in of women into formal financial activities has benefited specific groups of them, for many more, being drawn into the financial market system has been under exploitative conditions not of their own choosing.

Embedded liberalism: embedded gender

Unlike the classical Gold Standard, the post-war international financial order as constituted in the Bretton Woods system was geared to ensuring that domestic economic objects were not subordinated to international financial disciplines but had primacy over them. At the international level, Ruggie (1982) argued that capital controls, combined with the low level of cross-border flows, were designed so as to allow national authorities considerable autonomy in domestic and economic policy in that the scope for capital mobility and unfettered, self-regulating markets were substantially constrained in 'embedded liberalism'. The welfare nationalist forms of state (Cox, 1987), which were part of the post-war compromise, to all intents and purposes were a product of the social and political response to the harshness and economic depression of the 1930s. Literature on the post-1945 era focuses on the political construction which gave primacy to production over finance, and the consolidation of the political centre against right- and left-wing forces. Gill, for instance, describes the social conditions that gave rise to the (European) welfare state

> ...the social basis of part of the post war hegemonic settlement –
> 1945–7 – was a rough balance between the demands and pressure
> of internationally mobile economic forces and those of domestic social welfare. Vulnerable geographically immobile domestic groups and productive sectors were given protection that allowed time for social adjustment to demands of international competition. (1994: 169)

Within European social democracies, these social structures of accumulation were understood to rest on Fordist production and consumption structures, corporatism and Keynesian macro-economic management supported by a patriarchal welfare state. This period was judged to be one of unprecedented growth and prosperity in the West and Japan, where industrial growth was predicated upon cheap energy. Both the ideological dimensions implicit in Fordism and those institutionalised through welfare systems (in their various forms) had gendered implications which have their roots in the property of and the perceived role and nature of women – and so, of course, men. However, despite the universalistic claims of the welfare state and of development models, both contributed to the further ideological embedding of women into the domestic 'housewife' and 'carer' roles (Hughes & Lewis, 1998: 27). Hughes and Lewis have argued that with the social settlement of the British welfare state, motherhood came to be defined in terms of full-time childcare and homemaking, which was reinforced and reflected by the Family Allowance Act 1946 where married mothers were granted non-contributory allowances for all but the first child. Further, the norm of secure and permanent employment for the majority of household heads ('white, heterosexual, able-bodied males') was built into the structures of national insurance, pensions, family allowance, etc. There was a presupposed key role for women in supporting the male head of household (1998: 27).

Feminist critiques of the welfare state to some extent reflect many of the concerns of Marxism in that they see the state as consolidating unequal relations of power, namely those of men over women. Hughes states this partially reflected the patriarchal nature of the power interests involved in the post-war compromise (political parties, trade unions, corporate capital) in terms of the settlement over the family wage and full (male) employment. Pateman notes that 'class' was also constructed as a patriarchal category in that 'the working class was the class of working *men*' who were also full citizens in the welfare state, as opposed to women, whom she argues were not (Pateman, 1998). In this respect, not only did the welfare state reinforce women's identity as men's dependents both directly and indirectly, but its development presupposed that women were necessarily in need of protection by men and were dependent on them (1998: 232).

It can therefore be understood that, although it has been argued that the emergence of the welfare state saw the rewriting of social relations in capitalism, the script of gender relations remained very largely unaffected in that the material and substantive position of women in relation to access to and control of resources, including financial ones, remained unchanged. Within the private economic sphere, women were routinely refused mortgages and loans, or were granted these on special conditions requiring the signature of a male guarantor (J. Smith, 2001). There was a continuation of historically informed perceptions of the 'nature' of women and their ability (or perceived lack of it) to deal 'rationally' with financial matters. Development models were also infected by this masculinised hegemonic ideology, which resulted in development skewed in favour of men, as in usufruct land rights being replaced by private property as commodification progressed with women losing tradition property rights to men (Benería, 1999; Boserup, 1989; Kabeer, 1994). What is important here is to understand that 'embedded liberalism', whilst restraining (but not totally constraining) the mobility of financial markets, also reinforced existing subordinations of women in the North, whilst expanding and reproducing masculinised hegemonic ideological perceptions of the role and nature of women in the South. The impact of development strategies on men has had significantly different consequences than on women, with substantial evidence to indicate that women generally lost out in this process. Although the United Nations Decade for Women (1976–1985) called upon policy propositions to be initiated for the 'equitable integration' of women (although they had never been 'out' but invisible) in economic development during this period, Goetz stated

> ... these policies have unfolded in the context of a dominant western discourse about development that has reserved for itself the authority to define and name its epistemological categories: 'progress', 'modernisation', and its objects 'third world' and 'third world women'. (Goetz, 1981: 480)

Further, the diffusion of the ideological, historical and culturally specific notion of the nuclear family with its titular male head of household and the naturalised role of women, drawn from Western models of industrialization and modernization, was deemed rational and advantageous to the reproduction of the family unit. Such normative conventions, first promulgated through colonialism and immigrants of European descent, promoted the ideal 'of what it is to be a woman and her essential identity as wife and mother and had framed welfare strategies that were defined appropriate for impoverished "Third World" women' (Saunders, 2002: 2). Saunders further cites Boserup's identification of patterns that excluded women from the formal sector of the economy so that they were bound to a large extent to the subsistence and informal sectors. This very much echoes the discussion in the earlier chapters concerning women's historic exclusion from the 'formal' and relegation to the 'informal' as part of the process of the shift from feudalism to capitalism. Within the informal sectors, women were bound to a large extent to the subsistence and informal sectors where, in urban areas, women's economic activities were (and continue to be) focused on petty trading and prostitution with men disproportionately located in the formal waged section, with training privileges and access to credit (Boserup, 1989 cited by Saunders, 2002: 3–4).

Within the welfare approach to development, women were targeted as 'vulnerable groups' a concept which was then replicated within international development policy as a whole in the dual approach of financial aid for economic growth and relief aid for socially deprived groups. Therefore international economic aid prioritised government support for capital-intensive industrial and agricultural production in the formal sector, focusing on increased productive capacity of the male labour force, whilst ministries for social welfare gave lower priority to 'vulnerable' groups. The welfare approach, then, was based on three assumptions: that women were passive recipients of development rather than participants; that motherhood was the most important role for women in society and that child rearing was the most effective role for women in all aspects of economic development (Moser, 1992: 59–60). This was a clear reiteration of Western notions of women's place, role and activities within the private sphere defined by her reproductive capability. Gender relations were not questioned, nor were redistributional policies considered progressive or of universal applicability. This is what happened in terms of the development policies imposed from above, but not from the increasing opposition and agency which emerged from grassroots levels. It was further premised on Keynesian ideals and classical economics which reflected the 'embedded liberalism' consensus reached within Bretton Woods. The welfare approach to development was introduced in the 1950s and 1960s and was a component of many policy implementations, although its underlying rationale was linked to the residual model of social welfare first introduced by colonial authorities in many 'third world' countries prior to independence. (Wilensky & Lebeaux (1965) cited in Moser, 1992: 58).

However, with the contemporary reconstruction of global capital markets which as Pauly states, is intimately linked to the disruption of the post-war consensus in the 1970s, more particularly framed as 'the breakdown of Bretton Woods', financing in the North, was

> ... confronted the reality of open capital markets ... [so that] prominent bankers, and conservative politicians frequently underscored the internal 'discipline' on autonomous state action implied by international capital mobility. If that discipline implied cutting back the welfare states of the post-World War III era, they asserted, then so be it. (2006: 139)

The Washington Consensus enabled the mainstreaming of liberal economic ideology, becoming the 'development model' from the 1980s. As Thomas stated, over the past 50 years but more particularly in the 1990s, differentiation/stratification increased at the intrastate as well as interstate level for both 'First as for the Third World countries' (Thomas, 1999: 229). The dynamic, she continued, of economically driven globalisation led to a global reproduction of Third World social problems, while at the same time aggravating socio-economic divisions within weak states. 'Concentration of wealth, and social exclusion, seem to be part of a single global process' (1999: 229), and 'Social exclusion of the most vulnerable is intensifying: the old, the young, the disabled, ethnic minority groups, the less skilled, and across all these groups there is a bias against women' (1999: 231). In this respect, the post-war consensus, whilst constraining the power and reach of international finance, at the same time was instrumental in embedding specific gendered understandings of the role and nature of women, and although welfare and welfare policies in the North and South sought to stabilise societies whilst promoting economic growth, they did so at the continuing exclusion of women from formal markets, including financial ones. However, with global restructuring – a consequence in very large part of the crises of the 1970s – women in more recent years have been drawn into financial and credit relations on a global scale.

Globalisation and the global political economy

Within IR and GPE studies there are numerous contending discourses of and critiques on globalisation and it is not intended to deliberate on these here since this debate has been undertaken elsewhere.[31] However a brief overview of global restructuring and its relationship to the expansion of financial markets provides a background to the debate on whether such markets are structurally gendered. The increased reach, mobility and pace of financial markets since the 1970s has been a fundamental catalyst in contemporary global restructuring and 'one of the most spectacular developments in the world economy in recent years' (Helleiner, 1994: 1). Although there are various discussions as to the historical stretch of globalisation, it is generally agreed that global processes since the 1970s have seen a particular dynamic which resulted in the restructuring of both states and firms on a global scale. These processes have also been instrumental in reinforcing and enforcing specific changes within and between societies (Cox & Sinclair, 1997; Gill, 1994, 1997, 1998). As Gill states

> What is being attempted is the creation of a political economy and social order where public policy is premised upon the dominance of the investor and reinforcing the protection of his or her property rights. The mobile investor [has become] ... the sovereign political subject. (1998: 25)

Central to this (re)organisation of the global capitalist order have been the activities and global strategies of the multinational enterprise, including banking and finance, and advances in ICT. Indeed from a liberal economic or globalist[32] perspective, powerful institutional policy-makers such as Alan Greenspan (Kahn, 2000) have taken the definition of globalisation to mean the increasing interaction of national economic systems linked to technological progress and to government policies that have promoted deregulation and privatisation in markets around the world. In particular, techno-logical improvements have been held responsible for lowering trans-action and information costs, so promoting the efficient operation of market-based economic systems. In his report in the Economic Review, Kahn relates how the resulting expansion of markets has been associated with increased competition and reduced tariffs and trade barriers as well as 'other benefits'. These 'other benefits' achieved from globalisation, according to this report, have been caused by increases in foreign investment, in that fostering technology transfer, better training of labour in the host country and generating profits and tax revenues in the host country allows the foreign owners of capital to exploit economies of scale (Kahn, 2000: 5–13). The social and indi-vidual benefits on a world scale, in this view, include an increasing variety of goods and services offered through the market and this also furthers processes of integration. This understanding was also encapsulated in the Washington Consensus, which considered the best path to economic development, or transformation, was through financial and trade liberalisation, which international institutions were to persuade countries to adopt (Williamson, 1990). Once coun-tries adopted financial and trade liberalisation, transnational corpor-ations, financial institutions and actors such as banks, institutional investors and speculators would provide the engine for economic growth, a transformation from underdevelopment to 'development'. As has been argued in earlier chapters, this term 'transformation' or indeed 'transition' from one stage of capitalism to another, hides a gendered condition. It has to be remembered that the dynamics behind these actors and the ability to restructure in order to main-tain and increase profit accumulation and power have been depend-ent upon property being freed of its social relations in order to enable capital to be mobile and liquid, and for financial innovations to become commodities in their own right.

Major changes in the nature, structure and understandings of the now global financial system have seen the rise of the Euro markets (Abbot & Hampton, 1999; Burn, 1999), the demise of the post-war system of fixed exchange rates, market-oriented reform in domestic financial markets and the integration of many once-national capital markets across pol-itical and regulatory boundaries. Private firms have unrestricted access to transactional financial flows and this has led to increased pressure on governments to ease restrictions on business activity, especially for financial institutions, and to 'deregulate' domestic markets. During the 1970s and 1980s the liberalisation of capital flows and global financial integration led to an explosion in offshore activities which, Strange contends, led to the last vestiges of domestic policy autonomy (Strange, 1998). This more 'marketised' financial order, in combination with the liberalisation of trade, permitted owners of capital to choose from amongst a variety of economies offering incentives such as lower inflation, more advantageous interest rates, deregulated labour policies and less restrictive wage rates and hiring practices. Such shifts saw a dramatic reversal in the balance of public and private spheres, and in domestic and international economic management. Feminists have seen this emphasis on the formal spaces of globalisation as fundamentally masculinist in its exclusion of

> ...those economic, cultural, and political spheres (often casual or informal) operating in households and communities, in daily practices of caring, consumption, and religion, and networks of alternative politics where women's contributions to globalisation are often located. (Nagar et al., 2001)

This gendered process, within an increasingly globalised political economy, indicates the differentiated and unequal development which accompanies the gendered structures of global finance, and can be related closely to explanations of social exclusion. With the modernisation and dynamics of financial markets encroaching, deepening and expanding into the South, there are parallels with the shifts which took place within the earlier transition in the North, in that informal/ subsistence sectors are to be found more usually to be inhabited by women, whereas specific groups of men have been shown to be integral to the capitalist enterprise through this gendered dynamic. Yet despite the power dynamics and impact of the increasingly encroaching 'formal' and gendered financial markets into important aspects of states' functioning and thus societal security in far and distanciated spaces, the more traditional forms of women's informal economic and financial activity often remained the only source of resources particularly in times of crisis. To return to W. C. Jordan's statement

> Traditional forms and patterns of domestic credit – women in a prominent role as givers and receivers; small, short-term loans

at high annualised interest; face to face interaction; flexibility in relation to defaults; pawning; informal credit associations – survive in Third world societies, in immigrant communities in developed countries, and on the fringes of economic life – often inhabited by illegal immigrants and ethnic minorities – in highly industrialised and post-industrial societies. Every sharp economic crisis gives new life to these forms and patterns. Indeed, it is not likely that they will ever entirely disappear. (1993: 126)

Indeed, Jeff Powell has asserted that in the past two decades there has been a remarkable resurgence of non-state monetary systems, diverse in range but with characteristics in common in that they are interest-free monies created by non-state, not-for-profit actors. He states that these initiatives, like their predecessors, have emerged as a result of marginalisation from the capitalist economy. He cites the case of *Red del Tueque* in Argentina which grew substantially during recent periods of crisis. This system he considers is vital to its members' interests and although Powell does not link this specifically to gender, he does state that gender relations are being transformed through participation in the network. 'Women are assuming a role as a pivot between the formal economy, the informal economy and the barter economy' (2003: 619–649). In this respect, scholars from diverse approaches have considered these systems to be an integral part of their agendas for social change (Elson, 1999; Henderson, 1999; van Staveren, 1998). Henderson further argues that these offer an alternative agenda in anti-globalisation and anti-corporation debates.

Gendered markets

It is no longer possible, if it ever were, to treat the informal and formal spheres as separate entities. The reach and deepening of the formal aspects of global finance no longer allows us to see the 'often casual and informal' practices as something separate and apart from those activities grounded at the domestic, community and national level. An illustration of this is the blurring of the domestic daily practices of caring and consumption, the privatisation of welfare and the marketing strategies of credit organisations whether through supermarkets, catalogue companies or micro-credit schemes. The engines of growth have driven deep into society, enabled by trade and other forces of liberalisation, alliances formed and organisations transformed by the accumulation strategies of transnational corporations, financial institutions and actors such as banks and institutional investors. Formal credit markets are increasingly being linked to 'alternative' (informal?) micro-credit schemes, and multinational corporations increasingly sub-contract to companies who use informal markets or home working for cheap labour (Collins, 2003; Merc, 2003). Since the emergence of formal markets, informal markets have often underpinned and supported economic activity in the other sector. Further, feminists see the informal spheres as key sites for understanding globalisation processes 'in their own right' because 'it is precisely these spheres and activities that underwrite and actively constitute the public spheres of globalisation' (Nagar et al., 2001), with feminist academics and women's movements increasingly directing attention to the highly uneven and gendered impact of the current 'transformations'.

Euro markets/offshore banking provided the lever for financial deregulation and increased capital mobility, which led to enhanced freedom of capital to facilitate greater competition and, in keeping with neo-liberal economic theory, greater efficiency in the distribution of scarce resources. As has been stated earlier, this is associated with understandings of efficient markets in terms of achieving lower costs and more flexible adjustment processes in terms of production and services across the world economy. Such processes have been supported and enabled through the (neo) liberal economic character of the policies of states such as United States and Britain, international institutions such as the IMF and World Bank and transnational enterprises – engines of growth – whose interests are, in theory, supported by promoting a 'free' or 'freer' market economy. This assumption in itself is highly debatable but alas, cannot be dealt with here.[33] On the other hand, deregulation and increased capital mobility have led to a highly competitive global economy with increased instability and volatility, and associated escalation of risk and inequality on a global, as well as a local, scale (Helleiner, 1994; ILO (International Labour Organisation), 1998; Mitchie & Grieve Smith, 1999; Thomas, 1999). Susan Strange termed this instability 'casino capitalism', a phenomenon she linked to five trends of that time: innovations in the way in which financial markets work; the sheer size of markets; commercial banks turned into investment banks; the emergence of Asian nations as players and the shift to self-regulation by banks (1986: 10). Even before the present financial crisis began to unfold, critiques of 'casino capitalism' focused on the structure of markets and their relationship to social institutions where the instability and volatility of active markets can devalue the economic base of real lives or indeed can lead to the near collapse of national and regional economies. Iceland is a case in point (Iceland Government Information Centre, 2009). Although more recent data is difficult to access, an indication of the size and flow of foreign exchange transactions indicates that worldwide this reached $13 trillion a day in 1995 (a corresponding figure in the early 1970s being $18 billion) which is the equivalent to $313 trillion a year of 240 business days (Tobin, 1996 cited by Mitchie & Grieve Smith, 1999: 151). By comparison, the annual global turnover in equity markets in 1995 was $21 trillion, whereas the annual global trade in goods and services was $5 trillion (and total reserves of central banks around $1.5 trillion at the end of 1995) (Mitchie & Grieve Smith, 1999: 151).

At the time of editing, the world is in the process of coming to terms with a long-expected (in many academic quarters) credit crisis brought on ostensibly by the problem of the US sub-prime market. The consequences in terms of depth and reach of this crisis are still unfolding as is the gendered impact – and there will be one. For the past decade or so, worldwide there has been an increased promotion of credit at all levels of society – which is more accurately stated as the promotion of increased levels of debt and thus insecurity. The full force of this promotion of 'credit' is now coming home to policy-makers everywhere. In August 2007, central banks around the world had pumped some $323 billion into the system, (Teacher et al., 2007), with the US Federal Reserve and the European Central Bank, with Canadian, Swiss and British national banks putting forward a further $40 billion to lessen the fear of cash non-availability (Irwin, 2007) resulting from the apparent structural failure of neo-liberal deregulation's claim of free markets producing the best profits on the basis of little government interference. In the meantime, it has been reported that the number of house repossessions in Britain were set to rise to atleast 75,000 repossessions in 2009 (The Guardian, 2009). The Bank of England reported that the total personal debt in the UK in July 2007 was £1,355 on cards, mortgages and loans (BBC Business

News, 2008). In very large part, however, the risk and insecurities associated with the awarding of credit through financial markets is passed on to the recipients whilst the rewards in terms of high return accumulation remain with those who are in control of financial market activities.

States and international institutions have also been directly involved in the promotion of market-based micro-credit schemes as a means of alleviating poverty and social exclusion, as well as utilising credit in its many forms to promote consumerism as an essential mechanism for the promotion and maintenance of economic growth. It is only now that the risks involved in promoting this type of growth are truly becoming apparent for policy-makers and operators within financial markets more generally. Paterson (2002) has argued that the credit-driven nature of contemporary capitalism reinforces the importance of consumption, with levels of personal, corporate and state debt consistently rising. Some of this, he states, is to finance investment, but much is about financing consumption, and this consumption-credit connection is a key source of growth – and indeed now crisis – in contemporary economies. Consumer credit has also been seen as short-term substitution in lieu of a broad redistribution of new productivity gains:

> In the 1920s, the crisis of increased productive capacity and ineffective consumer purchasing power was met by the extension of consumer credit to unprecedented levels. The same phenomenon is occurring today. The productivity gains brought on by the information and telecommunications revolutions are finally being felt and, in the process, virtually every major industry is facing global under-utilisation of capacity and insufficient consumer demand. Once again, in the US consumer credit has become the palliative, a way to keep the economic engines throttled up, at least for a time. (Rifkind, 2000 cited by *Financial Times*, 2000)

For van der Pijl (1998), consumption is regarded as an inherent part of cycles of commodification and thus crucial to capitalist reproduction. For Sklair (2002) it is the culture-ideology of consumerism which is an essential element for the successful transition to capitalist modernisation and subsequent capitalist globalisation.

He cites Wells as stating that the concept of modernisation needed to be split analytically and replaced by the concepts of consumerism (the increase in consumption of the material culture of the developed countries) and producerism (the increased mobilisation of the society's population to work) (Wells, 1972: 47 cited by Sklair, 2002: 165). It is not intended to expand here on this aspect of credit in relation to sustaining growth in the economy since this is a complete research area of its own, particularly if using a gendered analysis. Indeed, the rise of consumerism in relation to women has a long history.[34] However, it is a strong indication of what structural forces in relation to financial markets and the economy, as well as at state levels have been at work in a highly competitive global economy so as to ease or further deregulate credit restrictions in order to make credit available – but not affordable – to those in need. If Matt Barrett, Chief Executive of Barclays Bank admitted that he did not use his company's credit card or anyone else's 'because it is too expensive' and urged his four children not to do so either, the ethics in promoting general credit availability seem highly questionable (*The Guardian*, 2003). Moreover, recent high levels of credit availability have required a cultural change in relation to people's acceptance of debt.

It is in this context that women, excluded for centuries from formal financial activity and credit markets, have more recently been brought into financial markets – more often at high cost, increased insecurity and risk to themselves and their families. The ideological framework for policies of deregulation, capital mobility and increased efficiency has evolved primarily around a neo-liberal set of theories, practices and assumptions, which are equated with competition, efficiency, progress and civilisation. Gill cites Samir Amin's notion of 'Eurocentrism' as being a claim to social hegemony of a set of particular culturally rooted practices and ideological/intersubjective understandings that are presented as having universal applicability. '[Eurocentrism] claims that imitation of the Western model by all peoples is the only solution to the challenges of our time' (Amin, 1989 cited by Gill, 1997: 5). In other words, inherent in globalising, free-market processes has been a set of associated assumptions and claims containing specific sets of beliefs, values, ethics and expectations, which have sought to impose or modify previously existing norms in society. In enriching Amin's notion of 'Eurocentrism' with Connell's concept of masculinised hegemonic ideology (1995: 77), the missing gendered dimension can be added to those globalising, free-market processes so as to provide a fuller and complementary understanding to 'social hegemony'. This sits well with Amin's concerns with 'Eurocentrism' since Connell contends that the foundation of contemporary hegemonic masculinity has its roots in the accumulation and concentration of wealth during colonial times (1995).

Those critical of changes in the financial system consider it to have promoted a more volatile, market-driven financial environment which has resulted in a 'hollowing out' of the state (Jessop, 1993; Strange, 1998) – a phenomenon which can be argued to have applied much earlier to many states in the South. Such arguments are concerned with the transformed role of the state to one of pursuing competitive political economic strategies in line with the competition state thesis (Cerny, 1995). The competition state thesis suggests that,

> The outer limits of effective action by the state ... are usually seen to comprise its capacity to promote a relatively favourable investment climate for transnational capital – i.e. by providing an increasingly circumscribed range of goods that retain a national-scale (or sub national-scale) public character or of a particular type of still-specific assets described as immobile factors of capital. Such potentially manipulable factors include human capital ...; infrastructure ...; support for a critical mass of research and development activities; basic public services necessary for a good quality of life for those working in middle- to high-level positions in an otherwise footloose environment ... firms and sectors; and maintenance of a public policy environment favourable to investment (and profit making) by such companies, whether domestic or foreign-owned. (Cerny, 1995: 611)

It should be noted that Cerny does consider the 'competition state' process to be profoundly paradoxical in (at least) three ways. First, globalisation can undermine both the domestic autonomy and political effectiveness of the state and at the same time lead to actual expansion of *de facto* state intervention and regulation in the name of competitiveness and marketisation. Second, states and state actors are among the greatest promoters of further globalisation as they attempt to cope more effectively with 'global realities'. 'In under-mining the autonomy of their own national models...they disarm themselves. And...[thirdly] states seem to be getting more and more socially fragile – thereby further undermining the capacity of polit-ical and social forces within the state to resist globalization' (Cerny, 2000: 300).

In other words, there is a structural component to the increased levels of competitiveness at a global level and this is being articulated through the activities and policies of states and firms and impacting on societies in very specific but diverse ways. This structural compo-nent includes seeking or opening up 'emerging markets' for further capital accumulation. The term emerging markets is used in relation to foreign capital flows from the North which, from the beginning of the 1990s, were once again directed to the South. Whereas such markets were previously termed 'less developed countries', a process of a rebranding took place and in the language of big business they became known as 'emerging markets' (Roberts, 1999: 18). In this pressure for multinational corporations, elites and financial institu-tions to seek further avenues and strategies for profit accumulation and power, increased networks or alliances between states and firms, and between firms have formed in a process which Dunning has termed alliance capitalism (Dunning, 1997), facilitated by ICT into 'global network society' (Castells, 1996).

Returning to Cerny's competition state thesis, the policies pur-sued by states in the past couple of decades or so have been in large part directed toward attracting FDI. Yet, in relation to the deregu-lated and highly mobile financial system, the assumption that the international mobility of short-term capital facilitates longer-term FDI and expanding trade in goods and services is countered by an increasing understanding that such economic expansion comes with new risks for governments, societies and individuals (Pauly, 2006: 139). Further, connections have been drawn between the principle of international capital mobility and various phenomena such as the retrenchment of national welfare states, monetary union in Western Europe, political and social crises in East Asia, traumatic systemic transformations in Russia and its neighbouring states and of course, the present financial and banking crisis. It has also led to the aban-donment of long-standing development models in Latin America and Africa. As a result of its increased volatility, the market-driven financial environment, with its associated contagion effects – and now the sub-prime and associated credit crisis of 2007–2009 while on the one hand having contributed significantly to the wealth and power of specific (male) groups and individuals, has on the other hand contributed to the increased risk and vulnerability of a high proportion of the population situated within and across societies (Pauly, 2006: 139).

There is therefore general recognition that the globalisation of financial processes has involved the spacial extension of areas of activity through the liberalisation of markets, as well as a deepening of market-led activities. Financial liberalisation has been posited as a desirable policy because like trade liberalisation, it is seen to lead to economic growth and stability. This is related to the neo-classical assumption that debtor countries should be exposed more directly to the exigencies of transnational finance so that such countries are forced to undertake market-based solutions to their current economic and political problems. Many scholars have emphasised the influence of neo-liberal ideology in determining the direction of globalisation, in particular its disciplinary nature, providing the direction for global transformatory processes since the 1970s (Cox, 1994; Gill, 1994, 1997; Marchand & Runyan, 2000). This has been related to the introduction by states of deregulatory policies, the liberalisation of domestic markets and the privatisation of state enterprises, either in terms of honing their competitive strategies or under the coercive influence of structural adjustment policies (Afshar & Barrientos, 1999; Thomas, 1999) which in turn have produced gendered results (Elson, 1995; Nahid & Gale, 2000; Osirim, 2003; Sparr, 1994). Developing countries, and those in transition, are incorporated into the global financial system but in a manner which is strongly hierarchical, gendered and uneven. In the 1990s, increased flows of credit have linked state markets more closely with world markets on some occasions, but on other occasions many have suffered from credit rating rationing.[35] The poorest countries have, however, remained, on the margins of private international finance and reliant on aid while the bulk of FDI is still directed towards the developed world. This may be seen as a form of global social exclusion.

In 1998, according to Held et al., some 90 countries were engaged in various forms of IMF structural adjustment programs (SAPs), partially as a result of the turbulence of the previous two decades. The drastic reversal of development in the 1980s, within which the oil and related debt crises were perceived to play a crucial role, saw repeated attempts at economic stabilisation and adjustment supported by the neo-liberal and free-market economic policies embedded within SAPs and supported by other interests, but these failed to produce the desired outcomes (1999: 201). The social and political implications were understood as threatening both at the local and the global levels with the financial system in crisis, and with an increase in social exclusion and violence (Escobar, 1995: 90).

Significant research has been carried out in relation to the gendered impact in times of crisis or austerity. It is the general position of women in society and their capacity to stretch their budgets to feed, clothe and care for their families, Enloe argues, which enables governments to retain their legitimacy:

> Thus the politics of international debt is not simply something that has an impact on women in indebted countries. The politics of international debt won't work in their current form unless mothers and wives are willing to behave in ways that enable nervous regimes to adopt cost-cutting measures without forfeiting their political legitimacy. (Enloe, 2001: 185)

As Elson and Çagatay so eloquently point out, in times of crisis it is women who are called upon to act as the heroes of everyday life, providing the ultimate social safety net for their families when all other forms of social security have failed. (Elson & Çagatay, 2000). Yet, as argued throughout, women's access and control of financial resources has been significantly curtailed by the encroachment of formal and gendered financial markets and the accompanying masculinised hegemonic ideology about the role and nature of women. It is recognised that patriarchy exists in many societies but with the increased institutionalisation of a market economy in finance and credit, the value system which accompanies it is to the detriment of women in particular. Whereas globalisation has given opportunities to certain groups of women to achieve greater personal autonomy, it is within an increasingly unequal and risk-laden environment. Accordingly, the statement by Gill that the limits of market civilisation became apparent as social atomisation and inequality intensified and the contradictions of a more crisis-prone form of global economic development became clear (Gill, 1997: 94) also requires a gendered qualification.

Gendered dimensions of global finance and insecurity

Since the substantive concern of this book is the apparent systematic exclusion of women from benefits that may have resulted from the enormous expansion in financial, monetary, investment and credit flow, it is also essential to consider the impact of global financial flows on and across societies. In the latter decades of the twentieth century (and into the twenty-first), it is generally recognised that the gap between the poorest and the richest countries has continued to widen and this has been linked to trade liberalisation (Pritchett, 1997). Within this general trend, the 1999 United Nations Human Development Report reveals that 'there is gender inequality in every society...including in political and professional life' (UNDP, 1999: 132). Yet with global finance so central to globalising processes, it is only recently that feminists and development theorists have begun to focus attention on the analysis of its gendered dimensions. These gendered dimensions, as van Staveren indicates, occur at 'the micro level (including the intrahousehold level); the meso level (industry, banking, government institutions, taxation); and the macro level (nationally as well as globally)' (2002). She further indicates that, based on other studies, the gendered effects of global finance are not very positive, with the explanations given as the lack of representation of women within financial institutions and governments, the increased gender gaps which global finance promotes, the instability induced by the prevailing gender structures in global financial markets and inefficient resource allocations in these markets instigated by gender discrimination (2002: 229–231).

In terms of finance, markets are understood as being structured sets of practices in which wealth and power are created, appropriated and then used in particular ways so that they become themselves structure of power. Further, the social actors within markets are assumed to be more usually private individuals and firms whose actions both collectively shape the structure of markets and are shaped by this collectively produced behaviour (Germain, 1997: 24). Where I depart from Germain is that, as has previously been argued, the sets of practices, which are instituted by those social actors involved in financial markets, are gendered and thus constitute gendered structures. These structures are more generally understood by many feminist scholars as translating into the marginalisation of women's issues in policy processes regarding government – and global institutional – lending, investment rules and private sector financial activities which have negative effects for and upon women. This has been the case with, for instance, SAPs. As a result of prolonged pressure from, in particular, women's movements, the World Bank came up with a Gender Mainstreaming Strategy, endorsed by Bank Executive Directors on 18 September 2001. This strategy's aims have been to streamline gender concerns into World Bank policies, starting with integration into Poverty Reduction Strategy Papers and Joint Staff Assessments. Further work involves conducting Country Gender Assessments (CGAs) in all actively borrowing countries, principally to identify gender-sensitive responses to poverty alleviation and economic growth to include consideration of male/female roles, allocation of resources and conferment of rights (World Bank, 2008b). This is laudable but it tends towards 'add women and stir', whilst the fundamental problem of using the one basic economic model as a universalising principle in terms of liberalisation remains.

This can be seen in terms of gender research arising from previous financial crises. At a critical level, Ling argues that in order to sustain Western capitalist hegemony in the global economy after the Asian financial crisis, the liberal international order embarked upon strategies which sought '... to (re)feminize Asia by discrediting the region's claim to a muscular, alternative capitalism', secondly to '(re)masculize the role of Western capital in the region by buying out Asian capital at bankrupt prices' and thirdly '(re)hegemonise relations in the region both domestically and internally by mimicking cold war power politics.' (Ling, 2002: 119). She further asks why stereotypes of masculinity and feminity still drive this competition. Although Ling is concerned with the way in which Asia firstly 'mimicked' the capitalism of the West but then changed substantively to incorporate aspects of its own institutional and cultural characteristics, it has become what she calls hypermasculine in its approach to capitalist competition with dire consequences internally for race and gender. Ling continues that the application of post-colonial theories of IR applied to the Asian financial crisis would discover that the hypermasculine, developmental state was regulating a hyperfeminised society under the rubric of national recovery; '... and depressed men exploiting women and other feminized subjects (children, minorities) for the health, wealth, and happiness of the patriarchal family-state-economy' (2002: 119–120). In extending Nandy's hypermasculine pathology[36] to the capitalist world economy, Ling suggests

> Hypermasculine capitalism reconstructs social subjects, spaces, and activities into economic agents that valorise a masculined, global competitiveness associated with men, entrepreneurs, the upwardly mobile, cities and industrialisation. It assigns a hyper-feminized stagnancy to local women, peasants, the poor and agrarian production. (Ling, 2002: 119)

It is both interesting and relevant to note that such characteristics of masculinism outlined by Ling are clearly reflected in work such as McDowell's on the cultural practices embedded with in the City of London, a highly symbolic site of global financial power. In seeking to explore the gendered character of workplace relations McDowell brings clearly to the fore the territory's hostility for those whose identities are marginalised by the implicit and valorised masculinity of City financial culture. An illustration of this is McDowell's contention that it is male power which is implicitly and explicitly reinforced. It is reinforced implicitly in many of the micro-scale interactions in organisations such as in workplace talk and jokes, for example 'men see humour, testing camaraderie and strength...women often perceive crude, specifically masculine aggression, competition, harassment, intimidation and misogny' (1997), and it is explicitly reinforced in the formal structures of institutions and their recruitment, promotion and appraisal mechanisms.

Although Ling's understanding of the way in which Asia has undertaken a process of hypermasculinity appears to be specific, to some extent it reflects the changing role of states as a reaction to global competition. If global competition is reduced to understandings of profit accumulation, this in turn raises questions as to the ways in which the role and nature of other states change also, so as to provide a stable environment for accumulation in the context of international competitiveness, and whether others adopt masculine characteristics in order to do so. In treating women as an emerging market, financial markets are imposing the values of wants instead of needs through consumerism and profit requirements instead of resources for sustainable social reproduction. States are complicit in this venture by promoting consumerism, not least, through credit. To a certain extent, such processes may be discerned in relation to, for example, shifts in the provision of social services and welfare (broadly defined) across societies, resulting in growing evidence of increased social fragmentation, disintegration and the uneven distribution of resources within and between states, all of which has a gendered dimension. The Human Development Report 1999 set out six areas of insecurity which are said to pervade society: jobs and income, health, cultural, personal, environmental and political and community. The report sets out both the growing inequalities between and within states that result in 'The erosion of family and community solidarity' and the gendered nature of these changes in that 'globalization has given rise to ambiguous and at times contradictory effects on gender equality' (UNDP, 1999: 83). This gendered dimension can be related to the rise of the discourse of 'social exclusion' and 'poverty alleviation' particularly in relation to women. The resolution to this exclusion and poverty alleviation has been to construct policies to draw the poorer sections of societies globally into the provision of financial resources and credit as forms of welfare from private institutions as opposed to state provision. Relatively little research has been undertaken into the 'financialisation' of economies in terms of its gendered impact – the one obvious example here is pension provision through the private sector. As Condon so aptly states, the discourse of 'retirement' itself has a gendered content in that 'what is being referenced is retirement from the productive labour force, not the ongoing work of social reproduction for which women take significant responsibility' (2007: 95). In other words, there is a gendered dimension to the impact of financial markets and the imperatives of finance capital – whether in crisis or not.

Marginalisation and the socially excluded

Global restructuring has been associated with states introducing deregulatory policies, the liberalisation of domestic markets and the privatisation of state enterprises, which have gone hand in hand with the restructuring and/or privatisation of many aspects of social welfare. As a consequence, global restructuring within an increasingly competitive environment has led to a reconfiguration of practices which places certain groups within and across societies as being considered 'socially excluded' or severely marginalised, within reduced social and community safety nets. As is generally acknowledged, neither global finance, nor credit, trade and production, can be separated from its functioning, or the generation of insecurities and increased risk in and across societies. In this respect, such insecurities often provide opportunities for further accumulation for those in power. Whereas the feminisation or 'housewifization' of production (Boserup, 1989; Mies, 1999; Moghadam, 2000) has received much attention from feminists, the focus here is on the relationship of insecurities to the deepening circuits of credit that in gendered financial markets have led to the exclusion of women from the benefits that may have accrued with the expansion of credit and finance.

Structural adjustment policies include policies in public sector employment, limitations on food and agricultural subsidies, denationalisation of public sector enterprises and reductions in public expenditure, which together are envisaged as increasing global competition and efficiency. Policies include not only credit incentives to stimulate productive capacity, but tax holidays and trade and tariff reforms to encourage export production. Further, small-scale entrepreneurial activity – a crucial principle in neo-liberal economic theory – is also encouraged through a decentralisation of credit extension. Implicit in this approach is the assumption that increasing productive capacity will generate employment for those increasingly dispossessed of both land and other productive resources, consequently leading to economic growth. It must be emphasised that, historically, production has been seen as a male activity rather than as an access to resources including finance and credit, for the purposes of general reproduction, which is more narrowly defined as social reproduction – the sphere of female activity. Such shifts in development strategy involved 'short term' costs which, Feldman states, are recognised as bearing disproportionately on the poor (Feldman, 1992: 3). A disproportionate number of the poor are women. 'Protecting the vulnerable' and 'poverty alleviation' then become the policy goals rather than challenging the conditions that create a significant proportion of a society's impoverished members. Further, these strategies are thought to enable long-term growth with equity, but this is difficult to envisage when it has been argued that the 'level playing field' of economic liberalism has been constructed with built-in gendered, class and other structural obstacles such as inequitable ownership, access and control of resources. In this respect, it has been frustratingly difficult to find statistics indicating women's ownership of property in terms of land, a crucial asset in terms of raising finance and credit but also because of the various rights other than 'private' which can be applied to property. Further, even if women worldwide 'owned' property, economic growth dependent on ownership of resources/private property cannot take into account the needs of society or community. In other words, perceptions of the distribution of private property on an equitable gendered basis in diverse societies raises other problems.

The key point here is that responsibility for making ends meet without control over resources is a source of constant insecurity, risk and anxiety for many women across the world. It is they who ultimately have to devise household survival strategies but it is their husbands or other males who control access to major and crucial resources. As Elson argues, there is evidence to show that in both developed and developing countries, through a wide spectrum of class positions and even in very poor households, men tend to maintain a personal allowance largely spent on luxuries such as alcohol, cigarettes, gambling and socialising. (Elson, 1992, Elson & Çagatay, 2000). This is also born out by research undertaken by financial and other firms in the North in terms of strategising their marketing towards poor but profit-making sectors. As discussed previously, the site of the household, for Wallerstein (1984, 1992) has been seen as problematic for capitalism, not least as the site of conflicting values and unequal ownership and control of resources. In this arena, the benefits of a market economy are limited because unequal gender relations structure the reproduction of human resources and because the reproduction and maintenance of human resources cannot directly and immediately respond to market signals '...as long as human beings are regarded as having an intrinsic and not merely instrumental value' (Elson, 1992: 37). Yet ultimately liberal economic theory takes as its goal increased economic growth through participation in the free-market system which it contends leads to increased standards of living – it is not seen as a zero-sum game but one in which global welfare can be seen as a benefit to all.

It often argued, in particular, by economists, that access to credit on market terms is a crucial resource for any group: whether individual, firm, community or state, it is an absolute necessity, and for women in particular, a means of 'empowerment' through entering into economic market activity. Yet on the other hand, it can be seen as intensifying the possibilities of and deepening the effects of insecurity and risk. With the costs of living in an increasingly competitive global political economy being born by those with the fewest resources, and with retrenchment and ideological shifts in welfare provision in both the North and the South, international institutions, states and non-governmental organisations (NGOs) are now involved in strategies of 'poverty alleviation' and 'social inclusion'. Within this discourse since the late 1990s, income maintenance and financial inclusion have become key development goals, with empowerment of the individual a stated objective. This shift in discourse can be recognised in the World Bank's World Development Report of 2008, calling for a concerted attack on world poverty, with an entire section devoted to empowerment. Empowerment, as defined by the World Bank, is

> ... the process of increasing the capacity of individuals or groups to make choices and to transform those choices into desired actions and outcomes. Central to this process are actions which both build individual and collective assets, and improve the efficiency and fairness of the organizational and institutional context which govern the use of these assets. (World Bank, 2008a)

This concurs with Parpart et al.'s statement that the World Bank and mainstream development agencies see empowerment as a mechanism for improved efficiency, whereas alternative agencies 'claim it as a metaphor for fundamental social transformation' (2002: 41). With the increased freedom and mobility of financial markets having seen a restructuring of the state in both the North and the South, with consequences for the provision of welfare, there has been an increased move towards an income maintenance system which combines an increased emphasis on individual moral responsibility with the aim of reducing state expenditure. This has been seen as the way forwards from a state of social exclusion to one of social inclusion and finance, credit and financial services through the market are promoted as the way in which this may be achieved. However, since fundamental social transformation would appear the only proposition which would enable a more equitable society in terms of gender, rather than drawing women into gendered markets, such a strategy of promoting social inclusion and empowerment would seem counter-intuitive.

7
Deepening the Circuits of Credit: Gender and 'a Deeper Share of Wallet'

Restructuring on a global scale has resulted in some recognition of the need to alleviate poverty, much of which is recognised as being of a gendered nature. This has seen processes which are placing an increased emphasis on the interactive nature of households, security and the economy in terms of the intrusion of credit relations and other financial services. Although in different locations and spaces it takes on different forms, there is a general pattern of drawing women into relations of credit and finance as a way of achieving income maintenance. This can be related to the shift in political discourses since the 1980s, from a collectivist social democratic ideology to that of an individualistic neo-liberalism, which Cutler states leads to a redefinition of the political problem 'Inequality leaves the stage because its resolution requires distribution. Its replacement is "exclusion" which becomes in effect a problem of lifestyle...and part of "inclusion" is the individual management of risk as a member of the workforce' (Cutler & Waine, 2001: 113). Access to employment is then defined as the means of escaping from welfare dependency, poverty alleviation or 'underdevelopment' and developing economic solvency and independence. In the North this tends to be structured around the possibility of regulated markets rather than state provision of, for example, pensions. Welfare is increasingly commodified and sold to the consumer as 'financial products' while access to employment itself is now seen as a core aspect of welfare. Reliance on the private sector for provision of financial products, including pensions, is often subject to the vagaries of stock markets leading to increased insecurities. In this respect over the past 20 years or so not only has the state become embedded in a globalised financial environment where government decision-making is vulnerable to financial markets, but financialisation has fashioned that environment, influencing the order of, and pressures involved in, such participation. The various elements of financialisation cover a range of neo-liberal doctrines such as deregulation, privatisation, user pays and the rise of pension funds as well as changes in ICT and its various contributions to financial innovation (Greenfield & Williams, 2007). With a shift in the state's policies has come the move from 'welfare to workfare', with welfare provisioning increasingly being seen in terms of making access to 'financial products' and bank accounts more attainable for all (Leyshon & Thrift, 1997: 7). And here the financial service sector is clearly an integral part of global financial markets as a provider of pensions and other forms of 'security', not least since the largest investors in financial markets are pension funds. In this respect, the boundaries of the different sectors within global finance are increasingly blurred and interdependent. However, the move from welfare to workfare, and welfare provisioning through the market, builds upon existing inequitable structures in society, particularly in regard to women's employment, and involves the promotion of commodities through financial markets. Although relating to Britain alone, a report undertaken to identify gender differences in wealth in Britain by Rowlingson et al. illustrates that economic inequality revealed in the analysis of income differences, accumulates over the life-course. They concluded

> ...typical female carer-dominated employment profiles – combined with the financial dependence on another income source which this type of working pattern entails – are continuing to damage women's chances of a decent income in their own right in the short term. In addition, in the medium term, they are depriving women of a savings safety net in their working lives. A longer term risk is that in a future Britain, where individuals will increasingly depend on private pensions rather than a state minimum, and one with a falling remuneration rate at that, the poverty which many women currently face in old age could very well persist. (1999)

Indeed it has been argued that the turn to financialised provision in pensions is creating new forms of gender inequality. Condon considers that the power of financial institutions resides in part in the ability to define the risk of financial problems in retirement and to offer their own, market-based solutions to these resulting in individual employees, particularly lower-income women, being governed more intensively than employers who are regulated less stringently (Condon, 2007: 100). Since in all countries of the world, women earn less than men, this is one illustration of how inequitable distribution of resources is reproduced through gendered structures and is indicative of the ways in which the different aspects of a capitalist society reflect the gendered nature of its material and substantive practices. Such policies are more usually seen in terms of the need to reduce state expenditure, and as a shift from the state as provider to the state as enabler. Despite recent resistance by social democratic states such as France and Germany to the encroachment on their welfare systems, they too are in the throes of change. Perhaps more accurately, it may be argued that the state's perceived inability to collect revenues for welfare and social provision from wealthy individuals and corporations in an era of capital mobility, offshore and global competition (Hampton, 2002; Oxfam, 2000) is a more convincing explanation than the domestic debate more often than not articulated in terms of availability of benefits not undermining incentives to work.

Further, the emergent liberal economic framework dominated by concern about individual moral responsibility for the maintenance of household income has been in tension with a conservative ideology which seeks to reinforce the centrality of women's 'natural' role within the family. This can be noted within the United States, where the 'moral majority's' reassertion of family values and the role of women within the family coincided with a continuing rise in women's employment and small improvements in women's earnings relative to men's (J. Clarke, 1994: 204). Within the United Kingdom, there have been similar and regular calls over the past 20 years by conservative interests to return to 'family values' (for example Daily Telegraph, 2008), with a particular culture of blame being laid upon single mothers. As stated by J. Clarke '...an increasing punitive public and political view of "welfare mothers" has transferred blame away from wider social economic and political circumstances onto an easier target' (1994: 205). In researching changes in the Canadian welfare system, Jenson states that such policies are supported by the idea that '... all able bodied people, and youth in particular, are effect-ively "undeserving" of social assistance if they do not try to retrain to participate more effectively in the job market and an underlying assumption that households are headed by male breadwinners' (Jenson & Sineau, 2001). Mies states that the effect of these eco-nomic policies has been a rapid process of pauperisation of women in Western economies '... in that they constitute the largest section among the "new poor" in the USA, in France, in England and West Germany' (Mies, 1999: 16). Although the research upon which Mies based her work was undertaken for the first edition of *Patriarchy and Accumulation* published in 1986, the 'feminisation of poverty' appears to have continued apace. This had then led to an increasing process of marginalisation of specific groups of women both in the North and the South within which class and ethnicity play a part. With increased emphasis on the market as provider, particularly in terms of financial provision, there was also a narrowing of resources, and in this case finance and credit, upon which women particularly in times of crisis and vulnerability could draw.

Social exclusion – financial exclusion

The notion of 'social exclusion' began making an appearance in US debates about single mothers and welfare dating from the late 1970s. It has since been taken up by policy-makers, bureaucrats and scholars worldwide, resulting in a mushrooming of a multitude of institutions focusing on social exclusion in order to set policies, undertake research or tackle what are perceived to be the base causes of this 'exclusion'. For instance, the World Bank uses the term when stating that it must ensure '... that actions taken today to promote development and reduce poverty do not result in environmental degradation or social exclusion'. The Social Programs Division of the Sustainable Development Department (SDS/SOC) of the International Development Bank seeks to

> ... support the Bank and its borrowing countries towards the goal of the inclusion and participation of all individuals ... regardless of race, ethnicity, gender or physical condition. SDS/SOC aims to give

technical support to the borrowing countries in their attempts to expand access to socially excluded groups to the services, physical conditions and legal rights necessary to live a decent life. (World Bank, 2006)

The British government set up a Social Exclusion Unit in 1998 and related social exclusion to '...what can happen when people or areas suffer from a combination of linked problems such as unemployment, poor skills, low incomes, poor housing, high crime, bad health and family breakdown' (Social Exclusion Unit, 2002). In this context, these dimensions of social exclusion are seen as typically interrelated, with each one increasing the likelihood of the others. Conventionally, such definitions equating 'social inclusion' with employment (thus production), marginalise other dimensions of 'exclusion' and so alternative understandings and routes to social reproduction. Economic exclusion is then being related to financial exclusion, which prevents certain groups in society from gaining access to the financial system, quite often in terms of what might be considered welfare provision. Financial exclusion has been defined as the inability of individuals, households, groups or communities to access necessary financial services in a manner suitable for their needs. Such exclusion is seen to come about as a result of barriers to access, discriminatory conditions, excessive prices, inappropriate marketing or self-exclusion as a result of negative experiences or perceptions (S. P. Sinclair/Centre for Research into Socially inclusive Services, 2002). This report was based on research in the UK and Scotland and assumed that financial exclusion is exclusively related to exclusion from mainstream financial services – as a consumer – rather than the underlying conditions which have resulted in, for instance, the difficulty or inability of women in particular, but also men, to afford or even obtain at low cost in times of hardship, sustainable pensions or other financial 'products'. This view of 'exclusion' is even more problematic when it is considered that secure employment – and so regular maintenance income – is grounded in a mythical 'golden age' whereas unemployment and underemployment in terms of 'flexible'/'feminisation' working practices are now increasingly the global norm.

Leyshon and Thrift also refer to financial exclusion as those processes relating to social exclusion that serve to prevent certain groups and individuals from gaining access to the financial system and although the criteria for exclusion may vary, gender plays an integral part of 'who gets what and when'. The costs of money (credit) within the financial system is calculated in relation to perceived risk and the higher this is perceived to be the more a borrower will pay (Leyshon & Thrift, 1997: 226). In utilising social exclusion in terms of poverty alleviation and so as an economic problem, the underlying political content of this 'condition' remains obscured. This discourse has now become internationalised – financial exclusion is now seen as a problem of poverty, rather than of the global structures of inequality and the of market as the solution.

The questions Jordan raised in seeking to develop an analysis of how poverty and social exclusion are related under present-day conditions, was of why these conditions appear in prosperous countries and why have they grown in poor ones at the present period; why neither the deregulatory free-trade policies of market-minded governments nor the more protective and solidaristic system of European states have been able to check their growth (1996: 4). Although this question was raised more than 10 years ago, the question is even more relevant today. He further goes on to state that

> Any theory that seeks to explain the relationship between individual need and social exclusion must necessarily analyse the economic of human collectivities. Individuals are most vulnerable when they have fewest personal capacities and material resources, and especially when they face the hazards of childhood, old age, sickness, disability or handicap. But none of these deficits and risks necessarily threatens their survival so long as they enjoy the protections afforded by members of an inclusive group that cooperates productively and redistributes its produce. Conversely, of course, a social formation that protects its vulnerable members may do so by exploiting or oppressing other members, notably women who might be better off under some other, more liberal, individualistic regime. (1996: 5)

The question raised by Jordan is of how human beings, interacting under conditions of scarcity in all kinds of collectivities from households to nation states, come to include some vulnerable individuals and exclude others from the benefits of membership, and at what costs to the rest of the members. However, Jordan's focus on 'from households to nation-states' does not to take into account the major changes in the nature and structure of the international system since the 1970s, nor how notions of 'vulnerability' – and how the need for 'protection' – have historically been thrust upon some – women and children – and not others.

Social exclusion, financial exclusion and poverty are therefore intimately related. In 2001, BRIDGE reported that a substantial body of literature exists which demonstrates the ways in which men and women experience poverty differently, such that women's poverty status cannot be 'read off' the concept of the 'household'. This report further raised the question of whether gender discrimination intensifies or diminishes with poverty, so raising concerns regarding emancipation or empowerment. More crucially, it emphasised the problem that by focusing on the perception of the 'feminisation of poverty', such research '...informs poverty-reduction approaches which target resources at women – in particular micro-credit interventions – without attempting to change the underlying conditions of "the rules of the game"' (BRIDGE, 2001: 5). This is precisely what the vast majority of policies currently undertaken both in the North and South, particularly those of states and international agencies, seek to do in opening up possibilities of access to credit at what would be considered exploitative rates of interest. Again, I refer to Cunningham's quote, 'At its most basic assumption, credit is when you can afford the loan and debt is when you cannot' (Cunningham, cited in Barty-King, 1991: vi).

Social inclusion – financial inclusion

The definition of financial exclusion as the inability to access the necessary financial services in an appropriate form sees this rather narrow understanding as a result of problems of access, conditions, prices, marketing or self-exclusion in response to negative experiences or perceptions (S. P. Sinclair, 2002). Leyshon and Thrift go further in stating that financial exclusion refers to those processes that prevent poor and disadvantaged social groups from gaining access to the financial system which

> ...has important implications for uneven development because it amplifies geographical differences in levels of income and

economic development. In recent years the financial services industry in the United States and in Britain has become increasingly exclusionary in response to a financial crisis founded in higher levels of competition and extreme levels of indebtedness. (1995: 312–341)

The more negative view may understand such policies as being more in line with Gill's statement that older forms of social protection have been replaced with a more individualist, self-help system '... in which people [stand] naked in the context of the harsh new marketplace' (1997: 94). Whereas Gill sees this as a regressive process, in an upbeat report by the Financial Services Authority (FSA), the benefits of the past 20 years are seen to have resulted in 'the problem of financial exclusion' which has '... ironically, resulted from increased inclusion that has left a small minority of individuals and households behind' (FSA, 2000). Such a situation is then related to '... gradual reform of welfare [that] has put more onus on individuals to make their own provision privately rather than rely on the state.' (FSA, 2000) This seems to place the onus of being socially excluded on the 'small minority of individuals and households' who, it appears, will continue to suffer social exclusion.

Here again it must be emphasised that gender relations were also crucially significant in the 'organisation and reorganisation' that took place with the emergence of a market society in the seventeenth and eighteenth centuries and were consolidated in the nineteenth. During the emergence of capitalism, men became the beneficiaries of new property forms, including the increasingly sophisticated credit and financial mechanisms that enabled alienated communal, household and women's property to be utilised by them in the form of liquid and mobile capital. In seeking to understand the 'financial exclusion' of the majority of the world's women from the benefits, but not the costs, of global finance, it is necessary to look back to the changes in social relations in specific locations as a result of the temporally and spatially uneven and differentiated process of expansion of financial markets on a global scale. However, in this more recent period of restructuring, there is a clear and specific strategy for financial actors to treat women as an emerging market for finance, credit and financial services – and consequently as a potential market for significant profit. Increasingly women have been drawn into the disciplinary structures of finance and credit at the lowest rungs of society. Although it can be argued that people should take responsibility for the large amounts of debt they now find themselves enmeshed in, the strategies that have been utilised by financial companies, supported by governments, to persuade them to avail themselves of credit are exceedingly sophisticated and in and of themselves can be argued to be significant structural elements in the process of profit accumulation.

Segmentation is widely used as a marketing tool and since it is contended that women with inadequate incomes are being targeted by financial companies, as well as states, I can do no better than to set out the introductory paragraph to *The Journal of Segmentation in Marketing Innovations*[37] which stated

> Identification and Targeting ... is a new bi-annual journal devoted to stimulating through and enhancing the practice of market segmentation and target marketing .... Articles will be about new segmentation methods, industry-specific applications, research techniques, market definition, niche, marketing, computer-related applications (e.g. databases, census data, syndicated services, etc) consumer and business segmentation, global segmentation, demographics and psychographics and other pertinent topics. (2002)

It is here where Gill's argument concerning the increasing use of 'surveillance and sorting techniques for maximising knowledge about, and influence over workers, savers and consumers – for example credit card holders' (Gill, 1997: 45) takes on crucial importance in bringing specific groups of people into circuits of credit and finance. It is an asymmetrical process and although it may bring benefits to an increasing number of individuals within a specific sector of society, it also feeds off specific groups, drawing them into increased levels of debt, vulnerability and risk. More importantly, the underlying structures which have resulted in whole swathes of the world's population being without adequate resources are not addressed. A more detailed exploration of women's entry into credit markets is therefore required.

Women as emerging markets

A deeper share of wallet (itself a rather gendered term) is a recognised marketing term used to direct strategies towards extracting an increasingly large proportion of an individual or household's income in order to increase profit margins. This strategy has been progressively directed at women within households with low incomes, who have, however, been acknowledged to be a fruitful market with relatively high gain, but low risk. Germain cites Braudel as stating that the forces which shape the practices associated with wealth creation are 'most naturally at home in the realm of capitalism' and 'often organised as institutions engaged in the trade and production of goods and services for a mass or world market'. He states that for Braudel, this is the home of accumulation on a world scale, where capitalists seek to reproduce their capital by engaging in speculative ventures attended by high levels of risk (Braudel, 1982: 622 cited by Germain, 1997: 20). At the same time such forces have, as is being argued here, generated excessive financial risk, which is almost exclusively a male activity 'decision makers in finance, men undertake larger financial transactions, and men are the main speculators' (van Staveren, 2002: 234).

At the present time, the latest financial crisis of 2007–2009, which centres on the London and New York financial system continues unfold and cause havoc across the world. Will Hutton writes

> No longer are these discrete financial markets; financial deregulation and the global ambitions of American and European banks…. are one system that operates around the same principles, copying each other's methods, making the same mistakes and exposing themselves to each other's risks…. the collapse of the American housing market, the explosive growth of American home repossessions and the discovery that 'structured investment vehicles' (SIVs), the toxic newfangled financial instruments that own as much as $350bn of valueless mortgages, are not American problems. They are ours too. (Hutton, 2007)

In terms of academic research, it is too soon at the time of writing to gauge the gendered impact – but there will be one. The indications are already there. A report in the New York Times in January 2008 cited in the ABA Journal states that women – and in particular black women – are the more likely victims of the sub-prime mortgage crisis in the US. Further

> While some of the disparity can be accounted for by factors such as the lower incomes earned by women, overall, compared to men, it appears that discrimination especially against women who are also members of racial minority groups – may also be a factor. (Neil, 2008)

The article continues with an acknowledgement that the disparity between men and women actually goes up as income rises: even amongst those defined as high earners, black women in particular were up to five times more likely than men to receive sub-prime mortgages. The newspaper notes that since sub-prime mortgages – high-cost loans made to borrowers with questionable credit qualifications and with interest rates at least three points above prime – are more likely than standard mortgages to be repossessed, so it is likely that women are disproportionately represented among homeowners facing foreclosure. The persons who carry the consequences of global financial crisis are predominantly females, who provide the unpaid care that keeps families and communities going (Elson, 2001; van Staveren, 2002). As Elson argues, there is evidence to suggest that women are more risk averse than men, and for this reason, are often reluctant recipients of credit (2001), findings which are supported by research by S. P. Sinclair for the FSA (2002). This is partially as a result of the fear and risk of being unable to repay loans when ultimately they are responsible for household food and welfare security. 'Women tend to have liabilities in the form of obligations to children which cannot easily be liquidated' (Elson, 2001).

Gill, in utilising the myth of the Panopticon to relate to those individuals and populations that are integrated into the privileged corporate circuits of production, consumption and finance, states that

> In the context of the wider global political economy these [integrated] people represent less than 10 per cent of the world's population. The rest of the world's population – that is the vast majority – is in effect excluded from these islands of normalized

affluence, since they do not represent opportunities for exploitation and profit. (1997: 52)

Although it is agreed that the vast majority of the world's population is being 'in effect' excluded from 'these islands of normalized affluence', they still represent opportunities for exploitation and profit. It is therefore more questionable whether it is from this section of society that a counter-movement will emerge as suggested by Gill and others. Since much of the previous discussion has explored the reasons why women have historically been left out of financial activity, it is now important to consider the notion that a significant but specific segment of those excluded from the 'culture of contentment' (Galbraith, 1992 as cited by Gill, 1997) – situated within the 'other third of the population increasingly marginalized' – far from being a threat to 'the privileged circuits' (Gill, 1997: 52) have now been drawn into credit markets at high cost, and thus high risk, to themselves, but at relatively low risk and high gain to those involved in deepening the circuits of credit at the lowest levels of society. In other words, it is necessarily a gendered process, not least since by far the largest group within this 'segment' being drawn into the 'disciplinary structures' of the financial and credit structures at the lowest rungs of society are women. And by far the most powerful group involved in the deepening of the circuits of credit – and indeed involved in the deepening of risks relating to potential financial crisis – are men. It is contended that for the vast majority of these women (although certainly not all) such processes have increased their and their households' vulnerability to risk '... particularly in an era which has seen the de-socialising of risk for a majority of the population' (Gill, 1997: 52). At the same time, financial innovations designed to decrease the levels of risk for businesses involved in unstable global markets continued apace, although there may be a period of reflection now that the dangers for the global economy of securitisation have come home to roost. It has been recognised for many years, particularly in the area of development and micro-credit, that poor women in terms of borrowing present lower risk and high social returns as an outcome of resources (UNDP, 1999), such information having been incorporated into 'property' in the form of databases to enable the innovation of techniques for maximising knowledge by financial (and other) concerns. This is above and beyond the more usual credit rating knowledge systems such as Standard and Poor and Moody's Investor Services, which have received critical attention for their ability to assert considerable disciplining power, not least over national as well as local governments (Cooley, 2003; Dieter, 2005; T. Sinclair, 1994).

Credit and poverty alleviation

Building upon the knowledge that women represent lower risks in terms of borrowing, in the South and North micro-credit and credit systems have increasingly been seen by governments and other institutions as a panacea for poverty alleviation. In the North, there has been a growing understanding by marketing strategists of credit companies and various businesses that integrate, then prioritise, credit facilities over their core business (such as catalogue companies), that these general and gendered characteristics associated with risk can be incorporated into targeting strategies to penetrate areas previously considered unprofitable. In other words, catalogue companies may be perceived as direct marketing channels for products but it is their credit facilities which are now core and integral to their profit-making activities and provide a way for lowerincome households to buy products for the family. This is also where a blurring of boundaries can be seen, not only in the perceived separation of the domestic and international processes and businesses, but also in mainstream understanding of global financial markets, which separates 'wholesale purveyors' of credit and finance with institutions formerly never conceived of as banks or financial institutions.

The present proliferation of types of financial instruments has led to the deepening of the commodification of finance (Scholte, 2000) in terms of 'bond and money markets, ... and has been joined by floating-rate bonds, repurchase agreements, asset-backed securities ... [and] new forms of financial derivative' (Scholte, 2000: 117 drawing from the Financial Times, 19 June 1997: 20). The blurring of boundaries which has also emerged with the increased commodification of financial mechanisms and products has led to some interesting but profitable institutional fusions. Whilst, as Scholte states, 'Many of today's retail banks have become financial supermarkets, offering a dizzying array of savings and borrowing instruments ...' (Scholte, 2000: 117), retail supermarkets have indeed become financial banks. An illustration of this is Sainsbury's Bank, which went into operation in February 1997. It boasts more than 1.7 million customers in the UK, with its 'speedy growth' being related to 'a mixture of keenly priced credit products' and its branches are 'where we go...to go shopping' so that 'picking up a loan with your shopping is as physically easy as it is financially attractive'.[38] Sainsbury's promotes savings accounts, ISAs, flexible mortgages, credit cards, loans and home, travel, pet and car insurance.

To return to catalogue companies and sub-prime lending, a report of Palmer and Conaty for the The New Economics Foundation (NEF) (2002: 2) stated that sub-prime lending is targeted at people who are unable to obtain mainstream credit (for instance, bank loans or the major credit cards) because of, for instance, social exclusion. Such inability may be caused by bad credit ratings or the inability to raise possessions or property as security against a loan. As the availability of mainstream credit has risen to unprecedented levels since the late 1970s (although this may well change for a while after the present turmoil has settled), so the availability of credit to the financially excluded has risen. The report continues

> Unsecured credit from doorstep lenders, high street retail chains and catalogue companies is now readily available to many who fall foul of the computerised credit check.... For many the rising availability of consumer credit, combined with society's growing moral acceptance of debt, has been empowering. The trappings of consumerism...are within the reach of more people than ever before. But for those left behind, whose lives involve more basic needs such as food, school uniforms or a Christmas present, credit can lead to an inescapable cycle of indebtedness. Predatory lending not only devastates individual families and households. It is systematically stripping the wealth and assets of some of the country's poorest neighbourhoods. (NEF, 2002: 2–3)

In support of its claims, the NEF cites research by the Credit Union Services which indicated that in three streets with a total of 40 households in an estate in Newcastle upon Tyne, £240,000 was being paid each year to high-cost lenders. Of this, more than £120,000 was paid in interest charges alone. The weekly income of the households was approximately £230 a week which meant, if taken nationally, that this added up to a huge transfer of resources and potential assets from poor communities to the directors and shareholders of loan companies (NEF, 2002: 20).

So-called 'domestic' transactions dealing with 'national' high street retail chains with store cards (such as Dixons and Debenhams) and catalogue companies (such as Great Universal Stores) which rely on credit for much of their value added rather than the goods sold, are firmly linked to global finance. It is here that the blurring of boundaries and definitions takes place. GE Capital, a wholly owned subsidiary of General Electric Company is described as 'a global company providing financial services for consumers and businesses' (Press Release from GUS on Experian, 24 April 2001), whose Card Services division provides the credit and other facilities which support the store (credit) cards for 'national' high street chains and catalogue companies, including those mentioned above. These store cards are renowned for being one of the most expensive forms of credit and are structured as revolving lines of credit, term loans, factoring, and/or securitisation facilities for credit. GE Capital is also described as a 'private lender' in its position on a task force set up by President Bush which included representatives of the World Bank and '...private lenders such as GE Capital...' (Financial Times, 2001). Further, it is also named as a bank, or at least is affiliated to a company, GE Capital Bank, in several European countries, such as Germany, Austria and Switzerland. The key point is to show that circuits of credit are operating either explicitly, or as with GUS, indirectly and covertly (that is to say without the customers full knowledge that the mark-up is credit related), in alliances through the everyday lives of people, often specifically targeting those who are socially and financially excluded from society and thus unable to obtain credit elsewhere, with transfers of wealth moving from the local, to the global at great cost to specific groups in societies. This process appears to be a reversal of the gendered nature of property and financial markets but is actually based on a confirmation of gender subordination within society.

Such networks of power can be explained as a functioning of alliance capitalism (Dunning & Boyd, 2003; Phillips, 2000). This has been defined by Phillips as 'an organisational logic', whereby the operating unit is not the firm but the business enterprise itself – projects organised across individual firms or formal alliances into extensive network relations. This can also be understood as a product of increasing and intensifying processes of competition resulting in

...the increasing organisation of business activities into an enterprise not run by individual firms or even multinational corporations but by international networks constituted through a variety of actors and institutions continuously adapting to support the environments and markets in which the enterprise itself operates. (2000: 44)

Although it is not intended to go further into the workings of alliance capitalism here, it is stressed that many of these networks are indeed informal and, on occasions, secretive alliances. It is entirely appropriate here to illustrate this by outlining the activities of a particular US-based company. This firm created an alliance of consumer data to be used for marketing and has created a pool of customer information. Companies provide a monthly 'top up' of their full customer transactional databases. Once companies have started adding their customer details to the 'pool', they then qualify to buy additional names from this firm for marketing; this provides them with names of new people who have similar profiles to their original customers. In other words, this is a network – and alliance – of 'cross-pooling' of customer databases. Profiling of customers includes geographical location and band, profitability, propensity to buy, amount spent and type of product and identification of what products and brands this customer is likely to purchase. The sophistication of marketing strategies belies the claims of straightforward consumer choice. Marketing has become something of a science involving research into 'consumer and business segmentation, global segmentation, demographics and psychographics and other pertinent topics', and a science of which the average consumer has little understanding.

Psychographics is the term used in marketing to describe the identification of a particular audience based on psychological characteristics, determined by standardised tests. The purpose of such identification of characteristics is to affect a person's purchasing behaviour based on their lifestyle. One major player in this industry states that its Financial Strategy Segment Grouping is a person-level segmentation developed to help financial services companies target their financial services products and services. It classifies adults in Great Britain into 31 distinct financial lifestyles, including such categories as Golden Empty Nesters, Provincial Privilege, Fledgling Nurseries, Burdened Optimists, Dinky Developments, Families on Benefits and Greenbelt Guardians. These are further grouped so as to describe 'their typical product holdings, behaviour and future intentions'.[39] The information that this segmentation is built upon can be seen as reinforcing Ritzer's crucial point that with the aid of the credit card industry, as well as advertising and marketing industries, capitalism has discovered new ways of acquiring more of the consumer's resources, 'even resources the consumers did not yet have' (1995: 19). Lastly, such developments are highly dependent upon the new ICTs and its associated networks.

In the UK, Abacus Alliance boasts that it operates the UK's largest transactional cooperative database with more than 620 members contributing more than 420 million transactions (Abacus Alliance, 2009). Its database is said to account for all principal consumers within the UK. The US company holds more than 90 million households on file and tracks more than 3 billion transactions. This enterprise now operates in Japan and has more European operations planned. Expedia, has started its own version of such an alliance called Club Canvasse 'the essential data co-operative for everyone involved in the home shopping industry.... With over 220 of the UK's leading home shopping companies already pooling customer transactional data, we hold information on the buying habits of over 12 million multi-buyers, providing a clear picture of your best prospects and customers' (Experian, 2007). It is a global firm with offices located in 38 countries and, not surprisingly, considers itself to be a global information services company. Its vision is for 'Experian's people, data and technology to become a necessary part of every major consumer economy around the world' (Experian, 2007). With such a depth of knowledge and sharing – and indeed potential global sharing – of customer profiling based to a large extent on psychological profiling, it is very difficult to argue that power relations between firms and consumers are equal in the market place.

It is appropriate here, in identifying the depth of marketing strategies, to consider the term 'emerging market', which is often used in relation to developing countries where financial markets are perceived to be opportunities for expansion. Michael Porter has advanced the idea of inner cities being future 'emerging markets' in relation to revitalisation through market-led strategies (M. Porter, 2001). In this context, the use of the term 'women as an emerging market' is allegorical in describing a sector, within and across societies, inhabited by very largely – but not only – poor women, in which financial interests perceive a possible market where credit can be offered, at low risk and sufficiently high gain. To return to Gill's contention that those excluded from 'islands of normalized affluence' (1997: 52) do not present opportunities for exploitation and profit, this has not been considered necessarily to be the case (if it ever was) since there has been a process of increasing penetration of market-led financial activities into those very areas of poverty and destitution, in pursuit of profit. This penetration has been represented as an offer of inclusion to 'normalised affluence' but it is a subordinated affluence at the margins of society. As has been stated earlier, the targeting of these areas in terms of potential credit consumers can be at the instigation of states, international institutions, firms or NGOs.

In many cases, financial markets cannot be seen as separate and apart from the majority of financial and micro-credit schemes – often termed 'alternative' even if they are market-led – which have mushroomed at the local or 'grassroots' level in the past decade or so. Increasingly, these schemes are being associated with commercial concerns and on occasions financial inclusion sought (by way of the purchase of 'financial products') through the private sector. As indicated by Mordoch, credits to developing countries from institutions such as the IMF and, to a lesser extent, the World Bank have added to the domestic money supply. This affects governments' consumption and investment and foreign-exchange fluctuations. Domestic credit schemes, more particularly in relation to developing countries, are often supported through bilateral development cooperation and the World Bank, so creating indirect dependency on global sources of finance. Mordoch states that 8–10 million households were estimated to be borrowing from micro-credit programmes in 1999 (1999: 1569), while other organisations such as Global Envision have put the figure in 2002 at 30 million (Global Envision, 2006). Financial globalisation involves not only FDI but also the buying and selling of stocks, international loans and aid, and involves relationships between multinational banks and micro-finance organisations. As conditions for loans, the IMF and World Bank require countries to adopt SAPs and open their borders to foreign trade and investment, privatise state-owned industries and deregulate (Pyle & Ward, 2003: 468).

Gill's argument concerning the increasing use of 'surveillance and sorting techniques for maximising knowledge about, and influence over workers, savers and consumers – for example credit-card holders' (1997: 51) takes on crucial importance in bringing specific groups of people, including women, into circuits of credit and finance. This process, although it undoubtedly brings benefits to some, also draws groups into increased levels of vulnerability, debt and risk, whilst still leaving them as 'the other third of the population ... increasingly marginalized' (Gill, 1997: 52). The underlying structures which have resulted in many groups within this sector being without adequate resources are not addressed. Further, many women are increasingly being drawn into circuits of credit and finance without even being aware of the true nature of the exploitative relationships they have entered, for instance through the marketing practices of catalogue companies. The shift in the activities of such companies in recent years from providers of clothing and household goods to providers of credit is not transparent, in that the provision of household goods is secondary to profit accumulation through credit facilities. Such shifts in the nature of companies require a re-evaluation of our understanding of the organisation of those institutions involved in credit and finance today. The major catalogue companies, for instance, whose target market is women from low income households, are shifting marketing strategies from the traditional agency based structure where profit was gained through the tangible product, to one where up to 33 per cent is built into the cost of goods to cover credit facilities. Here it is relevant to note that Great Universal Stores (GUS), one of the largest catalogue companies in Europe, until 2006 owned one of the fastest growing credit rating agencies, Experian. This credit rating agency describes itself as an organisation that: '... enables organizations to find the best prospects and make fast, informed decisions to improve and personalize relationships with their customers'. As discussed previously, it does this by combining sophisticated and intelligent decision-making software and systems with some of the world's most comprehensive databases of information on consumers, businesses, motor vehicles and property.

Credit cards have been used as an illustration of how global processes have detached financial activities from territorial space and as an indication of the non-territoriality of global finance. Scholte has written 'the geography of...credit cards...has little to do with territoriality and several credit cards like Visa, MasterCard and American Express can be used for payments at countless establishments in almost every country across the planet' (2000: 48). In these various ways, he states, money – that is, credit – has become detached from territorial space. This may be so, but the transactions still occur in some territorial space. However, vast numbers of people in the developing world do not have credit cards (yet) but Rosenau also treats the credit card as a metaphor to represent the effect of globalisation on the production and distribution of wealth and the spread and growing uniformity of consumer tastes (Rosenau, 1999: 310). The globality of these credit card transactions is not necessarily only in their increasing stretch, in that in seeking to explain the deepening of the processes of globalisation within territorial space, we should again return to those 'emerging markets' to be found at the lowest levels of society. This can be linked to David Harvey's suggestion that place-bound identities might actually have become more rather than less important in a world of diminishing territorial barriers (1993: 4 cited by Scholte, 2000: 48–49). Here, it might be argued that there has been a gradual deepening of financial global processes to those areas previously perceived as not worthy of exploitation and that targeting has been focused on those sections of society whose territorial space is restricted and confined by poverty. Further, the notion of 'consumer choice' in a free market for those living in poverty is nonsensical, since they are severely constrained to those one or two products offered to them on highly inequitable and extortionate terms. In a so-called 'information society', as stated previously, highly focused and psychological marketing methods, based on extraordinarily detailed databases are available to businesses – at a price –making for highly asymmetrical relations within the market. This is particularly so in the areas of finance and credit.

Ritzer states that the positive contributions are that credit cards permit people to spend more money than they have, thus allowing the economy to function at a much higher and faster level than it might if it relied solely on cash and cash-based instruments. In this connection, there is a tendency to put problems on individuals, blaming them for conditions that are thought to exist within the individual. However, ultimately he considers that individuals have been 'victimised by a social and financial system that discourages savings and encourages indebtedness' (1995: 7–8). 'Credit cards become instruments of bondage locking people into a lifetime of indebtedness. Moreover, they embed people in consumer society' (1995: 11–12) – indeed the circuits of debt of Barty-King. Credit cards have been said to perform two functions: first they may be used as a transactional medium, as a substitute for cash and cheques; and second they may be used as credit, as a substitute for other forms of short-term, small-value credit (Gill, 1997: 63). There is, however, a third function: Richard Fairbank, chairman and Chief Executive Officer (CEO) of CapitalOne credit card company stated

> Credit cards aren't banking – they're information. When we started this company, we saw two revolutionary opportunities: we could use scientific methodology to help us make decisions, and we could use information technology to help us provide mass customisation. (CapitalOne, 2002)

In the short term, it is small-value credit which is attractive to a high percentage of the targeted group of women who have very little recourse to credit other than traditional sources of family and social networks or moneylenders who charge extortionate rates of interest. However, the informational understanding of credit cards is also crucial to understanding the whole process of targeting by, and the deepening of, this side of financial markets. Today, there are many highly skilled professional women who are able to take advantage of the increasing variety of financial products, including credit cards. In targeting women in the lowest income sectors of society, credit organisations bring women and men into circuits of credit in very specific gendered ways so as to 'gain a greater share of wallet'. Since women are known to spend more of their resources on household and family, marketing strategies are aimed at credit for domestic goods rather than luxuries in this sector. Such organisations rely on databases and credit scoring facilities to enable them to target the key elements of their base not only for creditworthiness, but also for those who are unable to gain credit anywhere else, particularly housewives and women without an independent income.[40] The target here would be the long-term retention of low income, low credit scoring groups so as to gain 'a greater share of wallet' and ensure long-term credit is maintained on the card at high interest. Women make up the majority of this group since, just like their counterparts in developing countries, they are being perceived as low risk in terms of regular payback – more so than men – yet are charged at premium interest rates because of the perceived risk of lending to low income groups. Thus the family and household become the focus of offers from these credit organisations. Such organisations, concentrating on the low income sectors of society may actively decline the professional, highly paid recruit since there is anecdotal evidence to suggest that these are less likely to maintain a credit balance and will thus incur no interest charges and so profit. Such anecdotal evidence gained credence in 2008 as the financial crisis started to unfold when credit cards were withdrawn from 'good customers'. Neil Munroe, external affairs director at credit reference agency Equifax is quoted as remarking 'But I think consumers also need to recognise that lenders need to be able to make money as commercial organisations and, therefore, they will also look at customers from a profitability perspective' (*Insley*, 2008).

Although the provision of credit to low income groups can be seen as beneficial, particularly to women who are unable to obtain credit elsewhere, again it is very largely women involved in social reproduction at the lowest income levels of society who are being drawn in to the disciplinary structures of finance and credit, so increasing their and their households' vulnerability to risk. These groups are the least able to afford a significant proportion of their scarce resources to be handed over in unproductive interest payments to wealthy financial organisations. It is also understood that actors in global markets are not influenced by social or other values in terms of so-called vulnerable groups. That is the problem of provision by markets and the problem of states utilising marketisation for social provision. Should default occur, it can have disastrous consequences because of the lack of resources to fall back on. As stated earlier, in an era which has seen the desocialising of risk for the majority of the population (Gill, 1997: 52), women can be seen as presenting opportunities for exploitation and profit which in most cases, have the potential to leave women marginalised, open to further vulnerabilities and still very largely socially excluded. This also can be argued to be the case in relation to poverty alleviation programmes in the South, more particularly, micro-credit schemes.

Micro-credit schemes

With the deepening of financial markets through liberalisation, the growth of household credit has been encouraged for both household enterprise and the acquisition of household goods. Dymski, in drawing on the East Asia financial crisis, considers the price of the gains is greater household risk because of the greater cash flow dependence and financial fragility which ensues '... financial crises can force households to bear heavier adjustments costs than would be otherwise felt, and these costs may well be borne disproportionately by women who become more economically vulnerable as a result' (Dymski & Floro, 2000: 1270–1271). Women are generally more economically vulnerable because of the gendered maldistribution of property and resources and the uses to which such resources are more generally utilised within the household. This is of central importance when considering credit as a means of supporting activities in relation to social reproduction and consequently social development, and the deepening levels of risk and insecurity across the world.

The World Bank set out estimated figures that in 2001, 1.1 billion people had consumption levels below $1 a day and 2.7 billion lived on less than $2 a day. It further stated that these figures are lower than earlier estimates, indicating that some progress has taken place, but that they still remain too high in terms of human suffering. (World Bank, 2008b). Households headed by women tend to have lower incomes and are therefore more likely to have incomes per person lower than $1. Whether households are headed by women or men, gender relations affect intrahousehold resource allocation and use. This distribution of poverty in terms of gender is confirmed by Williams who stated that most of the 24 per cent of the world's population who live on incomes of less than $1 a day are women, who also constitute the backbone of the unpaid, and growing pool of the paid workforce underpinning trade liberalisation and FDI. He further states – with echoes of Enloe and Elson above – that women are the major cushion for domestic adjustment (Williams, 2000). Research has indicated that trends in the recent period of globalisation has had gendered effects on the division of labour including the effects of trade, production and finance on women's roles (Marchand & Runyan, 2000; Pyle & Ward, 2003: 461). Besides these gendered effects, as set out in previous chapters, it has been argued that globalisation of finance and credit also developed as a matter of gendered causes. The 'micro-impacts' (Pyle & Ward, 2003: 461) have been investigated in relation to gendered production networks including export production, sex work, domestic service and micro-finance income generation. There are related patterns here with the feminisation of the workforce in industrialised countries following the breakdown of Bretton Woods, with its delinking of social goals and the period of capital market liberalisation involving the restructuring of states and of the activities of transnational enterprises across the world. These patterns can be recognised from Guy Standing's assertion that 'Radical changes in labor market relations, involving erosion of protective and pro-collective labor regulations, decentralization of wage determination, erosion of employment security and a trend (away from) statutory regulation of the labor market' (1999: 584) has led to production systems becoming 'feminised', relying on forms of labour that result in greater insecurity and inequality for workers (1999: 583–602). These processes are integrally related to the activities of global financial markets and multinational enterprises in the restructuring of manufacturing, service and finance sectors and this has resulted in production being reorganised across successive tiers of countries, not least through the establishment of informal networks of subcontractors (Pyle, 1999). While it is widely acknowledged that women act as providers of last resort and may benefit from access to financial resources in times of need, historically access to formal credit for women has been severely restricted because of a variety of social, legal, ideological and financial constraints. Not the least of these restrictions has been women's inequitable access to property either as a result of, or compounded by, ideological and substantive changes in understandings of property forms as a result of the emergence of capitalism and expansion and internationalisation of legal, ideological and administrative processes. Increasing focus on women's access to credit (resources) as a development strategy has occurred in a period when the gap between poverty and wealth has increased and been recognised as a global problem, more specifically in relation to social instability. At the same time, state restructuring has taken place more particularly in relation to strategies of welfare which have left women in an increasingly insecure and risky environment. As has been argued earlier, the answer in both the North and the South with regard to poverty alleviation is no longer seen in terms of welfare or welfarism, but in terms of access to financial resources.

In discussing the marginalisation of the analysis of gender inequality, Dunaway has stated that the pro-capitalist development paradigms discovered women and co-opted them all over the world (2001: 2–29). Since the 1970s, there has been increasing focus, particularly by the North, on credit and income generating programmes in the South as a way of generating sustainable livelihoods and these have more particularly since the 1990s been targeted at women. A high proportion of micro-finance schemes are directed at enhancing the earning potential of both women and men and are based on micro-credit programmes which '... promise the possibility of cost recovery; as low-income borrowers demonstrate their repayment capacity at market rates of interest, donors can satisfy their ambitions for financially sustainable development' (Goetz & Gupta, 1996: 45–46). Interest in this form of poverty alleviation followed the perceived success of the Grameen Bank, which promoted 'the breaking of the vicious cycle of poverty through the voluntary formation of small groups at grassroots level to provide mutual and morally binding group guarantees in place of the collateral which is required by conventional Banks' (Grameen Bank, 2002). The Grameen Bank works on the assumption that if credit is accessible to individual borrowers, they will be able to identify and engage in viable but simple income generating activities. Although women were not initially the target recipients of this scheme, Grameen states that today 90 per cent of borrowers are women since they have proved to be

> ... not only reliable borrowers but astute entrepreneurs. As a result they have raised their status, lessened their dependency on their husbands and improved their homes and the nutritional standards of their children. (Grameen Bank, 2002)

In other words, it is a strategy that relies on success being 'measurable' but, as Jackson (1998) points out, gender and poverty are two distinct forms of disadvantage and tackling one does not necessarily mean tackling the other.

The more general institutionalisation of micro-credit programmes has taken place through organisations such as the United Nations Capital Development Fund (UNCDF), which supports a variety of initiatives that 'facilitate the provision of financial services to the poor'. These initiatives include investments in micro-finance institutions

(MFIs), technical services such as MFI appraisals and project design and learning agendas and capacity building through the Special Unit for Microfinance (SUM). Its remit is to incorporate

> ...those elements into new programmes....the growth of effective microfinance institutions that have transparent track records and solid institutional and financial performance in reaching poor clients, particularly women, on a sustainable basis. SUM also fosters an understanding of microfinance best practices and assists UNCDP and other UN agency country offices worldwide to incorporate. (UNCDF, 2002)

It should be noted that micro-credit programmes such as those modelled on the Grameen Bank and others which are run on a 'sustainable basis' exact extortionate interest rates from their borrowers – the Grameen Bank, for instance, has interest rates of over 30 per cent (Weber, 2001). Here, I take extortionate interest rates to be those which exact scarce resources over and above that required to repay the original loan from those in need for the requirements of community and social reproduction. Credit functions as a way of allocating financial resources to those in need of capital and current neo-classical economic theory suggests that credit is not something which should be given for free. Without the incentive of interest rates, it is assumed that the efficiency of the market in the distribution of scare resources will be impaired. Interest rates are justified on the grounds of 'the time preference of money', in that those who are willing to give up consumption today by saving money should be compensated for this temporary loss of money. As research by Hulme and Mosely indicates, although within such programmes there seems to be a tendency for default rates to be greater among the very poor, there seemed to be little doubt that between programmes, the poor have higher repayment rates than the rich. Examples given are Grameen Bank, BancoSol in Bolivia and BKK in Indonesia, all of which are aimed at very poor borrowers but have higher repayment rates than any less developed country's (LDC) commercial bank. One of the reasons given for this is that schemes targeted on the poor are more effective at reaching women borrowers, and they have a better repayment record than men (Hulme & Mosely, 1996: 37). Such schemes, it was concluded, did not substantially reduce the vulnerability of borrower groups to sudden falls in income and produced few benefits for the poorest of the 'core poor'. There was little evidence that such schemes increased the political leverage of poorer people and the cases compared were best treated as financial institutions striving to alleviate material poverty. 'They are not social movements promoting the empowment of subordinate classes [and one assumes women] as some have mythologized' (1996: 205).

Further research has indicated that not all in need are afforded credit facilities: in some instances problems have arisen in relation to increased violence against women, and men are known to have coerced their wives in to obtaining credit on their behalves. Goetz's study of micro-credit schemes in Bangladesh (1996) sought to understand whether women were empowered through activity in micro-credit schemes. Goetz argued that the implementation of credit schemes and the projects' decision-making processes perpetuates the historical forms of dominance and subordination. This resulted in women being worse off in terms of both access to credit and more generally in participation in development organisation. The discriminatory policies, Goetz maintains, may be explained by the official objectives, which lay emphasis on commercialisation and the use of economic criteria for project success (Goetz & Gupta, 1996: 145). In seeking to evaluate the conflicting evaluations in relation to micro-credit schemes and its empowering impact, Kabeer (1998) raised the problem that 'empowerment' itself is a highly contested concept which varies across class, time and space. Ultimately Kabeer argued that since there are so very few choices for women because of gender barriers, purposeful interventions which can help direct resources to women, thereby overcoming traditional barriers to entrepreneurial potential, must be welcomed on grounds of efficiency and equity. Although this may be considered an interim measure Nan Dawkins Scully of the Women's Microcredit accountability NETwork states that as long as micro-enterprise development is offered as a substitute for meaningful social development '...it will only impede progress toward finding real answers to the very real problem of poverty in the South'. A similar understanding of various processes aimed at 'financial inclusion' in the North may come to a similar conclusion, in that it only when the underlying gendered structures of exploitation and the historical maldistribution of resources based on property relations are addressed, will it be possible to find real answers to the very real problems of poverty and social development and indeed empowerment.

A more general critique of the micro-credit approach to poverty reduction has been undertaken by Heloise Weber, who argues that there is a disjunction between these discourses and the actual social experiences associated with micro-credit schemes. Weber argues that one explanation for this inconsistency lies in understanding the strategic embedding of the micro-credit and poverty reduction agenda in the global political economy. By stating that micro-credit performs a 'dual function' in the global political economy by, on the one hand, facilitating financial sector liberalisation and, on the other, providing a 'political' safety net in the context of the implementation of SAPs or the implementation of neo-liberal political prerogatives generally she asserts 'the strategic embedding of microcredit in the global political economy provides a substantial explanation for understanding the disjunction between the asserted normative claims and its actual experiences' (2004: 357–386).

Such processes can be seen to have parallels in the rhetoric and policy changes in the North which seek to address issues of poverty reduction to the socially excluded through the promotion of financial products and services via the market mechanism, by way of addressing those aspects of welfare which in previous decades had been the responsibility of the state. In other words, there has been an increasing commodification of social welfare in the expectation that those low income sectors of society, within which women form a significant proportion, can find welfare and security by entering into market relations, including those of a financial nature. This process has enabled the intensification of the liberalisation of markets, not least through deepening circuits of credit, particularly if it is accepted that financial markets have blurred boundaries and have deepened their activities into areas of poverty, specifically for profit. This too, then, can be seen to provide a 'political' safety net in the context of the restructuring of the state and the implementation of neo-liberal prerogatives generally, whilst offering little in the way of empowerment or increased access and control over financial resources and related political and social power. There is never any consideration put forward to rectify the underlying structures which have resulted in a maldistribution of, and access to, resources – in other words, rectification of the very unlevel playing field imposed by the historical emergence of gendered financial institutions based on private property. Until such time as analyses of financial markets and their place in the global political economy take into account the profoundly gendered nature of their foundations, entering into credit relations based on specific and gendered free-market ideologies and structures for the most part will continue to result in changing, costly but continuing combined, differentiated and uneven development, particularly in terms of risk and insecurity for societies across the world, as the present financial crisis continues to illustrate so profoundly.

Notes

1. Such as the infamous US sub-prime mortgages, which had been bundled together and resold in financial markets.
2. Seager contends that only 1 per cent of agricultural land is owned by women, although women provide a high proportion of agricultural labour across the world and even in industrialised countries, she states that women have far lower home ownership than men. More generally in gender literature, the figure of women only owning 2 per cent of the world resources is often cited with little evidence in support other than the Declaration of UN Year of Women and Development Report 1975. This source also supplies little evidence for these figures and thus such statistics must remain highly questionable although not the underlying premise of highly skewed distribution of resources based on gender.
3. Youngs directs us to Murphy and Tooze's (1991) discussion of 'common sense' which helps us to understand the tendency of assumptions of dominant theoretical perspectives to go unquestioned.
4. Author's italics.
5. These were contained in Lectures on Jurisprudence. See Nyland (1993). In these Lectures, Smith remarked that 'the laws of most countries being made by men generally are very severe on the women, who can have no remedy for this oppression' yet as Dimand et al. state, in contrast to John Stuart Mill, Smith 'was not moved by this insight to oppose the legal oppression of women or the lack of political representation that gave rise to it, nor even to make any reference in print to the legal position of women' (2004: 232).
6. See http://www.worldbank.org/gender, http://www.un.org/womenwatch/ianwge/collaboration/summary1999.htm
7. Within the context of this chapter, and as a starting point, it is intended to use the terms 'formal' and 'informal' markets in a very general way for the purposes of discussion, since it is recognised that there is no clear dividing line in function between formal and informal economic spheres. However, in the conventional formula, the formal sector refers to that economic zone that is legally sanctioned, regulated through state intervention, whereas the informal sector typically refers to irregular exchanges outside legal sanction without state regulation of any sort.
8. An example here is research which has shown that women tend to spend more of their available resources towards the upkeep of the family in both the developed and developing world, whereas a higher proportion of men's income is directed at personal pursuits.
9. For further comments on the failure of IR and IPE to engage with gender and feminist research, see Stienstra (2000), Youngs (2004), Waylen (2004) and Zalewski (1998).

10. Author's italics.
11. Original italics.
12. Author's italics.
13. It is not clear from the context of Peterson's work whether she is stating that it is only with the rise of capitalism that women became transmitters of property but women, through marriage, have long performed the role of transmitter of property and wealth. For instance, the *oikos* in ancient Greek city states was perpetuated through marriage and production of legitimate children (Pomeroy, 1997: 24). In Sparta concerns were raised during the periods of Kings Ageis IV and Cheoens regarding the inequities of wealth where women, especially members of the royal family owned two-thirds of public land and a major portion of private land. This wealth had been gained through dowry and inheritance, with heiresses and wealthy widows sought for marriage. Further the programmes of Ageis and Cheoens claimed to have restored the polity by multifaceted but essential requirement of the redistribution of land when women agreed to contribute property for redistribution, with the state the ultimate 'owner' of land (Pomeroy, 1997: 64). However, it may be argued that the methods of transmission changed as a result of the emergence of capitalist organisation.
14. Although not dealt with directly here, the evolution and construction of political thought and its impact on (male) citizenship has received considerable critique by feminists (Mouffe, 1996; Prokhovnik, 1998; Reiger, 2000).
15. Author's italics.
16. There are many women who would recognise such a statement today as constituting a most powerful weapon of control, by which the value of men and women is measured in terms of accountable economic/financial worth and not by other productive/social reproductive contributions, which cannot be measured in these terms.
17. Author's italics.
18. For an in-depth account see B. Anderson and J. Zinsser's excellent *A History of Their Own: Women in Europe from Prehistory to the Present* Vol. 1 and 2.
19. Author's italics.
20. 'Some say I preach merely the homilies of housekeeping or the parables of the parlour,' she said in 1982. 'But I do not repent. Those parables would have saved many a financier from failure and many a country from crisis.'
21. Indeed since the 1980s there has been a shift from understandings of rights to universal welfare to welfare consumerism which has been utilised by various states in the North (and some in the South) to including a discourse of social and financial inclusion as a remedy to poverty alleviation – see Chapter 5.
22. Author's italics.
23. Author's italics.
24. Author's italics.

25. Clark provides wide-ranging evidence drawn from original documents for this period. One of her conclusions drawn from her research was that it was significant that men at that time did not regard marriage as necessarily involving the assumption of a serious economic burden, 'but on the contrary, often considered it to be a step which was likely to strengthen them in life's battles' (1919: 39).

26. However, married women as consumers were not averse to utilising devises in order to evade the strictures of coverture (Finn, 1996: 703–704).

27. Three hundred years on, at a forum on poverty which I attended in Britain, this same statement was made by several women giving evidence on the lack of sources of credit open to them in times of dire need. After borrowing from kin, family and friends, pawnbrokers and door-to-door money lenders with exorbitantly high interests rates are the only options open to many of today's inner city poor. See also Palmer, H. with Pat Conaty (2002).

28. This has an interesting and telling parallel with findings from research into micro-credit schemes today, more specifically in the South.

29. As an anecdotal footnote, at a recent Poverty Forum in London attended by diverse groups and representatives of credit organisations, I spoke to the representative of the British Pawnbroker's Association (a pawnbroker himself) and asked whether he knew that in the fifteenth, sixteenth and seventeenth centuries, the majority of pawnbrokers were women. I asked what he thought the percentage was now and his reply – after a short pause – was 'We do have a high percentage of women *working for us* now'.

30. Hansard Written Answers for 5 February 2002, Column 911W.

31. For extensive and varied discussions of globalisation, see L. Sklair (2002), Held et al. (1999), Scholte (2000) and Waters (2001).

32. 'Globalist' a term used by Held, Rosenau and McGrew denotes those who consider globalisation is the reality – positivists consider it is a good thing whilst the pessimists consider such a condition is leading to deepening inequalities.

33. For a more detailed consideration of regulatory transformations and associated issues, see Assassi, L., Nesvetailova, A. and D. Wigan (2007) *Global Finance in the New Century: Beyond Deregulation*, Houndsmill: Palgrave Macmillan.

34. For an excellent exposition of this connection see De Grazia, Victoria and E. Furlough (1996) *The Sex of Things: Gender and Consumption in Historical Perspective*, Berkeley, LA, London: University of California Press.

35. For discussion of credit rating processes, see T. Sinclair, 'Passing judgement: credit rating processes as regulatory mechanisms of governance in the emerging world order' (1994).

36. Nandy contends that that in many of the Eastern civilisations, in spite of patriarchal elements, there is a perceived continuity between the masculine and the feminine, and between infancy, adulthood and old age. In some cases, Nandy contends, it is a reaction to the colonial culture,

which assumed '...clear breaks between the male and the female, the adult and the children, and the adult and the elderly, and then used these biological differences as the homologues of secular political stratifications. In the colonial ideology, the colonizer became the tough, courageous, openly aggressive, hypermasculine ruler and the colonised became the sly, cowardly, passive-aggressive, womanly subject. Likewise, the culture of the colonizer became the...mature, complete, adult civilisation while the colonized became the mirror of a more simple, primitive, childlike cultural state' (1987: 38).

37. Now discontinued.
38. ⟨http://www.bank.org.uk/sainsburys-bank/⟩.
39. From a confidential source.
40. This information has been supplied in confidence by a management consultant.

Bibliography

Abacus Alliance. http://www.abacusalliance.com/ Retrieved 12 February 2009.

Abbott, J. P. and M. Hampton (1999). *Offshore Finance Centres and Tax Havens: The Rise of Global Capital*. Basingstoke, Macmillan.

Afshar, H. and S. Barrientos (1999). *Women, Globalization and Fragmentation in the Development World*. Basingstoke, Macmillan.

Allen, T. and A. Thomas, Eds. (2000). *Poverty and Development into the 21st Century*. Oxford, Oxford University Press.

Amin, A., B. Gills, R. Palan and P. Taylor (1994). 'Editorial: Forum for heterodox international political economy.' *Review of International Political Economy* 1(1): 1–12.

Anderson, B. S. and J. P. Zinsser (1989). *A History of their Own: Women in Europe from Prehistory to the Present, Vol. 1*. London, Penguin.

Anderson, B. S. and J. P. Zinsser (1990). *A History of their Own: Women in Europe from Prehistory to the Present, Vol. 2*. London, Penguin.

Angela, C. (2007). 'Resistance, regulation and rights: the changing status of Polish women's migration and work in the "new" Europe.' *The European Journal of Women's Studies* 14(1): 37–50.

Anon. (1735). *The Hardships of the English Laws in Relation to Wives*.

Anon. (1777). *The Laws Respecting Women, as they Regard their Natural Rights, or their Connections and Conduct*, vi. London.

Ardener, S. and S. Burman, Eds. (1996). *Money-Go-Rounds: The Importance of Rotating Savings and Credit Associations for Women*. Oxford and Washington, DC, Berg.

Aslanbeigui, N. and G. Summerfield (2000). 'The Asian crisis, gender and the international financial architecture.' *Feminist Economics* 6(3): 81–104.

Assassi, L., A. Nesvetailova and D. Wigan (2007). *Global Finance in the New Century: Beyond Deregulation*. Houndsmill, Palgrave Macmillan.

Austin, L. M. (1987). 'Ruskin and his ideal woman.' *South Central Review* 4(Winter): 28–39.

Babcock, B. A., Ed. (1975). *Sex Discrimination and the Law: Causes, and Remedies*. Boston, MA, Little Brown and Co.

Bagehot, W. (1905). *Lombard Street: A Description of the Money Market*. London, Henry S. King and Co.

Bailey, J. (2002). 'Favoured or oppressed? Married women, property and "coverture" in England 1660–1880.' *Continuity and Change* 17(3): 351–372.

Bakker, I. (1994). *The Strategic Silence: Gender and Economic Policy*. London, Zed Books.

Bakker, I. (2000). 'Who built the pyramids.' Paper presented at *British International Studies Association Conference*, Edinburgh.

Bakker, I. (2003). Neo-liberal governance and the reprivatization of social reproduction: Social provisioning and shifting gender orders. *Power,*

Production and Social Reproduction. I. Bakker and S. Gill (Eds). Basingstoke, Palgrave Macmillan: 66–82.

Balogh, T. (1947). *Studies in Financial Organization*. Cambridge, Cambridge University Press.

Barty-King, H. (1977). *The Baltic Exchange*. London, Hutchinson.

Barty-King, H. (1991). *The Worst Poverty: A History of Debt and Debtors*. Wolfeboro Falls, NH, Allan Sutton Publishers.

BBC Business News (2008). 'Chancellor Warns of Personal Debt.' Retrieved 8 May 2008, from http://news.bbc.co.uk/1/hi/business/6992450.stm

Benería, L. (1999). 'Globalization, gender and the Davos man.' *Feminist Economics* 5(3): 61–83.

Benería, L. (2003). *Gender, Development and Globalization: Economics as if People Mattered*. London and New York, Routledge.

Benería, L. and S. Feldman (1992). *Unequal Burden: Economic Crises, Persistent Poverty, and Women's Work*. Boulder, CO, San Francisco, CA, Oxford, Westview Press.

Benería, L., F. Maria, C. Grown and M. MacDonald (2000). 'Globalization and gender.' *Feminist Economics* 6(3): 7–18.

Bhagwati, J. (1985). *Essays in Development Economics, Vol. 1: Wealth and Poverty*. Oxford, Blackwell.

Blackstone's Commentaries on the Laws of England, Book the Second, Chapter the eighth: Of freeholds, not of inheritance, II, 134 note p, [Internet] The Avalon Project, (1996–2007), Yale Law School. Retrieved 10 December 2004, from http://www.yale.edu/lawweb/avalon/blackstone/blacksto.htm

Bohstedt, J. (1988). 'Gender household and community politics: Women in English riots 1770–1810.' *Past and Present* 120: 88–122.

Boserup, E. (1989). *Women's Role in Economic Development*. London, Earthscan.

Braudel, F. (1979). *Civilisation and Capitalism 15th to 18th Centuries: The Perspective of the World*. New York, Harper and Row.

Braudel, F. (1982). *Europe: The Wheels of Commerce at the Highest Level*. London, Collins.

Braunstein, E. and G. Epstein (1999). Creating international credit rules and the multilateral agreement on investment: What are the alternatives? *Global Instability: The Political Economy of World Economic Governance*. J. Mitchie and J. Grieve Smith (Eds). London and New York, Routledge: 119–137.

Breckinridge, S. P. (1906). 'Legislative control of women's work.' *The Journal of Political Economy* 14(2): 107–109.

Brenner, R. (1977). 'The origins of capitalist development: Critique of neo-Smithian Marxism.' *New Left Review* 104: 25–92.

Brereton, B. (1998). 'Gendered testimonies: autobiographies, diaries and letters by women as sources for Caribbean history.' *Feminist Review* 59: 143–163.

Brewer, J. and S. Staves, Eds. (1995). *Early modern conceptions of property*. London, Routledge.

Bridenthal, R., S. M. Stuard, and M. E. Wiesner-Hanks, Eds. (1998 3rd edn). *Becoming Visible: Women in European History*. Boston, MA, Houghton Mifflin Co.

BRIDGE (2001). Briefing paper on the 'Feminisation of poverty', Institute of Development Studies, University of Sussex.

Brown, S. (1988). 'Feminism, international theory and international relations of gender inequality.' *Millennium* **17**(2): 461–475.

Burback, B. R., O. Núñez, and B. Kagarlitsky, Eds. (1997). *Globalization and its Discontents.* London, Pluto Press.

Burch, K. (1998). *Property and the Making of the International System.* London, Boulder, CO, Lynne Reinner.

Burn, G. (1999). 'The state, the City and the Euro markets.' *Review of International Political Economy* **6**(2): 225–261.

Business News, Online (2008). Surge in US home repossessions. Retrieved 28 May 2008, from http://news.bbc.co.uk/1/hi/business/6957738.stm

Butler, M. (1991). Early liberal roots of feminism: John Locke and the attack on patriarchy. *Feminist Interpretations and Political theory.* M. L. Shanley and C. Pateman (Eds). Cambridge, Polity Press.

Cagatay, N. (2000). Introduction. *World Development* (July). **28**(7): 1145–1156.

Callinicos, A. (1994). *Marxism and the New Imperialism.* London, Bookmarks.

Cameron, R. and V. I. Bovykin (1991). *International Banking, 1870–1914.* New York, Oxford University Press.

CapitalOne (2002). 'Press Release.' Retrieved 14 February 2002, from http://CapitalOne.ca/canada/about/press_clips.shtml

Castells, E. (1996). *The Rise of Network Society.* Oxford, Blackwell.

Cerny, P. (1993). 'Plurilateralism: Structural differentiation and functional conflict in the post-cold war era.' *Millennium: Journal of International Studies* **22**: 27–51.

Cerny, P. (1995). 'Globalisation and the changing logic of collective action.' *International Organization* **34**(2): 595–625.

Cerny, P. (2000). Political globalization and the competition state. *Political Economy and the Changing Global Order.* R. Stubbs and G. Underhill (Eds). Oxford, Oxford University Press.

Charles, N. and C. A. Davies (2000). 'Cultural stereotypes and the gendering of senior management.' *The Sociological Review* **48**(4): 544–567.

Chen, M., J. Vanek, F. Lund, J. Heintz with R. Jhabvala, C. Bonner (2005). *Progress of the World's Women: Women, Work and Poverty.* New York, United Nations Development Fund for Women.

Clark, A. (1919). *Working Life of Women in the Seventeenth Century.* London, Routledge.

Clarke, J. (1994). 'An American welfare state?' *The United States in the Twentieth Century.* R. Maidment (Ed.). East Kilbride, Hodder and Stoughton/Open University: 204.

Clarkson, L. A. (1972). *The Pre-industrial Economy in England 1500–1750.* New York, Schocken Books.

CNN Money, (2007). 'Fortune Global 500.' Retrieved 2 June 2008, from http://money.cnn.com/magazines/fortune/global500/2007/

Cockerell, H. A. L. (1984). *Lloyd's of London: A Portrait.* Cambridge, Woodhead-Faulkner.

Cohen, M. (2002). 'Making microfinance more client-led.' *Journal of International Development* **14**: 335–350.

Collins, D. (2003). 'Stumbling our way toward a worldwide democratic-capitalist government: Globalization and sweatshops.' *Business Ethics Quarterly* **13**(3): 403–411.

Condon, M. (2007). 'The feminisation of pensions? Gender, political economy and defined contribution pensions'. *Global Finance in the New Century: Beyond Deregulation*. L. Assassi, A. Nesvetailova and D. Wigan (Eds). Basingstoke, Palgrave Macmillan: 89–101.

Connell, R. W. (1995). *Masculinities*. Ontario, Oxford University Press.

Cook, J., J. Roberts and G. Waylen (2000). *Towards a Gendered Political Economy*. Houndsmills, Basingstoke, Macmillan Press.

Coole, D. (1986). 'Re-reading political theory from a woman's perspective.' *Political Studies* **34**: 129–148.

Coole, D. (1993 2nd edn). *Women in Political Theory*. New York, Harvest Wheatsheaf.

Cooley, A. (2003). 'Thinking rationally about hierarchy and global governance.' *Review of International Political Economy* **10**(4): 672–684.

Cornish, W. R. and G. R. Clark (1989). *Law and Society in England 1750–1950*. London, Sweet and Maxwell.

Cox, R. (1987). *Production, Power and World Order: Social Forces in the Making of History*. New York, Columbia University Press.

Cox, R. (1994). 'Multilateralism and world order.' *Review of International Studies* **18**: 162–163.

Cox, R. (2006 3rd edn). Political economy and world order: Problems of power and knowledge at the turn of the millennium. *Political Economy and the Changing Global Order*. R. Stubbs and G. Underhill (Eds). Oxford, Oxford University Press: 59–60.

Cox, R. and T. Sinclair (1997). *Approaches to World Order*. Cambridge, Cambridge University Press.

Cutler, T. and C. Waine (2001). 'Social insecurity and the retreat from social democracy: Occupational welfare in the long boom and financialization.' *Review of International Political Economy* **8**(1): 96–117.

Dailey, A. C. (1993). 'Review: Feminism's return to liberalism.' *The Yale Law Journal* **102**(5): 1265–1286.

Daily Telegraph, The (2008). Tory Party Conference: Commitment to family values gets best reception. *Daily Telegraph, The*. 1 October 2008.

Davidoff, L. and C. Hall (1987). *Family Fortunes : Men and Women of the English Middle Class, 1780–1850*. London, Hutchinson.

Dawkins Scully of the Woman's Microcredit accountability NETwork. Retrieved 14 February 2002, http://www.developmentgap.org/micro.html

Defoe, D. (1706). *Review of the State of the English Nation*. No. 7, 15 January. Reproduced by Arthur Wellesley Secord (1965): Vol. III, Book 6. New York, AMS Press.

De Goede, M. (2000). 'Mastering 'Lady Credit'.' *International Feminist Journal of Politics* **2**(1, 23 June 2000): 58–81.

De Grazia, V. (1996). Empowering women and citizen-consumers. *The Sex of Things: Gender and Consumption in Historical Perspective*. V. de Grazia and E. Furlough (Eds). Berkeley and Los Angeles, University of California Press: 275–285.

De Grazia, Victoria and E. Furlough (1996). *The Sex of Things: Gender and Consumption in Historical Perspective*. Berkeley, LA, London, University of California Press.

Delphy, C. and D. Leonard (1992). *Familiar Exploitation: A New Analysis of Marriage in Contemporary Western Societies*. Cambridge, Policy Press.

Dicken, P. (1998 3rd edn). *Global Shift*. New York, Guilford Press.

Dickenson, D. (1996). *Property Women and Politics: Subjects or Objects?* Cambridge, Polity Press.

Dickson, P. G. M. (1967). *The Financial Revolution in England*. London and New York, St Martin's Press.

Dieter, K. (2005). 'Holding global regulators accountable: The case of credit rating agencies.' *Governance* 18(3): 453–475.

Dimand, R. W., E. L. Forget, C. Nyland (2004). 'Retrospectives gender in classical economics.' *Journal of Economic Perspectives: American Economic Association* 18(1): 229–240.

Dunaway, W. A. (2001). 'The double register of history: Situating the forgotten woman and her household in capitalist commodity chains.' *Journal of World-Systems Research* 7(1): 2–29.

Dunning, J. H. (1997). *Alliance Capitalism and Global Business*. London and New York, Routledge.

Dunning J. and G. Boyd, Eds. (2003). *Alliance Capitalism and Corporate Management: Entrepreneurial Cooperation in Knowledge Based Economies*. Cheltenham, Edward Elgar.

Dymski, G. and M. Floro (2000). 'Financial crisis, gender and power: An analytical framework.' *World Development* 38: 1269–1283.

Earle, P. (1989). 'Female labour market.' *Economic History Review* **42**: 328–353.

Edelstein, M. (1982). *Overseas Investment in the Age of High Imperialism: The United Kingdom, 1850–1914*. London, Methuen and Co. Ltd.

Elias, J. (2005). 'Stitching-up the labour market.' *International Feminist Journal of Politics* 7(1): 90–111.

Elshtain, J. B. (1981). *Public Man, Private Woman: Woman in Social and Political Thought*. Princeton, Princeton University Press.

Elson, D. (1992). *Male Bias in the Development Process: an Overview*. Manchester, Manchester University Press.

Elson, D. (1993 2nd edn). *Male Bias in the Development Project*. Manchester, Manchester University Press.

Elson, D. (1994). Micro, meso, macro: Gender and economic analysis in the context of policy reform. *The Strategic Silence: Gender and Economic Policy*. I. Bakker (Ed.). London, Zed Books: 33–45.

Elson, D. (1995). 'Gender awareness in modelling structural adjustment.' *World Development* 23(11): 1851–1868.

Elson, D. (1999). Socializing markets, not market socialism. *Social Register 2000: Necessary and unnecessary utopias.* L. Panitch and C. Leyes (Eds). Woodbridge, VA, Merlin Press.

Elson, D. (2001). International Financial Architecture: A View from the Kitchen. *International Studies Association Annual Conference.* Chicago.

Elson, D. (2002). Gender justice, human rights and neo liberal economic policies. *Gender Justice, Development, and Rights.* M. Molyneux and S. Razavi (Eds). Oxford, Oxford University Press: 78–114.

Elson, D. and N. Çagatay (2000). 'The social context of macroeconomic politics.' *World Development* 23(11): 1851–1868.

Ely, J. W. (1992). *The Guardian of Every Other Right: a Constitutional History of Property Rights.* New York, Oxford University Press.

Enloe, C. (1989). *Bananas, Beaches and Bases: Making Feminist Sense of International Politics.* London, Pandora.

Enloe, C. (2001). 'Interview with Professor Cynthia Enloe, annual convention of the ISA in Chicago.' *Review of International Studies,* 27(4): 649–666.

Erickson, A. L. (1993). *Women in Property in Early Modern England.* London and New York, Routlege.

Erikson, A. L. (2005). 'Coverture and capitalism.' *History Workshop Journal* 59(1): 1–16.

Escobar, A. (1995). *Encountering Development: The Making and Unmaking of the Third World.* Princeton, Princeton University Press.

Esping-Andersen, G. (1999). *Title Social Foundations of Postindustrial Economies* Oxford, Oxford University Press.

Experian (2007). 'Which Club Has the Answers to All Your Home Shopping Questions? Experian Club Canvasse.' Retrieved 26 May 2008, from http://www.experian.co.uk/business/clubcanvasse/index.html

Feenstra, R. C., G. M. Grossman, and D. Irwin, Eds. (1995). *The Political Economy of Trade Policy: Papers in Honour of Jagdish Bhagwait.* Cambridge, MA, MIT.

Feis, H. (1934/1974). *Europe The World's Banker 1870–1914: An Account of European Foreign Investment and the Connection of World Finance with Diplomacy before the War.* Clifton, originally published by Council on Foreign Relations, Reprint Augustus M. Kelley.

Feldman, S. (1992). Crises, poverty and gender inequality: Current themes and issues. *Unequal Burden.* L. Benería and S. Feldman (Eds). Boulder, CO, Westview Press.

Fenton, L. (2005). 'Citizenship in private space.' *Space and Culture* 8(2): 180–192.

Ferris, P. (1985). *Gentlemen of Fortune: The World's Merchant and Investment Bankers.* London, Weidenfeld.

Financial Services Authority (2000). DOI: FSA/PN/093/2000. Retrieved 13 July 2009, http://www.fsa.gov.uk/pubs/consumer-research/crpr03.pdf

Financial Times (2001). *Financial Times.* London.

Finley, M. I. (1981). *Economy and Society in Ancient Greece.* London, Chatto & Windus.

Finn, M. (1996). 'Women, consumption and coverture in England c. 1760–1860.' *The Historical Journal* 39(3): 703–722.

Fletcher, A. (1995). *Gender, Sex, and Subordination in England, 1500–1800.* New Haven, CT, London, Yale University Press.

Floro, M. and G. Dymski (2000). 'Financial crisis, gender, and power: an analytical framework.' *World Development* 28(7): 1269–1283.

Folbre, N. and H. Hartmann (1988). The rhetoric of self-interest: Ideology and gender in economic theory. *The Consequences of Economic Rhetoric*. A. Klamer, D. N. McCloskey and R. Solow (Eds). Cambridge, Cambridge University Press: 184–199.

Forget, E. L. (1997). 'The market for virtue: Jean-Baptiste say on women in the economy and society.' *Feminist Economics* 3(1): 95–111.

Freeden, M. (1996). *Ideologies and Political Theory*. Oxford, Oxford University Press.

Fussell, E. (2000) 'Making labor flexible: The recomposition of Tijuana's Maquiladora female labor force.' *Feminist Economics* 6(3): 59–79.

Galbraith, J. (1992). *The Culture of Contentment*. London, Sinclair-Stevenson.

Geelink, A. (2001). 'Gender and globalization: Processes of social and economic restructuring.' *The European Journal of Women's Studies* 8(4): 511–513.

Germain, R. (1997). *The International Organization of Credit: States and Global Finance in the World-Economy*. Cambridge, MA, Blackwell.

Giddens, A. (1971). *Capitalism and Modern Social Theory: An Analysis of the Writings of Marx, Durkheim and Max Weber*. London, Cambridge University Press.

Gill, S. (1994). Structural change and global political economy: Globalizing elites and the merging world order. *Global Transformations: Challenges to the State System*. Y. Sakamoto (Ed.). Tokyo, New York, Paris, United Nations University Press.

Gill, S. (1997). Finance, production and panopticism: Inequality, risk and resistance in an era of disciplinary neo-liberalism. *Globalization, Democratization and Multilateralism*. S. Gill (Ed.). Toyko, New York, Paris, United Nations University Press: 51–76.

Gill, S. (1998). 'New constitutionalism, democratization and global political economy.' *Pacific Review* 10: 23–38.

Gill, S. (2000 2nd edn). Knowledge, politics and neo-liberal political economy. *Political Economy and the Changing Global Order*. R. Stubbs and G. Underhill (Eds). Oxford, Oxford University Press: 48–58.

Gill, S. (2002). Power and Resistance in the New World Order. *British International Studies Association Annual Conference*. London School of Economics.

Gill, S. and D. Law (1988). *The Global Political Economy: Perspectives, Problems and Policies*. Hemel Hempstead, Harvester.

Gilpin, R. (1987). *The Political Economy of International Relations*. Princeton, NJ, Princeton University Press.

Gilpin, R. (1996).'Economic Evolution of National Systems.' *International Studies Quarterly* 40: 411–431.

Gilpin, R. (2001). *Global Political Economy: Understanding the International Order*. Princeton, NJ, Princeton University Press.

Global Envision (2006). 'The Basics of Microfinance.' Retrieved 26 May 2008, from http://www.globalenvision.org/library/4/1061

Goetz, A. M. (1981). 'Feminism and the claim to know: Contradictions in feminist approaches to women in development.' *Millennium* 17: 477–497.

Goetz, A. M. and R. S. Gupta (1996). 'Who takes the credit? Gender, power and control over loan use in rural credit programs in Bangladesh.' *World Development* 24(1): 45–63.

Grameen Bank. (2002). Banking on the poor. Retrieved 14 March 2002, from http://www.grameen-info.org/index.html

Grameen Bank (2008). 'Grameen Bank: Banking for the Poor.' Retrieved 14 March 2002, from http://www.grameen-info.org/index.html

Grant, R. (1991). The sources of gender bias in international relations theory. *Gender and International Relation.*, R. Grant and K. Newland (Eds). Bloomington, Indiana University Press.

Grant, R. and K. Newland. (1991). *Gender and International Relations.* Bloomington, Indiana University Press.

Grant, R. and K. Newland. (1992). Introduction: Sources of gender bias in international relations theory. *Gender and International Relations.* G. R. K. Newland (Ed.). Milton Keynes, Open University Press.

Gray, M. (2000). *Productive Men, Reproductive Women: The Agrarian Household and the Emergence of the Separate Sphere during the Enlightenment.* New York and Oxford, Berghan Books.

Greenfield, C. and P. Williams (2007). 'Financialization, finance rationality and the role of media in Australia.' *Media, Culture and Society* 29(3): 415–433.

Griffin, P. (2007). 'Sexing the economy in a neo-liberal world order: Neo-liberal discourse and the (re)production of heteronormative heterosexuality.' *British Journal of Politics & International Relations* 9(2): 220–238.

The Guardian (2001). 'Sometimes I just feel like walking away. Marie Gill is one of seven women hoping that the House of Lords will save their homes from repossession by the banks.' 12 June 2001: 14–17.

The Guardian (2003). Barclays blows the gaff.

Guérin, I. (2006). 'Women and money: Lessons from Senegal.' *Development and Change* 37(3): 549–570.

GUS (2001). 'Press Release on Experian.' Retrieved 12 November 2004, from http:///www.gusplc.com/

Halcombe, L. (1983). *Wives and Property Reform of the Married Women's Property Law in Nineteenth Century England.* Oxford, Martin Robertson.

Hampton, M. H. (2002). 'Offshore pariahs? Small island economies, tax havens, and the reconfiguration of global finance.' *World Development* 30(9): 1657–1673.

Hardin, R. (1999). *Liberalism, Constitutionalism and Democracy.* Oxford, Oxford University Press.

Harding, S. (1986). *The Science Question in Feminism*, Milton Keynes, Open University Press.

Hartsock, N. (1983). *Money, Sex and Power.* New York, Longman.

Harvey, D. (1993). From place to space and back again. *Mapping Futures Local Cultures Global Change.* J. Bird, B. Curtis, T. Putnam, and L. Tickner (Eds). London and New York, Routledge.

Held, D., A. McGrew, D. Goldblatt, and J. Perraton (1999). *Global Transformations: Politics, Economics and Culture.* Cambridge, Polity Press.

Helleiner, E. (1994). *States and the Re-emergence of Global Finance.* Ithaca, NY, Cornell University Press.

Helleiner, E. (1995). 'Explaining the globalization of financial markets: Bringing states back in.' *Review of International Political Economy* 2(2): 315–341.

Henderson, H. (1999). *Beyond Globalization: Shaping a Sustainable Global Economy.* West Hartford, CT, Kumarian Press.

Hilton, R. (1990 2nd edn). 'Women traders in medieval England.' *Class Conflict & the Crisis of Feudalism.* R. Hilton (Ed.). London, Hambledon Press.

Hirschman, N. (1992). *Rethinking Obligation: A Feminist Method for Political Theory.* New York, Cornell University Press.

Hirst, P. Q. and G. Thompson (1998 2nd edn). *Globalization in Question: the International Economy and the Possibilities of Governance.* Cambridge, Polity Press.

Hobson, C. K. (1963). *The Export of Capital.* London, Constable.

Hoekman, B. and M. Kostecki (1995). *The Political Economy of the World Trading System.* Oxford, Oxford University Press.

Holderness, B. A. (1975). 'Credit in a rural community 1660–1800.' *Midland History* 3(2).

Holderness, B. A. (1976). 'Credit in rural society before the 19th century.' *Agricultural History Review* 24.

Hughes, G. and G. Lewis (1998). *Unsettling Welfare: the Reconstruction of Social Policy.* London, Routledge.

Hulme, D. and Mosley, P. (1996). *Finance against Poverty, Vol. 1.* London and New York, Routledge.

Hutton, W. (2007). The worst crisis I've seen in 30 years. The latest financial downturn is the final nail in the coffin of the conservative free-market world-view. *The Observer.* London, 4 November 2007.

Iceland Government Information Centre regarding the current financial circumstances in Iceland. The financial crisis in Iceland. Retrieved 12 February 2009, from http://www.iceland.org/info

ILO (1998). Women in the Informal Sector and their Access to Microfinance Social Finance Unit. *Inter-Parliamentary Union (IPU) Annual Conference.* Windhoek, Namibia, ILO Employment Sector, Social Finance Unit.

IMF (2008). Global Financial Stability Report. *IMF.* Washington, DC, International Monetary Fund.

Ingrassia, C. (1998). *Authorship, Commerce, and Gender in Early Eighteenth-Century England: A Culture of Paper Credit.* Cambridge and New York, Cambridge University Press.

Insley, G. (2008). Egg card cancellation won't effect your rating. *The Guardian.* London, 4 February 2008.

Irwin, N. (2007). Fed leads global bid to spur loans. *Washington Post,* 13 December 2007.

Jackson, C. (1998). Rescuing gender from the poverty trap. *Feminist Visions of Development: Gender Analysis and Policy.* C. Jackson and R. Pearson (Eds). New York, Routledge: 39–60.

Jacques, M. (2009). The new depression. *New Statesman,*12 February 2009.

Jennings, A. (1993). 'Public or private?' Institutional economics and feminism. *Beyond Economic Man.* M. Ferber and J. Nelson (). Chicago, University of Chicago Press.

Jenson, J. and M. Sineau (2001). *Who cares? Women's Work, Childcare, and Welfare State Redesign.* Toronto, University of Toronto Press.

Jessop, B. (1993). 'Towards a Schumpeterian workfare state? Preliminary remarks on post-Fordist political economy.' *Studies in Political Economy* **40**: 7–39.

Jones, G. (1993). Multinational banking strategies. *The Growth of Global Business.* H. Cox, J. Clegg and G. Ietto-Gillies (Eds). London, Routledge: 38–61.

Jordan, B. (1996). *A Theory of Poverty and Social Exclusion.* Cambridge, Polity Press.

Jordan, W. C. (1993). *Women and Credit in Pre-Industrial and Developing Societies.* Philadelphia, PA, University of Pennsylvania Press.

The Journal of Segmentation in Marketing Innovations (2002). Retrieved 23 January 2003, from http://www.ualverta.ca/~ppopknows/journals/jsm. htm

Kabeer, N. (1994). *Reversed Realities: Gender Hierarchies in Development Thought.* London, Verso.

Kabeer, N. (1998). 'Money can't buy me love? Re-evaluating gender, credit and empowerment in rural Bangladesh.' *Discussion Paper 363,* Institute of Development Studies.

Kahn, G. A. (2000). 'Global economic integration: Opportunities and challenges – a summary of the bank's 2000 symposium.' *Economic Review – Federal Reserve Bank of Kansas City* **85**(4): xvii–xxix.

Katherine, R. (2002). 'Social capital, microfinance, and the politics of development.' *Feminist Economics* **8**(1): 1–24.

Kempton, E. and C. Whyley (1999). *Kept Out or Opted Out? Understanding and Combating Financial Exclusion.* Bristol, University of Bristol, Polity Press.

Keohane, N. (1982). Speaking from silence: Women and the science of politics. *A Feminist Perspective in the Academy.* E. Langland and W. Cove (Eds). Chicago, IL, University of Chicago Press.

Kofman, E. and G. Youngs (1996). *Globalization: Theory and Practice.* London, Pinter Press.

Kreps, B. (2002). 'The paradox of women: the legal position of early modern wives and Thomas Dekker's the honest whore.' *ELH* **69**(1): 83–102.

Kwolek-Folland, A. (1994). *Engendering Business: Men and Women in the Corporate Office 1870–1930.* Baltimore, MD and London, Johns Hopkins University Press.

Landes, D. S. (1969). *The Unbound Prometheus.* Cambridge, Cambridge University Press.

Langley, P. (2004). '(Re)politicizing global financial governance: What's "new" about the "New International Financial Architecture"?' *Global Networks: A Journal of Transnational Affairs* **4**(1): 69–87.

Laurence, A. (1994/1996). *Women in England 1500–1750 A Social History.* London, Weidenfeld & Nicolson.

Lemire, B. (1997). *Dress, Culture and Commerce: The English Clothing Trade before the Factory, 1660–1800.* London, Routledge.

Lemire, B. (1998). Petty pawns and informal lending: Gender and the transformation of small-scale credit in England circa 1600–1800. *From Family Firms to Corporation Capitalism: Essays in Business and Industrial History in Honour of Peter Mathias.* K. Bruland and P. O'Brien (Eds). Oxford, Oxford University Press: 112–120.

Lenin, V. I. (1916). *Imperialism: the Highest Stage of Capitalism.* New York, International Publishers.

Lerner, G. (1986). *The Creation of Patriarchy.* New York, Oxford University Press.

Levene, T. (2009). 'Repossessions Hit 12-Year High.' *The Guardian.* Retrieved 18 July 2009, from http://www.guardian.co.uk/money/2009/feb/20/repossessions-homeowners

Leyshon, A. and N. Thrift (1995). 'Geographies of financial exclusion: financial abandonment in Britain and the United States.' *Transactions of the Institute of British Geographers. New Series* **20**: 312–341.

Leyshon, A. and N. Thrift (1997). *Money and Space: Geographies of Monetary Transformation.* London and New York, Routledge.

Lindsey, C. and L. Duffin (1985). *Women and Work in Pre-industrial England.* Beckenham, Croom Helm.

Ling, L. (2002). Cultural chauvinism and the liberal international order: 'West versus rest' in Asia's financial crisis. *Power, Postcolonialism and International Relations: Reading Race, Gender and Class.* G. Chowdry and S. Nair (Eds). London, Routledge: 115–141.

Lloyd, J. M. (1995). 'Raising lilies: Ruskin and women.' *The Journal of British Studies* **34**: 325–350.

Lurie, G. (1974). *The Feminist Controversy in England 1788–1810.* New York, Garland Publishing.

Maclean, J. (1988). Belief systems and ideology in international relations: A critical approach. *Belief Systems and International Relations.* R. Little and S. Smith (Eds). Oxford and New York, Basil Blackwell Ltd: 57–84.

Macpherson, C. B., Ed. (1978). *Property Mainstream and Critical Positions.* Oxford, Blackwell.

Mahmud, S. (2003). 'Actually how empowering is microcredit?' *Development and Change* **33**(4): 577–605.

Mandelson, P. (2008). In defence of globalisation. *The Guardian*, 3 October 2008.

Mansbridge, J., Ed. (1990). *Beyond Self Interest.* Chicago, University of Chicago Press.

Marchand, M. and A. S. Runyan, Eds. (2000). *Gender and Global Restructuring: Sightings, Sites and Resistances.* London, Routledge.

Marx, K. (1990). *Capital: A Critique of Political Economy.* London, Penguin Classics.

Marx, K. and F. Engels (1958). *Selected Works in Two Volumes: Lawrence and Wishart.* Oxford, Oxford University Press.

Mary, B.-L. and A. J. Jerry (2003). 'Globalization, work hours, and the care deficit among stockbrokers.' *Gender & Society* **17**(2): 230–249.

Massey, D. (1994). *Space, Place and Gender.* Cambridge, Polity Press.

May, C. and S. Sell (2001). 'Moments in law: Contestation and settlement in the history of intellectual property.' *Review of International Political Economy* **8**(3): 467–500.

McDowell, L. (1997). *Capital Culture: Gender at Work in the City.* Oxford, Blackwell.

McDowell, L. and G. Court (1991). 'Missing subjects: Gender, sexuality and power in Merchant Banking.' *Economic Geography* **70**: 229–251.

McRae, M. and F. Cairncross (1991). *Capital City: London as a Financial Center.* London, Methuen.

Mendelson, S. and P. Crawford (1998). *Women in Early Modern England 1550–1720.* London, Methuen.

Merc, J. (2003). Codes of conduct and wages in the athletic footwear chain. Paper presented at Global Regulation Conference. University of Sussex, May 2003.

Merchant, C. (1980). *The Death of Nature: Women, Ecology and the Scientific Revolution.* New York, Harper Collins.

Mies, M. (1999 6th edn). *Patriachy and Accumulation on a World Scale: Women in the International Division of Labour.* London and New York, Zed Books.

Mill, J. S. and H. Mill (1970). *Essays on Sex Equality.* A. S. Rossi (Ed.). Chicago, Chicago University Press.

Mills, M. B. (2003). 'Gender and inequality in the global labor force.' *Annual Review of Anthropology* **32**(1): 41–62.

Mitchie, J. and J. Grieve Smith (1999). *Global Instability: the Political Economy of World Economic Governance.* Basingstoke, Routledge.

Moghadam, V. M. (2000). Economic restructuring and the gender contract: A case study of Jordan. *Gender and Global Restructuring.* M. H. Marchand and A. S. Runyan (Eds). London and New York, Routledge.

Mordoch, J. (1999). 'The microfinance promise.' *Journal of Economic Literature* **37**(4): 1569–1614.

Morton, F. (1964). *The Rothschilds: A Family Portrai.* London, Penguin.

Moser, C. O. N. (1992). Adjustment from below: Low income women, time and the triple role in Guayaquil, Ecuador. *Women and Adjustment Policies in the Third World.* H. Afshar and C. Denis (Eds). London, Macmillan.

Moser, C. O. N. (1993). *Gender Planning and Development.* London and New York, Routledge.

Mosley, P. (1996). 'Metamorphosis from NGO to Commercial Bank: The case of Bancosol' in *Metamorphosis From NGO to Commercial Bank: The Case of Banco Sol in Bolivia. Working Paper No. 4.* Institute for Development Policy and Management, University of Manchester.

Mosley, P. and D. Hulme (1998). Micro-enterprise finance: Is there a trade-off between growth and poverty alleviation? *Implications for Policy.* I. Matin and S. Sinha (Eds). Poverty Research Unit, University of Sussex.

Mouffe, C. (1996). *Dimensions of Radical Democracy: Pluralism, Citizenship.* London, Verso.

Muldrew, C. (1998). *The Economy of Obligation: the Culture of Credit and Social Relations in Early Modern England,* Basingstoke, Macmillan.

Munnell, A. H. (1980). The couple versus the individual under the federal personal income tax. *The Economics of Taxation.* H. J. Aaron and M. J. Boskin (Eds). Washington, DC, The Brookings Institution: 247–278.

Murphy, R. (2003). *Debt on Our Doorstep: the Case for an Interest Rate Cap: a Study Based on Provident Financial Plc.* London, Church Action on Poverty, New Economics Foundation.

Murphy, C. and R. Tooze (1991). *The New International Political Economy.* Boulder, Colorado, Lynne Reinner.

Murray, M. (1995). *The Law of the Father: Patriarchy in Transition from Feudalism to Capitalism.* London, Routledge.

Nagar, R. V. L., L. McDowell and S. Hanson (2001). Locating globalization: Feminist (re)readings of the subjects and spaces of globalisation. Paper given at Conference on Global Economic Change. Clark University.

Nahid, A. and S. Gale (2000). 'The Asian crisis, gender, and the international financial architecture.' *Feminist Economics* 6(3): 81–103.

Nandy, A. (1987). *Traditions, Tyranny and Utopias.* New Delhi, Oxford University Press.

Neil, M. (2008). 'Women got more subprime mortgages.' *ABA Journal Law News Now.* Retrieved 15 January 2008, from http://www.abajournal.com/news/women_got_more_subprime_mortagages/print/

Nelson, J. A. (1993). The study of choice or the study of provisioning? Gender and the definition of economics. *Beyond Economic Man : Feminist Theory and Economics.* M. A. Ferber and J. A. Nelson (Eds). Chicago, IL, University of Chicago Press: 23–36.

Nyland, C. (1993). 'Adam Smith, stage theory and the status of women.' *History of Political Economy* 25(4): 617–640.

O'Brien, R. and M. Williams (2004). *Global Political Economy: Evolution and Dynamics.* Basingstoke, Palgrave Macmillan.

OECD (2003). Retrieved 1 August 2003, from www1.oecd.org/dac/Gender

O'Hara, P. A. (1999). *Encyclopedia of Political Economy,* Vol. 2. London and New York, Routledge.

Okin, S. M. (1979). *Women in Western Political Thought.* Princeton, NJ, Princeton University Press.

Oliver, M., T. Shapiro and J. Press (1993). 'Them that's got shall get': Inheritance and achievement in wealth accumulation.' *Research in Politics and Society.* 5: 69–95.

Osirim, M. (2003) 'Carrying the burdens of adjustment and globalization: Women and microenterprise development in urban Zimbabwe.' *International Sociology* 18(3): 535–558.

OXFAM (2000). Tax Havens: Releasing the Hidden Billions for Poverty Eradication. *Oxfam Briefing Paper*. Oxford, OXFAM, Great Britain.

OXFAM (2009). 'Gender Equality.' Retrieved 2 February 2009, from http://www.oxfam.org.uk/resources/issues/gender/introduction.html

Palan, R. (2003). *The Offshore World: Sovereign Markets, Virtual Places, and Nomad Millionaires*. Ithaca, NY and London, Cornell.

Palmer, H. and P. Conaty (2002). *Profiting from Poverty*. London, New Economics Foundation.

Parker, G. (1977). The emergence of modern finance in Europe 1500–1730. *The Fontana Economic History of Europe*, Vol. 2. C. M. Cipolla (Ed.). London, Fontana.

Parpart, J. L., S. M. Rai, and K. Staudt (2002). *Rethinking Empowerment: Gender and Development*. Basingstoke, Routledge: 527–594.

Pateman, C. (1988). *The Sexual Contract*. Cambridge, Polity Press.

Pateman, C. (1998). The patriarchal welfare state. *Defining Women: Social Institutions and Gender Divisions*. L. McDowell and R. Pringle (Eds). Cambridge, Polity Press/Open University.

Paterson, M. (2002). 'Shut up and Shop! Thinking Politically about Consumption.' *The Globalsite*. Retrieved 28 October 2004, from http://www.theglobalsite.ac.uk/press/211paterson.htm

Paul, L. (2004). '(Re)politicizing global financial governance: what's "new" about the "new international financial architecture"?' *Global Networks: A Journal of Transnational Affairs* 4(1): 69–87.

Pauly, L. W. (2006). Capital mobility and the new global order. *Political Economy and the Changing Global Order*. R. Stubbs and G. Underhill, 3rd edn (Eds). London, Macmillan: 135–144.

Peiss, K. (1998). American Women and the Making of Modern Consumer Culture. Retrieved 30 February 2002, from http:www.//albany.edu/jmmh/vol1no1/peisstext.html

Peterson, V. S. (1992). *Gendered States: Feminist (Re)Visions of International Relations Theory*. Boulder, CO and London, Lynne Reider.

Peterson, V. S. (1997). Early and post-modern masculinism. *Innovation and Transformation in International Studies*. S. Gill and J. H. Mittelman (Eds). Cambridge, Cambridge University Press: 185–207.

Peterson, V. S. (2000). 'Rereading public and private: The dichotomy that is not one.' *SAIS Review* 20(3):11–29.

Pettman, J. J. (1996). Women and gender in the international political economy. *Worlding Women*. J. J. Pettman (Ed.). St. Leonards, Hllen and Unwin.

Phillips, R. (2000). Approaching the organisation of economic activity in the age of cross-border alliance capitalism. *Global Political Economy: Contemporary Theories*. R. Palan (Ed.). London and New York, Routledge: 36–52.

Pierenne, H. (1937). *Economics and Social History of Medieval Europe*. London, Keagan Paul.

Pirages, D. and C. Sylvester (1990). *Transformations in the Global Political Economy*. Houndsmill, Macmillan.

Polanyi, K. (1944). *The Great Transformation*. New York, Rinehart.

Polanyi, K. (1968). *Primitive, Archaic and Modern Economics: Essays of Karl Polanyi*. G. Dalton (Ed.). Boston, MA, Beacon Publications.

Pomeroy, S. B. (1975). *Goddesses, Whores, Wives and Slaves: Women in Classical Antiquity*. New York, Schocken Books.

Pomeroy, S. B. (1997). *Families in Classical and Hellenistic Greece: Representations and Realities*. Oxford, Clarendon Press.

Poovey, M. (1988). *Uneven Developments: The Ideological Work of Gender in Mid-Victorian Britain*. Chicago, University of Chicago.

Poovey, M. (1995). *Making a Social Body: British Cultural Formation 1830–1864*. Chicago and London, University of Chicago Press.

Porter, M. (2001). Retrieved 10 February 2004, from http://www.federalreserve. gov/DCCA?newsletter/2001/intercity.htm

Porter, T. (2005). *Globalization and Finance*. Cambridge, Polity.

Powell, J. (2003). 'Petty capitalism, perfecting capitalism or post-capitalism? Lessons from the Argentinean barter experiments.' *Review of International Political Economy* 9(4): 619–649.

Pressnell, L. S. (1956). *Country Banking in the Industrial Revolution*. Oxford, Clarendon Press.

Pritchett, L. (1997). 'Divergence, big time.' *Journal of Economic Perspectives* 11: 3–17.

Prokhovnik, R. (1998). 'Public and private citizenship: From gender invisibility to feminist inclusiveness.' *Feminist Review*. 60: 94–104.

Pyle, J. L. (1999). 'Recasting our understanding of gender and work during global restructuring.' *International Sociology* 18(3): 461–489.

Pyle, J. L. and K. B. Ward (2003). 'Recasting our understanding of gender and work during global restructuring.' *International Sociology* 18(3): 461–489.

Rankin, R. (2002). 'Social capital, microfinance, and the politics of development.' *Feminist Economics* 8(1): 1–24.

Ravenhill, J., Ed. (2008). *Global Political Economy*. Oxford, Oxford University Press.

Reeve, A. (1986). *Property*. Basingstoke, Macmillan.

Reiger, K. (2000). 'Reconceiving citizenship.' *Feminist Theory*. 1(3): 309–327.

Ricardo, D. (1871/1971). *Principles of Political Economy and Taxation*. M. Savy and P. Veltz (Eds). Harmondsworth, Penguin Books.

Richards, R. D. (1958). *The Early History of Banking in England*. London, Frank Cass and Co.

Rifkind, J. (2000). Another wolf at our door. *Financial Times*. London.

Ritzer, G. (1995). *Expressing American: A Critique of the Global Credit Card Society*. Thousand Oaks, Pine Forge Press.

Roberts, R. (1999). *Inside International Finance*. London, Orion Business.

Rosenau, J. N. (1999). 'People, nations, and credit cards: Major variables in an emergent epoch.' *International Politics* 36: 291–320.

Rosenblatt, G. and K. Rake (2003). *Gender and Poverty*. London, Fawcett Society.

Rowbotham, S. (1973). *Hidden from History: 300 Years of Women's Oppression and the Fight against It*. London, Pluto Press.

Rowlingson, K. C. Whyley, and T. Warren (1999). *Wealth in Britain: A Lifecycle Perspective*. London, Joseph Rountree Foundation, Policy Studies.

Ruggie, J. G. (1982). 'International regimes, transactions, and change: Embedded liberalism in the post-war economic order.' *International Organization* 36(2): 379–415.

Ruskin, J. [1865] (1909–1914). 'Essays: English and American.' *Harvard Classics*, Vol. 28 of 51. Charles W. Eliot (Ed.). New York, P. F. Collier & Son.

Russell, G. (2000). ' "Faro's daughters": Female gamesters, politics, and the discourse of finance in 1790s Britain.' *Eighteenth-Century Studies* 33(4): 481–504.

Ryan, A. (1987). *Property*. Minneapolis, MN, University of Minnesota Press.

Sainsbury's Bank (2003). 'Sainsbury's Finance.' Retrieved 2 February 2004, from http://www.sainsburysbank.co.uk/

Sampson, A. (1981). *'Who Keeps the World?' The Money Lenders*. New York, Penguin.

Saunders, K., Ed. (2002). *Feminist Post Development Thought: Rethinking Modernity Post Colonialism and Representation*. London, Zed Books.

Sayer, D. (1987). *The Violence of Abstraction. The Analytical Foundations of Historical Materialism*, Oxford, Blackwell.

Sayers, R. S. (1957). *Title Lloyds Bank in the History of English Banking*. Oxford, Clarendon Press.

Scholte, J. A. (2000). *Globalisation: a Critical Introduction*. Basingstoke, Palgrave.

Schwartz, H. (2000). *States and Markets*. London and Basingstoke, Macmillan.

ScienceDaily (2008). Testosterone levels predict city traders' profitability. *ScienceDaily*. 30 September 2008.

Seager, J. (1997). *The State of Women in the World Atlas*. London, Penguin.

Sen, G. and C. Grown (1987). *Development, Crises and Alternative Visions: Third World Women's Perspectives*. New York, Monthly Review Press.

Sequino, S., T. Stevens, M. A. Lutz (1996). 'Gender and cooperative behaviour: Economic man rides alone.' *Feminist Economics*, 1466–4372 2:1(March): 1–21.

Shanley, M. L. (1989). *Feminism, Marriage and the Law in Victorian England*. Princeton, Princeton University Press.

Sinclair, S. P. (2002). Financial Exclusion: an Introductory Survey, British Attitudes to Financial Services. Financial Services Authority. Retrieved 11 November 2002, from http://www.fsa.gov.uk/pages/search/index.shtml

Sinclair, T. (1994). 'Passing judgement: Credit rating processes as regulating mechanisms of governance.' *Review of International Political Economy* 1: 133–160.

Sklair, L. (2002 3rd edn). *Globalization: Capitalism and its Alternatives*. Oxford, Oxford University Press.

Smail, J. (2003). 'The Culture of Credit in Eighteenth-Century Commerce: the English Tile Industry.' *Enterprise and Society (Project Muse)* 4(2): 299–325.

Smith, A. [1776] (1991). *An Inquiry into the Nature and Causes of Wealth*. London, Everyman.

Smith, J. (2001). *Moralities: Sex, Money and Power in the Twenty-first Century.* London, Allen Lane, Penguin Press.

Social Exclusion Unit (2002). 'Social Exclusion.' Retrieved 28 February 2004, from http://www.neighbourhood.gov.uk/page.asp?id=630

Sparr, P. (1994). *Mortgaging Women's Lives: Feminist Critiques of Structural Adjustment.* London, Zed Books.

Spero, J. E. (1997 5th edn). *The Politics of International Economic Relations.* London, Routledge.

Squires, J. (1999). *Gender in Political Theory,* Cambridge: Polity Press

Standing, G. (1999). *Global Labour Flexibility: Seeking Distributive Justice 1999.* London and Basingstoke, Macmillan.

Stanfield, J. R. (1986). *The Economic Thought of Karl Polayni.* London, Macmillan.

Stanfield, J. R. (1999). Disembedded Economy. *Encyclopedia of Political Economy.* P. A. O'Hara (Ed.) London and New York, Routledge: 1.

Stanfield, J. R. and J. B. Stanfield (1997). 'Where Has Love Gone? Reciprocity, Redistribution and the Nurturance Gap.' *Journal of Socio-Economics,* **26**(2): 111–126.

Staves, S. (1990). *Married Women's Separate Property in England, 1660–1833.* Cambridge, Polity Press.

Staves, S. (1994). 'English chattel property rules and the construction of personal and national identity.' *Law and History Review* **12**: 123–154.

Steans, J. (1998). *Gender and International Relations: An Introduction.* Oxford, Polity Press.

Stienstra, D. (2000). Dancing resistance from Rio to Beijing: Transnational women's organizing and United Nations conferences. *Gender and Global Restructuring: Sightings, Sites and Resistances.* M. H. Marchand and A. S. Runyan (Eds). London and New York, Routledge.

Stopford, J. and S. Strange (1991). *Rival States, Rival Firms: Competition for World Market Shares.* Cambridge, Cambridge University Press.

Strange, S. (1986). *Casino Capitalism.* Oxford, Basil Blackwell.

Strange, S. (1988). *States and Markets.* London, Pinter.

Strange, S. (1990). 'Finance, information and power.' *Review of International Studies* **16**: 259–274.

Strange, S. (1998). *Retreat of the State.* Cambridge, Cambridge University Press.

Sweezy, P. (1976). The debate on the transition. *The Transition from Feudalism to Capitalism.* P. Sweezy et al. (Eds). London, Verso.

Strange, S. (2000 2nd edn). World order, non-state actors and the global casino: The retreat of the state? *Political Economy and the Changing Global Order.* R. Stubbs and G. Underhill (Eds). Oxford, Oxford University Press: 82–90.

Stubbs, R. and G. Underhill, Eds. (2000 2nd edn). *Political Economy and the Changing Global Order.* Basingstoke, Macmillan.

Stubbs, R. and G. Underhill, Eds. (2006 3rd edn). *Political Economy and the Changing Global Order.* Basingstoke, Macmillan.

Sweezey, P. and M. Dobb, Eds. (1978). *The Transition from Feudalism to Capitalism.* London, Verso.

Sylvester, C. (1994). *Feminist Theory and International Relations in a Post-Modern Era*. London, Routledge.

Teacher, D., A. Seager, K. Allen, and J. McCurry (2007). Central banks pour in billions – but global slide goes on. *The Guardian*. London.

Tebbutt, M. (1983). *Making Ends Meet: Pawnbroking and Working-Class Credit*. New York, St. Martin's Press.

Teschke, B. (1998). 'Geopolitical relations in the European Middle Ages: History and theory.' *International Organization* 52(2): 325–358.

Thatcher, M. (1982). 'News Archives.' Retrieved on 18 July 2009, from http://toolbar.google.com/archivesearch?q=%22prime+minister+thatcher%22%2B%22homilies%22&hl=en&ned=tus&scoring=t

Thomas, C. (1999). 'Where is the Third World now?' *Review of International Studies* 25: 225–244.

Tickner, J. A. (1991). On the fringes of the world economy: A feminist perspective. *The New International Political Economy*. C. N. Murphy and R. Tooze (Eds). Boulder, CO, Lynne Reinner.

Tickner, J. A. (1992). *Gender in International Relations: Feminist Perspectives on Achieving Global Security*. New York, Chichester, Columbia University Press.

Tilly, L. A. and J. W. Scott (1978). *Women, Work and Family*. New York, Holt Rinehart and Winston.

Tully, J. (1993). *An Approach to Political Philosophy: Locke in Context*. Cambridge, Cambridge University Press.

United Nations Capital Development Fund (UNCDF) (2002). 'Special Unit for Microfinance.' Retrieved 14 March 2002, from http://www.uncdf.org/sum/index

United Nations Capital Development Fund (2005). Retrieved 14 March 2005, from http://www/uncdf.org/sum/index.html

United Nations Development Report (UNDR) (2003). *Human Development Report 2003: Millennium Development Goals: A Compact Among Nations to End Human Poverty*. New York, Oxford University Press.

United Nations Human Development Report (1999). 'Globalization with a Human Face.' Retrieved 28 June 2004, from http://hdr.undp.org/en/reports/global/hdr1999/

UNDP (2003). *Women's Political Participation* 327–320, UNDP.

UNIFEM (2005). 'Reducing Women's Poverty and Exclusion.' [Internet] Retrieved 2 February 2009, from http://www.unifem.org/gender_issues/millennium_development_goals/

Valodia, I. (2001). 'Economic policy and women's informal work in South Africa.' *Development and Change* 32(5): 871–892.

van der Pijl, K. (1998). *Transnational Classes and International Relations*. London, Routledge.

van der Pijl, K. (2004). *Global Regulation: Managing Crises after the Imperial Turn*. Basingstoke, Palgrave.

van Staveren (1998). *Robinson Crusoe and Silas Marner, or Two Stories on the Gendered Monetary Economy*. Brussels, WIDE.

van Staveren, I. (2001). 'Gender biases in finance.' *Gender and Development* 9(1): 9–17.

van Staveren, I. (2002). Global finance and gender. *Civil Society and Global Finance*. J. A. Scholte and A. Schnabel (Eds.). London, Routledge: 228–246.

Vargas, V. (2003). 'Feminism, globalization and the global justice and solidarity movement.' *Cultural Studies* **17**(6): 905–920.

Vickers, J. (1991). *Women and the World Economic Crisis*. London, Zed Books.

Walby, S. (2000). 'Gender, globalisation, and democracy.' *Gender and Development* **8**(1): 20–28.

Wallerstein, I. (1980). *The Capitalist World Economy. The Modern World System.* Cambridge, Cambridge University Press.

Wallerstein, I. (1984). *Politics of the World-economy: the States, the Movements, and the Civilizations.* Cambridge, Cambridge University Press.

Wallerstein, I. (1991). Labour-force formation in the capitalist world-economy. *Race Nation and Class.* É. Balibar and I. Wallerstein (Eds). Oxford, Blackwell: 107–112.

Wallerstein, I. (1992). 'The West, capitalism, and the modern world-system.' *Review* **15**(4): 561–619.

Waring, M. (1989). *If Women Counted: a New Feminist Economics.* London, Macmillan.

Warren, T., K. Rowlingson, and C. Whyley (2004). 'Gender and wealth inequality.' *Radical Statistics* **75**: 49–54.

Waters, M. (2001). *Globalization.* London, Routledge.

Waylen, G. (2004). 'Putting governance into the gendered political economy of globalization.' *International Feminist Journal of Politics* **6**(4): 557–578.

Waylen, G. (2006). 'You still don't understand: Why troubled engagements continue between feminists and (critical) IPE.' *Review of International Studies* **32**: 145–164.

Weber, H. (2001). 'The global political economy of microcredit.' Paper presented at *The Global Constitution of Failed States Conference*, University of Sussex.

Weber, H. (2002). 'The imposition of a global development architecture: The example of Microcredit.' *Review of International Studies* **28**(3): 537–555.

Weber, H. (2004). 'The new economy and social risk: banking on the poor.' *Review of International Political Economy* **11**(4): 356–386.

WEDO (2002). *The Numbers Speak for Themselves.* New York, Women's Environment and Development Organisation.

Whitehead, A. (1984). Men and women, kinship and property. *Women and Property: Women as Property.* R. Hirschon (Ed.). London and Canberra, Croom Helm: 123.

Whitworth, S. (2000). Theory and exclusion: Gender, masculinity, and international political economy. *Political Economy and the Changing Global Order.* J. Stubbs and G. Underhill (Eds). Oxford, New York, Oxford University Press: 88–102.

Wiesner-Hanks, M. E. (1998 3rd edn). Spinner out capital: Women's work in preindustrial Europe. *Becoming Visible: Women in European History.* R. Bridenthal, S. M. Stuard and M. E. Wiesner-Hanks (Eds). Boston, MA, Houghton Mifflin Co.

Williams, M. (2000). Mobilizing international resources for development – foreign direct investment and other private flows, and trade. Financial for development. DAWN. New York, United Nations.

Williamson, O. E. (1985). *Contractual Man' in The Economic Institutions of Capitalism*. New York and London, Free Press.

Williamson, J. (1990). What Washington means by policy reform. *Latin American Adjustment: How Much Has Happened?* Washington DC, Institute for International Economics.

Wiltenburger, J. (1993). 'Disorderly women and female power in the street literature of early modern England and Germany.' *Renaissance Quarterly* 46(3): 627–629.

Wolock, N. (1994). *Women and the American Experience*. New York, McGraw-Hill Inc.

World Bank (2000). *Consultation with Civil Society Organisations: General Guidelines for World Bank Staff*, Washington, DC, NGO and Civil Society Development Unit, The World Bank.

World Bank (2002). *Consultation with Civil Society Organisations: General Guidelines for World Bank Staff*. Washington, DC, NGO and Civil Society Development Unit, the World Bank.

World Bank (2006). 'Focus on Sustainability.' Retrieved 18 July 2009, from http://siteresources.worldbank.org/ESSDNETWORK/Resources/481106-1129303936381/1777397-1129303967165/intro.html

World Bank. (2008a). 'Empowerment.' Retrieved 26 May 2002, 2008, from http://lnweb18.worldbank.org/ESSD/sdvext.nsf/68ByDocName/WhatIs Empowerment

World Bank (2008b). 'Overview: Understanding Poverty.' Retrieved 26 May 2008, from http://web.worldbank.org/WBSITE/EXTERNAL/TOPICS/EXT POVERTY/0

Wright, S. (1985). 'Churmaids, huswyfes and hucksters': the employment of women in Tudor and Stuart Salisbury. *Women and work in preindustrial England*. C. Lindsay and L. Duffin (Eds). London, Indiana University Press.

Youngs, G. (1999). *From International to Global Relations: A Conceptual Challenge*. Cambridge, Polity Press.

Youngs, G., Ed. (2000a). *Political Economy, Power and the Body: Global Perspectives*. Basingstoke, Macmillan.

Youngs, G. (2000b). Breaking patriarchal bonds: Demythologizing the public/private. *Gender and Global Restructuring*. M. Marchand and A. Sisson Runyan (Eds). London, Routledge: 44–58.

Youngs, G. (2004). 'Feminist international relations: A contradiction in terms? Or: why women and gender are essential to understanding the world "we" live in.' *International Affairs* 80(1): 75–87.

Zalewski (1998). 'Where is woman in international relations? "To return as a woman and be heard."' *Millennium. Journal of International Studies* 27(4): 847–867.

Ziegler, P. I. (1988). *The Sixth Great Power: Barings, 1762–1929*. London, Collins.

Index

accumulation, 4, 6, 8, 19, 26, 30, 45, 49, 63, 80–1, 96–7, 111, 167
  colonialism, 81, 128
  and Fordism, 134
  gendered, 9, 30, 34
  household, 102
  and ideology, 84
  and power, 81, 132, 139, 144, 147, 154
  societal need, 123
Abacus Alliance, 174
ale-selling, 99
alliance capitalism, 147, 172–3
Anglo-Saxon value system, 124, 127
annuities, 64, 67, 76, 79, 123
Baltic exchange, 121
Bank of England, 71, 79, 93, 95, 143
bankers, 35–6, 92, 121, 125, 137
  colonial, 128
  Florentine, 70
  international, 125
  London, 93
banking, 70, 71–2, 74, 82, 93–4, 98, 103, 107, 119, 120, 121–5, 178
  crisis, 147
  families, 121
  offshore, 142
banks, 16, 36, 37, 70, 87, 89, 121–3, 131, 139, 142, 143, 167, 170, 171
  multinational, 175
Barclays Bank, 121, 145
barter systems, 109
British capital, 122
business, 143, 166, 169, 177
  and gender, 118, 126
  loans, 117
  strategies, 170, 172–3, 176

business and finance, separation of, 62–3
114, 115
women and, 100, 106, 107–9
capital mobility, 16, 133, 137, 142, 145, 147, 160
Capitalide, 178
casino capitalism, 94, 142–3
catalogue companies, 11, 141, 170–2, 176
circuits of credit, 20–1, 132, 158, 159–79, 181, 183, 185
City financial culture, 152
City of London, 3, 19, 36, 73, 93, 115, 119, 120–1, 122–5, 152
city states, Greek, 188
civil society, 24–5, 39, 40–1, 44–5, 48, 51, 55, 65
clothing trade, 99, 176
colonialism, 127–9
  bankers, 128
  and gender identity, 136
  masculinised hegemonic ideology, 129
  post-colonial, 128
  pre-colonial, 128
  property rights, 127
commercial activity, women's, 31, 34, 62, 99, 110
commodification, 15, 20, 65, 80, 84–6, 135
  of financial property, 60, 76, 170
  property forms, 51
  see also property
  of socio-economic relations, 28
  of welfare, 20, 185
common law, see women and common law
communal property, 54, 55, 63, 111